The Political Costs of the 2009 British MPs' Expenses Scandal

The Political Costs of the 2009 British MPs' Expenses Scandal

Edited by

Jennifer vanHeerde-Hudson

Senior Lecturer in Political Behaviour, School of Public Policy, Department of Political Science, University College London, UK

First published 2014 by
PALGRAVE MACMILLAN

Palgrave Macmillan in the UK is an imprint of Macmillan Publishers Limited,
registered in England, company number 785998, of Houndmills, Basingstoke,
Hampshire RG21 6XS.

Palgrave Macmillan in the US is a division of St Martin's Press LLC,
175 Fifth Avenue, New York, NY 10010.

Palgrave Macmillan is the global academic imprint of the above companies
and has companies and representatives throughout the world.

Palgrave® and Macmillan® are registered trademarks in the United States,
the United Kingdom, Europe and other countries.

ISBN 978–1–137–03454–0

This book is printed on paper suitable for recycling and made from fully
managed and sustained forest sources. Logging, pulping and manufacturing
processes are expected to conform to the environmental regulations of the
country of origin.

A catalogue record for this book is available from the British Library.

Library of Congress Cataloging-in-Publication Data
The political costs of the 2009 British MPs' expenses scandal / edited by
   Jennifer vanHeerde-Hudson, Senior Lecturer in Political Behaviour, School of
   Public Policy, Department of Political Science, University College London, UK.
      pages cm
   Includes bibliographical references and index.
   ISBN 978–1–137–03454–0
   1. Great Britain. Parliament. House of Commons—Salaries, etc.   2. Great Britain—
   Officials and employees—Salaries, etc.   3. Political corruption—
   Great Britain—History—21st century.   4. Independent Parliamentary Standards
   Authority (Great Britain)   5. Great Britain—Politics and government—2007–
   I. VanHeerde-Hudson, Jennifer, 1972– author, editor of compilation.
   JN581.P65 2014
   364.1′3230941090511—dc23   2014021114

Contents

Tables and Figures

Tables

Figures

Acknowledgements

I am grateful to the contributors to this volume for sharing their time and expertise; without them there would be no book. I'd like to thank the editors at Palgrave for their help and advice along the way, especially Andrew Baird and Amber Stone-Galilee. I came to London ten years ago on a one-year contract to teach research methods; ten years later, I am still here. Part of the reason is that I've had the privilege of working at the Department of Political Science at UCL and with many great colleagues – past and present. In many ways, it has been both home and work. The other reason I am still in London is because of David and Madeleine – the best way to start and end each day.

Contributors

Nicholas Allen is Senior Lecturer in Politics at Royal Holloway, University of London and received his PhD from the University of Essex in 2008. His research interests include the British prime ministers, parliamentary misconduct, public attitudes towards political ethics and the changing British constitution. He is co-editor of *Britain at the Polls 2010* and over a dozen articles and chapters on political misconduct and elite and public attitudes towards right and wrong. His work on perceptions of political misconduct (with Sarah Birch) has been supported by the British Academy and the Economic and Social Research Council (ESRC).

Sarah Birch is Professor of Comparative Politics at the University of Glasgow. Her current research has two main foci: attitudes towards public ethics and electoral integrity. She has published articles in journals including *Comparative Political Studies, European Journal of Political Research, European Political Science Review, Political Studies* and *Electoral Studies*. She is the author (with N. Allen) of *Ethics and Integrity in British Politics: How Citizens Judge Their Politicians' Conduct and Why It Matters*. She was elected a Fellow of the British Academy in 2013.

Justin Fisher (AcSS) is Professor of Political Science and Director of the Magna Carta Institute at Brunel University and is joint editor of the *Journal of Elections, Public Opinion and Parties*. In recent years, he has acted as an advisor and consultant to the Electoral Commission, the Committee on Standards in Public Life, the Council of Europe, the Hayden Phillips review of Party Finance and the Public Administration Select Committee. He has recently completed an ESRC-funded project analysing constituency campaigning at the 2010 general election (with Ed Fieldhouse and David Cutts).

Oonagh Gay is Head of the Parliament and Constitution Centre (PCC) in the House of Commons Library. She has worked in the library since 1983 as a researcher specializing in several aspects of parliamentary reform, parliamentary standards, electoral law, public administration and devolution, before becoming Head of the PCC in 2004. She has published a variety of research during her time at the House of Commons

Library and has co-edited her most recent publication *Conduct Unbecoming: The Regulation of Parliamentary Behaviour* with Patricia Leopold. She is also an Honorary Senior Research Fellow at the Constitution Unit, UCL and a member of the Study of Parliament Group and the Association of Electoral Administrators.

Jennifer vanHeerde-Hudson is Senior Lecturer in Political Behaviour, Department of Political Science, University College London and Director of the UCL-IOE Q-Step Centre. Her research has been published in *Party Politics, British Journal of Political Science, Political Studies, Journal of Elections, Public & Parties* and *European Journal of Marketing*, and has been supported by the Nuffield Foundation, Leverhulme Trust and ESRC.

Ron Johnston (OBE, AcSS) is Professor of Geography at the University of Bristol and is one of the world's foremost experts in political geography. His recent work has examined spatial variations in voting, the impact of local campaigns and the process of constituency definition. He has published extensively and has been recognized by the Royal Geographical Society with a Victoria Medal (1990) and received a lifetime achievement award from the Association of American Geographers (2009).

Valentino Larcinese is Senior Lecturer in Public Policy and Public Choice in the Department of Government, LSE. His research interests include political economy, information and mass media, and taxation and public spending. His recent work has examined the MPs' expenses scandal and media bias and has been published in leading journals *Public Choice, Journal of Theoretical Politics* and *Political Studies*.

Charles Pattie is Professor of Political Geography at Sheffield University where he also received his PhD. His research interests include electoral geography, electoral redistricting, parties and party campaigning, citizenship and participation and the politics of devolution in the UK. He is one of the UK's most prolific scholars publishing nine books and over 100 academic articles, appearing in *Political Geography, Electoral Politics, Political Behavior, British Journal of Political Science* and *Party Politics*.

Indraneel Sircar is Research Assistant for the EU Compliance in Bosnia-Herzegovina and Serbia Project (ECoBHAS) based at the Department of Politics, Queen Mary University of London. He received his PhD in political science from the London School of Economics in 2006. His research interests include the politics of the European Union and the dynamics of party politics. His work has appeared in *Party Politics* and *European Union Politics*.

Jessica Tarlov earned her PhD from the London School of Economics in 2013. Her PhD research addresses the effect of political scandal on individual MPs' general election vote share and decision to stand down from Parliament, and analyses individual MP accountability in light of the strength of party politics in the UK. She is currently a Political Strategist at Douglas Schoen LLC where she oversees publications, polling and messaging.

Nick Vivyan is Lecturer in Quantitative Social Research in the School of Government and International Affairs at the University of Durham. Nick's current research focuses mainly on the link between legislators and their constituents in representative democracies. His ESRC-funded initiative will generate and validate new estimates of political opinion in Westminster Parliament constituencies and then use these estimates to examine whether Members of Parliament are individually responsive to political opinion in their constituencies. His recent work has been published in the *European Journal of Political Research, Political Studies* and *Electoral Studies*.

Markus Wagner is Assistant Professor in Quantitative Methods at the Department of Social Sciences at the University of Vienna. He received his PhD from the London School of Economics in 2009. His doctoral research concerned the interconnections between policy areas and how these influence party ideologies and positional change and his research on voting behaviour is focused on the role of political issues in determining vote choice. His research has been published in the *Journal of European Public Policy, Party Politics, Acta Politica* and *Electoral Studies*.

Orlanda Ward is an ESRC-funded PhD candidate in the Department of Political Science/School of Public Policy at University College London. Her research interests span many aspects of political behaviour and political communication, with particular focus on gender and politics. Her PhD research analyses news media coverage of female and ethnic minority political candidates during the UK 2010 and US 2012 general election campaigns. Prior to commencing her PhD, she worked for several NGOs and a front bench MP.

Ben Worthy is Lecturer in Politics, Birkbeck, University of London. He received his PhD from the University of Manchester and is co-author (with R. Hazell and M. Glover) of *Does FOI Work? The Impact of the Freedom of Information Act 2000 upon British Central Government*. He has authored a number of journal articles examining the workings of the Freedom of Information Act 2000 on Parliament and local government. This body of research has been supported by the ESRC.

Tony Wright is Professor of Government and Public Policy at UCL and Professorial Fellow in Politics at Birkbeck, University of London. A former member of Parliament, he chaired the Select Committee on Public Administration for over a decade, and chaired the Select Committee on Reform of the House of Commons in the wake of the parliamentary expenses scandal. He is currently a member of the board of the Independent Parliamentary Standards Authority. Before entering the Commons in 1992, he was Reader in British Political Thought at the University of Birmingham; and has authored or edited many books on politics, most recently *Doing Politics* (2012) and *British Politics: A Very Short Introduction* (2nd ed, 2013).

1
The 2009 British MPs' Expenses Scandal: Origins, Evolution and Consequences

Jennifer vanHeerde-Hudson and Orlanda Ward

This chapter introduces the British MPs' expenses scandal: its origins, evolution and consequences. We argue that despite some early predictions, the scandal was limited in its impact: the purported 'revolution' never occurred. We briefly review the comparative literature on the political impact of scandal, which illustrates why the effects of scandals are usually limited and reasons why voters may choose not to punish malfeasant politicians. We situate this scandal against other international scandals, highlighting similarities and differences in the effects of scandal depending on cultural contexts. The chapter illustrates the *mediated* nature of the scandal and how it is best understood as comprised of not only the acts of politicians themselves, but as a series of moves and counter-moves by the press and other actors.

Introduction

On 8 May 2009 the *Daily Telegraph* began publishing un-redacted expenses claims made by British MPs. The revelation of parliamentary expenses showed how, and the extent to which, some MPs took advantage of an unregulated expenses system – a system designed by, and vigorously protected against outside interference, by MPs themselves. The expenses regime was intended to cover the costs of performing parliamentary duties: operating costs for running constituency offices (including staff salaries, rent, computers, etc.) and communications and travel as part of their parliamentary duties. The regime also included Additional Costs Allowances (ACA),[1] worth up to £24,000 annually, to reimburse MPs for the expense of staying away from their primary home while performing their parliamentary duties.

It was, predominantly, MPs' ACA claims that captured media headlines and public attention in the weeks that followed the *Telegraph's* initial disclosure. Both the public and pundits revelled in, and were reviled by, some of the now (in)famous claims made: a duck house, a trouser press, chocolate bars, plasma TVs, a riding lawn mower, jellied eels, moat cleaning, light bulbs, dog food, Kenyan carpets, and hanging baskets and potted plants. However, it was the practice of 'flipping' or switching an MP's designated second home (which was eligible for ACA expenses), that revealed the extent to which the expenses regime could be manipulated to maximize personal gain. MPs reaped the benefits of renovating and maintaining their properties at taxpayers' expense: mortgage interest on second homes was tax deductible and many were sold on at a profit with MPs pocketing any subsequent capital gains.

The first few days of the *Telegraph's* revelations started with members of the then governing Labour Party, senior ministers in particular, but after a few days switched its attention to senior Conservatives and Liberal Democrats before turning to rank-and-file members of all political parties. What quickly became apparent was the degree to which Members were implicated. This was not a scandal limited to a few 'bad apples', but rather, engulfed many in the House of Commons. Its institutional nature dictated that media and public scrutiny could not simply focus on individual cases of wrongdoing, but was compelled to consider the rules and regulations – established by MPs themselves – governing parliamentary expenses.

The institution-wide focus revealed that while many were implicated in the scandal and charged in the court of public opinion as having abused the system, very few MPs had engaged in outright *illegal* behaviour. Of the millions of claims made, the vast majority were made within 'the rules', a point many an MP was quick to cite as justification for their behaviour. Yet in attempting to direct attention away from individual cases of purported wrongdoing and towards the institution itself, MPs placed the expenses regime on the front line. With the public eye centred firmly on life inside the Commons, the intensity and secrecy with which Parliament sought to protect the expenses regime from external scrutiny was revealed. The next section briefly outlines the emergence and evolution of the expenses scandal, showing how repeated efforts were made to exempt the expenses regime from efforts to make the system more transparent and accountable.

A scandal unfolds: A brief chronology

Few outside of the Westminster Village could claim to know much about MPs' pay and expenses before May 2009. However, that changed markedly with the disclosure of MPs' expenses claims by the *Telegraph*. The revelations resulted in a perfect storm that dominated media coverage in the weeks that followed (vanHeerde-Hudson 2011) and, save for the handful of journalists heavily involved in preparing the data for publication, few could have predicted the fallout from the disclosure and the fury of the British public (Winnett and Rayner 2009). But for many in the Commons, parliamentary expenses had been an issue of concern and contention dating back as early as 2004, when Heather Brooke, an investigative journalist, began making requests to the Commons' Data Protection Office to release information concerning MPs' expenses.[2] Later that year the Commons did publish the information, broken down by office, travel and ACA claims, but the aggregated nature of the report meant that the details of MPs' individual claims remained hidden from public view (Winnett and Rayner 2009).

By 2005, Brooke's requests had company, as two other journalists, Ben Leapman and Jon Ungoed-Thomas, made similar requests to the Commons' new Freedom of Information (FOI) Office. All three were rebuked, often with personal involvement from then Speaker Michael Martin – citing the costs of preparing the reports and concerns over Members' privacy – which ultimately contributed to his resignation in May 2009. Undeterred, appeals were filed with the Information Commissioner, Richard Thomas, in 2006.

Meanwhile, some in the Commons didn't intend to wait for the Information Commissioner's decision. Conservative MP for Penrith and the Border, David Maclean, sponsored a bill that would have exempted Parliament from FOI, thereby ensuring secrecy for MPs' expenses (Barrett and Bloxham 2010). The bill ultimately failed and in 2007 the Commissioner ruled that ACA claims should be published, disaggregated by the various categories, but without detailed receipts. This partial release of information satisfied neither side and appeals were lodged with the Information Tribunal, the appellate body on FOI requests. In February 2008 the Tribunal upheld the Commissioner's decision; it also went further, suggesting that allowances should be published except in cases where protecting them was 'absolutely necessary'. It was also at the Tribunal's hearing that the controversial 'John Lewis List' was made public for the first time (see Worthy, Chapter 2).

In the following months, the issue of expenses was actively being played out in Westminster, featuring in a few newspaper headlines, but with no real splash or indication of what was to come. And once again, Parliament intervened, this time appealing the Tribunal's decision to the High Court. However, in May 2008 the Court upheld the Tribunal's decision and ordered the publication of detailed expenses claims. The Commons indicated that it would do so by October of 2008, but this was pushed back several times with little to no explanation from Commons officials. But the all-quiet was soon explained as Parliament, led by the Leader of the House of Commons, Harriet Harman, made a final attempt to exempt the House from FOI legislation. However, the bill quickly ran into trouble, with many MPs fearing the legislation looked 'as if they had something to hide' (Winnett and Rayner 2009: 29). The bill failed and Parliament reluctantly agreed to disclose detailed information on expenses in June 2009.

Parliament's publication of expenses claims was spectacularly thwarted by the *Telegraph's* acquisition of a disk containing millions of non-redacted claims dating back to 2004. The disk was sold to the *Telegraph* for £300,000 by John Wick, a former SAS officer, on two conditions: 'first, that the *Telegraph* had to publish details of expenses immediately, and second, that the alleged abuse of expenses would not be used for partisan purposes, but would expose what was believed to be systematic abuse of parliamentary allowances' (Winnett and Rayner 2009, vanHeerde-Hudson 2011: 245).[3]

In the days and weeks following the *Telegraph's* revelations, there was little talk or focus on issues save for parliamentary expenses, as each new allegation and response contributed to a seemingly unending saga. Life inside the Commons was increasingly unbearable, as many Members anxiously reviewed their own claims, awaiting their turn to answer for perceived excesses (Winnett and Rayner 2009; see Wright, Chapter 3). Only a few scandals in history had shaken the political foundations of the country so intensely, and none in living memory. Former Prime Minister Gordon Brown called it the 'biggest parliamentary scandal for two centuries'.[4] In an effort to respond to the crisis, party leaders uniformly condemned the abuses, a handful of MPs were deselected by their parties and a record number of MPs announced their retirement. The Independent Parliamentary Standards Agency (IPSA) was created to oversee the investigation into MPs' expenses and to design and administer a new expenses regime.

Properly understood then, the expenses scandal and the public anger that arose as a result, was not about castigating politicians as criminals or indeed criminal behaviour in the true sense of the word; only a handful of MPs were charged with criminal wrongdoing.[5] It was the intentional lack of transparency and accountability that governed the parliamentary allowances scheme that was widely perceived to be the real offence. That MPs had deliberately sought to keep expenses details from being disclosed and were essentially free to regulate their own activities, reinforced for many in the public the belief that politicians are subject to a different set of rules and standards and increasingly 'out of touch' with the lives of 'ordinary' British citizens.

The consequences and fallout from the scandal were expected to be severe. Survey data from May to June 2009 showed that only a small percentage of the British public had not heard of the scandal and most were angry about it (YouGov 2010) and trust, while historically low, had fallen further as a result of the scandal (Hansard Society 2010). Public opinion of politicians also fell: 50% of the public thought that MPs: spend their time furthering personal and career interests (Hansard Society 2010); are unprincipled (47%); are more interested in serving their own personal interest (66%); are dishonest (48%); and are out of touch with the day-to-day lives of their constituents (70%) (YouGov 2010). How would the expenses scandal change the political landscape if citizens and voters acted on their anger and distrust? What impact would the scandal have in the short and long term? This volume aims to answer these and other questions.

Aims of the volume

The aim of this volume is to comprehensively examine the 2009 British MPs' expenses scandal, its anatomy, evolution and consequences. In the chapters that follow, the authors consider the scandal across a number of domains: the scandal's origins in FOI legislation; how MPs viewed the expenses regime and their efforts to protect it; its impact on turnout, vote choice and retirement; public perceptions of MPs' involvement in the scandal and on their reputations; evidence of media bias in reporting the scandal; and the efforts to reform the expenses regime and unintended consequences of reform efforts in the wake of the scandal.

More generally, the volume considers two views that have emerged concerning the impact of the scandal. The first view holds that while the scandal was a significant political event, similar to scandals elsewhere, it would not have a significant impact on British political life. Any evidence of short-term falls in trust and confidence in parties and politicians would likely return to previous levels as memory of the scandal faded. This view did not discount institutional reform to the expenses regime itself, but more generally didn't see the expenses scandal as a catalyst for fundamental change to the way of doing politics.

The second view saw the expenses scandal as a political earthquake that shook Westminster to its core, the consequences of which would be instant and irrevocable.[6] Bell (2012: 2–3) has described it as a 'revolution', providing a permanent change to the way we do politics in Britain. Given the intense media scrutiny, and public fury that followed the *Telegraph's* revelations, it was more than credible that the expenses scandal was the juggernaut needed to clean up British politics.

Here, we assess the evidence for both views. Was the MPs' expenses scandal a revolution, as purported by Bell (2009), or was the impact relatively limited, as consistent with the general findings from the comparative literature on scandal? Our findings show that the revolution never happened: with a few exceptions where we see significant scandal effects, the full force of public anger never really took hold, particularly in electoral terms. The most significant impact of the scandal is IPSA: an independent body created to both regulate and administer a new expenses regime; however, even its long-term existence is not assured (see chapters 9 and 10).

The volume draws on contributions from a range of outstanding UK and international academic and non-academic experts. Each chapter provides original research drawing on a rich range of data and a variety of methodological approaches. Care has been taken to translate findings from quantitative approaches so that they are widely consumable. Each of the chapters focuses primarily on the British MPs' expenses scandal, and where appropriate, consideration is given to scandals elsewhere. In this vein, a secondary aim of the volume is to consider the expenses scandal comparatively, drawing on the findings regarding scandals in other countries and contexts to see where there are similarities and/or differences. This is not to say the method is comparative; we aim only to view the British scandal in light of the comparative literature.

The scandal: Legacy and aftermath

This volume looks at the impact of the scandal some five years after the initial publication of parliamentary expenses, and while the intensity and scrutiny of the initial episode no longer exists, a line has not yet been drawn under it. Fortunately, it does not render this analysis premature; rather, it points to the continued saliency of parliamentary expenses for the British public, the consequences of rapid reform in the wake of the scandal and the inherent difficulties in balancing two competing objectives – facilitating MPs' abilities to perform their parliamentary duties and ensuring accountability and value for money in the use of public monies, particularly in the context of the current economic climate. And with some distance between the onset and today, we can consider it in light of its short- and medium-term consequences.

As recently as May 2013, Peter Oborne argued that MPs had not learned lessons from the 2009 scandal as evidenced by their continued criticism of IPSA, the body in charge of regulating the new expenses regime, and 'failing to accept [its] authority' (Oborne 2013; see also Gay, Chapter 9). And it was not just MPs' dissatisfaction with IPSA that yielded headlines, but expenses-related behaviour: claiming expenses for business-class flights despite being against the rules (Watts 2013); claiming expenses for learning their respective partner's languages (Brocklebank 2013); and perhaps most importantly, in taking advantage of a 'loophole' in the new regime that allowed MPs to rent taxpayer-funded homes to each other (Hastings 2012). With regards to the latter, Speaker John Bercow suffered some of the same criticism as that of his predecessor, Michael Martin, when he was accused of attempting to block moves to publish the names of MPs' landlords under a FOI request (Unlock Democracy 2012). Speaker Bercow argued that releasing the names of the 27 MPs who rented to one another was not feasible given 'security concerns', but critics responded that these could be alleviated by simply blacking out the addresses of the properties in question.

The legacy of the British expenses scandal, in conjunction with the global economic downturn, appears to have inspired similar debates in other national and supranational parliaments. For example, in October 2011, MEPs voted to freeze their expenditure allowance despite proposals by some MEPs to reduce it. This followed a decision in the previous June where the European Parliament ordered the publication of details of MEPs' expenses. In France, National Assembly members voted in July 2012 against plans for external scrutiny of their £5,000 monthly expenses[7] allowances, despite evidence of abuse: Pascal Terrasse, Member for Ardèche, claimed expenses for his family holiday, and Christian Blanc, State Secretary for the Paris region, claimed some 12,000 for Cuban cigars.[8] In late 2012 Canada was engulfed in its own expenses scandal, focusing predominantly on the living and travel expenses of senators. One senator, Pamela Wallin, has been accused of claiming parliamentary expenses while carrying out personal business. Although the scandal is thus far limited to a handful of senators, recent (June 2013) polling data shows that '86 per cent of respondents – including overwhelming majorities in all regions and across all age groups and party affiliations – feel it's likely that MPs and senators are claiming improper expenses. Of those, 56 per cent feel it's very likely.'[9]

In Italy, a rash of current scandals has raised concerns that Italian politics is still plagued by levels of institutional corruption similar to that of the Tangentopoli scandal of the 1990s. Roberto Formigoni, Governor of Lombardy, himself under investigation for accepting paid vacations from a healthcare lobbyist, 'dismissed the entire city government of Reggio Calabria to stave off infiltration by organized crime and surrendered his own government after accusations of vote-selling and more than a dozen regional lawmakers embroiled in scandal'.[10] At the national level, Italy's provision of both salary and expenses is among the highest in the West. Italian politicians can claim for 'meals in lavish restaurants, cosmetic dentistry, private cars and chauffeurs, and police protection – including outriders stopping traffic to let them through' (Malone 2011). The degree of abuse is thought to be so extensive, that the scandal that engulfed British politicians would be seen as 'amateur' (Malone 2011).

Thus, expenses-related scandals are, and remain, an important and salient issue in many countries. The next section considers the cross-national literature on scandals and their impact on political life before considering in more detail the explicitly mediated nature of the MPs' expenses scandal, a feature of nearly all modern political scandals. The final section outlines the contributions of each of the chapters presented in this volume.

The political impact of scandal

Knowledge of the political impact of scandals comes largely from studies of the US and UK, although there is a growing literature looking at scandal cross-nationally. The literature on the impact of scandal and shows that, despite a great deal of public knowledge/awareness of scandal and condemnation of politicians' behaviour, scandals are rarely the electoral and political earthquakes they are initially thought to be.

In the UK, scandals involving public figures have generally been labelled with the term 'sleaze', although Dunleavy and Weir (1995) delineate different types: alleged financial wrongdoing (including improprieties regarding lobbying, quangos, honours, 'jobs for the faithful', company directorships and party fundraising); unconventional sexual behaviour; and salary increases for 'fat cats' in the privatized public utilities. Thompson (1997) also distinguishes scandal by type: those involving sex, those involving money (usually fraud or corruption) and those involving an abuse of power, although modern scandals frequently blur these boundaries. For example, in 1963 UK Secretary of State for War, John Profumo, who was married, had a brief sexual relationship with Christine Keeler. The scandal around his extra-marital affair was compounded by the allegation that Keeler had a relationship with a Soviet attaché, and her relationship with Profumo – during the peak of the Cold War – was a means to access top-secret British military intelligence. More recently, former US presidential candidate John Edwards admitted to a sexual relationship with Rielle Hunter, with whom he also had a child, while married to Elizabeth Edwards. This sexual scandal also became a financial one when Edwards was later charged with violating US campaign finance law for using campaign funds to cover up his relationship with Hunter.

Delineating the type of scandal matters because the impact or effect of scandal varies depending on both its type and the cultural context. In the US, moral violations have been shown to result in the most severe electoral consequences and conflict of interest the least, 'bringing about essentially no retribution' (Peters and Welch 1980: 703). However, with respect to the 1997 UK general election, Farrell *et al.* (1998: 88) find that 'financial and sexual scandals were of about equal importance in the minds of voters, although neither resulted in any major shifts in votes'. They go on to point out however, that prior to the 1990s, 'almost all British scandals were concerned with sex, not money, while the opposite was closer to the truth in the US (King 1986). It may be that voters punish the types of scandals they are least familiar with in their particular polity.' (1998: 91) Drawing on these insights then, we would expect to find significant effects of the expenses scandal on electoral outcomes; however, as shown in chapters 4 and 5, the effects are relatively muted.

Research into the effects of political scandal on politicians' electoral success or failure reports mixed findings, but overall tends to suggest that effects are limited (Alford *et al.* 1994; Jacobson and Dimock 1994; Farrell *et al.* 1998). Several theories have been suggested to account for the low impact of scandal on vote share, including uninformed voters (Klasnja 2011), cognitive dissonance (Dimock and Jacobson 1995) and implicit trading (Rundquist *et al.* 1977) Together, these suggest that while better informed voters may sometimes be less likely to vote for corrupt politicians, partisan and issue-based priorities often take precedence over scandal in determining vote choice. Herrick (2000) argues that the minimal effect of scandal on incumbents' chances of re-election is often due to members' degree of electoral security. While association with scandal tends to lead to a decline in vote share, this regularly fails to do away with members' majorities altogether.

For example, the British 1997 general election followed a torrent of sleaze allegations directed at the incumbent Conservative Party and saw a landslide win for New Labour. That year, average Tory vote loss across all seats was 11.8%, compared to 13.5% in Conservative constituencies where the MP had been subject to an allegation of sleaze (Farrell *et al.* 1998: 789).[11] However, the net electoral effect of sleaze allegations was much reduced when comparing predicted and actual electoral outcomes. While sleaze played a partial role in motivating defections by Conservative voters in 1997, 'it was overshadowed by other issues, such as economic management and, most important of all, education' (Farrell *et al.* 1998: 90).

Similar findings have been reported relating to the 1992 US House Bank scandal. Despite public expectations of disastrous consequences for those caught up in the scandal, Alford *et al.* (1994: 799) find 'practically no effect of the scandal on reelection. While numerous challengers used the issue in their campaigns and many political observers braced for the impact of the Banking scandal, the issue did not appear to resonate with voters.' At the 1992 US congressional elections, over 80% of offending incumbents were re-elected (Alford *et al.* 1994; Dimock and Jacobson 1995). Furthermore, the majority of those who failed to secure re-election ran in re-drawn districts and five had to contend with fellow incumbents (Alford *et al.* 1994: 789). Ahuja *et al.* (1994: 920) conclude that for the few who were ousted, 'it was usually because they were opposed by a politically experienced, well-financed challenger not a novice' (see also Abramowitz 1991). Therefore, had redistricting and the associated quality of challengers not been factors, the number of check-kiting incumbents gaining re-election may have been even higher.

The effects of individual (rather than institution-wide) scandals are also somewhat limited. The average loss in vote share for US House incumbents facing allegations or charged with corruption has remained relatively low: between 6 and 11% from 1968 and 1978, and at 9% from 1982–1990 (Welch and Hibbing 1980; 1997). Welch and Hibbing (1997) also show that during the period 1982–1990, the vast majority, 75%, of corruption-charged US House Representatives competing in general elections were successfully re-elected. However, 25% lost, compared to just under 3% of other incumbents. So while the loss in vote share wasn't substantial, it was enough to have a sizeable effect on re-election rates compared to 'clean' politicians. Welch and Hibbing suggest therefore that 'the common wisdom that corrupt politicians continue to go unpunished is not altogether on target' (1997: 237).

Electoral security, seniority and incumbent advantage do help to protect scandal-ridden incumbents from electoral defeat however. Peters and Welch (1980: 704) note that seniority provides 'a larger cushion against retribution than that possessed by the more junior candidate'. Similarly, Herrick (2000: 96) finds electoral security to be the most significant factor affecting whether or not members accused of unethical behaviour can survive an election cycle. Herrick notes that while institutional power, media coverage, the political climate and the member's age also impact upon their electoral prospects, the size of the swing necessary to oust them tends to be the most decisive factor. Peters and Welch (1980) and Nyblade and Reed (2008) also show that scandal-ridden incumbents who choose not to stand down are insulated by seniority and incumbent advantage. Therefore, while the negative effect of scandal on vote share is apparent, it often fails to be strong enough to result in a defeat of scandal-ridden members who chose to run for re-election.

The electoral effects of political scandal have also been found to differ along partisan lines. Peters and Welch (1980: 703) find that from 1968 to 1978, Democrats were more likely than Republicans to be charged with corruption, and lost almost twice as many votes as corruption-charged Republicans. Conversely however, Welch and Hibbing (1997: 237) find that from 1982 to 1990, all else being equal, Republicans were be more likely than Democrats to be charged with corruption and were also harder hit at the polls.[12] Clarke *et al.* (1999) also find that Republicans were more affected than Democrats following the House banking scandal, a finding echoed by Banducci and Karp (1994). Partisan variation in the electoral effects of scandal may reflect many factors, including differences in the mediation of scandal and in the trade-offs made by voters of varying partisan affiliations.

The electoral consequences of scandal can also been seen in its effect on turnover or members' decisions to retire.[13] Clarke *et al.* (1999) note that at the 1992 congressional elections, 66 members of the House of Representatives retired, constituting the highest number of retirements since the end of World War II. Of these, 53 did not seek another elective office (Clarke *et al.* 1999: 81). They find that in addition to scandal effects, political and economic factors also exerted significant influence on individual decisions to run and thus turnover (see also Kiewiet and Zeng 1993; Groseclose and Krehbiel 1994). And again, differential partisan effects were observed. Although representatives for both parties were equally implicated in the scandal, trouble with the economy, a partisan climate hostile to Republicans and time-limited claims on retirement income made Republicans more likely to retire in 1992. So while the scandal led to an increase in turnover, thus narrowing the pool of scandal-ridden incumbents seeking re-election to those with greater chances of success, the phenomenon was moderated by other factors which encouraged certain groups to cut their losses.

While these factors help to explain why scandal often fails to result in electoral defeat, three additional factors relating to characteristics or behaviours of voters themselves – information levels, cognitive dissonance and trading, – may also serve to limit electoral accountability. Klasnja (2011) finds that less-informed voters are more likely to vote for incumbents accused of corruption and argues, therefore, that an increase in political awareness may serve to reduce support for malfeasant incumbents. This is supported by Chang *et al.* (2010), who argue that mediation of a political scandal may constitute the necessary spark to hold those implicated accountable. Their study of judicial investigations of malfeasance among deputies in the Italian lower house over the course of 11 post-war elections found that while all legislatures included deputies charged with malfeasance, a dramatic rise in press coverage in the 1990s preceded the ousting of the previously immune corrupt legislative elite, concluding that 'this change in the informational environment was crucial to the change in voter behavior' (Chang *et al.* 2010: 213). The authors theorize that one consequence of mediation is that as corruption increases in salience, voters are alerted to the level of shared anti-corruption sentiment among them, and act to hold politicians accountable.

Dimock and Jacobson (1995) however, observe a more perplexing pattern of behaviour in their study of voter reactions to the US House Bank scandal:

> Fortunately for members who had written bad checks, voters who knew about the transgression were least disposed to be outraged by it, while the voters most disposed to outrage were also most inclined to believe the guilty were innocent. The explanation for these curious patterns is that voters who faced the option of condemning an incumbent they otherwise appreciated or dismissing the offense as inconsequential often chose the latter course. The damage was also moderated by partisanship; voters of the incumbent's party showed a strong tendency to err in the incumbent's favor in assessing involvement in the scandal. The classical theory of cognitive dissonance readily explains both phenomena.
>
> (Dimock and Jacobson 1995: 1143)

Therefore, knowledge of a scandal may not always lead to a straight-forward decrease in approval or likelihood of voting for malfeasant politicians.

Finally, Rundquist *et al.* (1977: 956) propose a theory of implicit trading to describe why informed voters continue to vote for malfeasant candidates: 'if candidate corruption is treated like any other component in the voter's choice between two candidates, it follows that there are conditions under which a rational voter would knowingly support corrupt candidates'. This is supported by Farrell *et al.* (1998) who find that British voters in 1997 prioritized education issues over sleaze allegations in casting ballots. Rundquist *et al.* (1977) suggest that a strategy for corrupt politicians would then be to take distinct positions on substantive issues in order to encourage implicit trading with specific constituencies. On balance however, the literature suggests that the electoral success of both incumbents and challengers associated with scandal may not simply be attributable to voters' lack of knowledge, but also to their partisan and issue-based priorities. Therefore while knowledge may be a necessary condition for voters to seek electoral retribution, it does not appear to be sufficient.

A plague on your houses: Evidence of minor party gains from scandal?

It is worth pausing for a moment to consider how this scandal affected minor parties' fortunes post 2009 in Britain. As the evidence above suggests, mainstream parties and politicians do not seem to suffer electorally in the medium to long term, which may not be surprising given that many were implicated. But what, if anything, happens to minor party support in the short to medium term? Is there any evidence that minor parties' fortunes are helped by 'a plague on all your houses' sentiment by the public?

The minor party story in Britain post 2010 general election has been that of UKIP. Clearly positioned as the antithesis to the 'Westminster-insider', UKIP has experienced surge in popularity and in terms of electoral support. In the European Parliament elections in June 2009, one month following the break of the scandal, UKIP won only seven seats – not much evidence the voters were turning to an anti-establishment, anti-expenses party.

Since then, UKIP's popularity and electoral fortunes have blossomed. In the May 2013 local county council elections, UKIP won over 140 seats and fielded 1,700 candidates, three times the number that stood in 2009. They've also increased their vote share in nearly every by-election since

2010, notably placing second in Barnsley Central with 12% and Newark with 26% of the vote. In the 2014 European Parliament elections, UKIP came first, winning 27.5% of the vote, taking support not just from the Tories, but across all three major parties. But is UKIP's increased popularity the result of abandoning the main three parties over expenses or does it reflect UKIP's long-standing anti-EU, anti-immigration stance under 'austerity'?

One way of getting at this is to look at what UKIP was talking to voters about in the run up to the 2010 general election. In terms of its manifesto, UKIP argued for the right of the public to recall MPs, including those who abused expenses. But much of the language around recall was couched in references to bureaucracy, both Whitehall and Brussels, and giving power back to local people; hardly taking expenses head on.

There is some evidence, however, that UKIP was talking to voters about expenses as seen in a review of UK national newspapers in the month prior to the 2010 election. Just over one in five articles (23%) mentioned UKIP or party leader Nigel Farage and expenses. However, by comparison, 54% of all articles mentioned either Europe or immigration. The reality of austerity and the economic downturn, the re-emerging split within the Conservative Party over Europe, and Ed Miliband's low popularity, rather than expenses, are more plausible factors in explaining UKIP's rise in popularity. In sum, there is little evidence to support the premise that the expenses scandal had an impact on the party system more generally, despite the success of one anti-system party.

The negative effects of scandal on trust and confidence

Outside the electoral arena, scandal has also been shown to negatively affect public trust and confidence. Unsurprisingly, scandal has been found to harm the overall reputation of both the individual politicians and the institutions implicated in scandal (Patterson and Magleby 1992; Hibbing and Theiss-Morse 1995). For example, both the House Banking scandal and the 1976 'Koreagate' scandal – in which it had emerged that members of Congress had taken bribes from South Korean businesspeople acting on behalf of the Korea Central Intelligence agency, with the intention of influencing US policy in the context of uneasy relations between the two countries – coincided with two of the lowest recorded approval ratings of Congress (Patterson and Magleby 1992; cited in Herrick 2000: 97). British public attitudes towards MPs following the expenses scandal were remarkably cynical:

40% of respondents report not trusting MPs to put the national interest first and a majority believing MPs never tell the truth (*The Telegraph* 13 December 2010). The Hansard Society's Democratic Audit of Political Engagement (2010: 32), however, points out that the expenses scandal didn't contribute to a 'collapse in trust' because trust was already so low. Instead, the scandal 'confirmed and hardened the public's widely held skepticism about politicians rather than changed their views'.

In Italy, the aftermath of the Tangentopoli or 'bribesville' scandals was a somewhat more dramatic 'citizenship revolt', leading to a 'massive vote against state funding of parties, the collapse of the traditional parties in local elections and the accompanying hemorrhage of membership' (Pujas and Rhodes 1999: 49). While the severity of public response to scandal may vary, the negative effects of malfeasance on trust have also been shown to extend beyond Western democracies. Chang and Chu's (2006) study of five Asian democracies (Japan, the Philippines, South Korea, Taiwan and Thailand), also found a consistent 'strongly corrosive effect of corruption on citizens' trust towards political institutions' (265).

The breadth or reach of a sandal, for example whether institutional or individual in nature, has important implications for blame attribution and accountability. Alford *et al.* (1994: 790) distinguish between the effects of individual and institutional scandals on voter evaluations of candidates, noting that voters 'discount the culpability of their own members for a scandal that is perceived as attached to an institution'. This mirrors the overall gap in evaluations of individuals in institutions, seen in positive evaluations of local representatives despite negative evaluations of Congress as a whole (Fenno 1975; Parker and Davidson 1979). Alford *et al.* (1994: 790) contend that the diffuse nature of the House Bank scandal explained how it impacted on attitudes towards Congress without causing great harm to individual members. Furthermore, in individual terms, while the activation of a politician involved in a political scandal has been found to decrease judgements of trustworthiness of politicians in general (assimilation effect), it also *increases* judgements of other specific politicians not involved in the scandal (contrast effect) (Schwarz and Bless 1992; Bless and Schwarz 1998; Bless *et al.* 2000). These findings, however, are mediated by level of expertise or information. Régner and Floch (2005: 259) show that when taking account of political knowledge, 'expertise', assimilation and contrast effects are present among young adults in France with a rich political knowledge, but tend not to be seen among those with poorer knowledge. Therefore, the impact of scandal on confidence and trust in individuals and institutions is not always straightforwardly negative, and mirrors wider patterns of conflicting attitudes towards politicians individually and collectively.

Some cases, such as the expenses scandal, constitute clear-cut examples of institutional scandal given the uniformity of the type of allegations made (if not the degree of impropriety) and the implication of all main political parties; however, others are less clear cut. For example, the wave of Tory 'sleaze' preceding the 1997 UK general election was the result of diverse individual activities constituting several types of scandal, but 'the number of cases of reported corrupt activities by Conservative politicians, and their prominence in the media, made the issue a national, collective one' (Farrell *et al.* 1998: 92). Arguably, it was the way in which these activities were presented collectively as a 'wave' by the British press, which transformed the relatively unconnected behaviour of specific individuals into an institutional scandal tainting an entire political party. Had the same behaviour been mediated differently it may have resulted in different outcomes in perceptions of both individual politicians and parliament as a whole. Farrell *et al.* (1998: 92) also argue that while sleaze was viewed as a national, party-wide issue in Britain in 1997, the 1992 House Bank scandal was conceived differently in the US, 'whose individualistic political culture attributes blame for corruption to the candidate, and only rarely to a party as a whole across the country'. Thus, the conception and mediation of a scandal as individual or institutional may depend both on political culture and media landscape.

A decline in diffuse party/political support?

Thinking about the medium to long term, what evidence is there that the expenses scandal has impacted diffuse support for the political system, if at all? Have parties, politicians and political institutions lost legitimacy in the eyes of the public? Data and research on the long-term effects of scandal are extremely limited. This is unsurprising given that confounding variables pose serious challenges to measuring the causal impact of the scandal in the short term, and even more so in the long term. Even the best research designs will have difficulty teasing out a range of factors which may have influenced support for and engagement with the political system post 2009: the financial crisis, BBC/Savile inquiry, press intrusion and Leveson inquiry, bankers' bonuses, and the 'Etonization' of the front bench in government, among others.

Castells (2007: 244) has argued that the 'crisis of political legitimacy in most of the world cannot be attributed exclusively, by any means, to scandal politics and to media politics. Yet, scandals are most likely at the very least a precipitating factor [...] in rooting skepticism vis-à-vis formal politics in the long term'. Perhaps the greatest long-term effect of the MPs' expenses scandal, compounded by the succession of scandals in public institutions that followed, has been what might be termed a crisis of engagement.

The most recent Hansard *Audit* (2013: 1) found that 'just 41% of the public now say that in the event of an immediate general election they would be certain to vote – a decline of seven percentage points in a year and the lowest level in the debate of the Audit'. The authors contend that, 'combined with the low turnout levels at recent local elections and the disastrous turnout at the polls for Police and Crime Commissioners in November 2012, these findings are deeply worrying for the health of our democracy' (ibid.: 1).

Party political membership has also suffered as a result of the scandal, but it follows a long-term trend dating back to the 1950s. Political commentators predicted a decline in support for Britain's largest political parties and the evidence suggests this has been the case. In 2011, the BBC noted that, 'there are more members of the Caravan Club, or the Royal Society for the Protection of Birds, than of all Britain's political parties put together'.[14]

However, the news is not all bad with respect to party membership. The number of Labour Party members has fluctuated more so than Conservative or Liberal Democrat numbers (House of Commons Library, 2012), and while the trend remains negative, Hansard *Audit* (2010: 108) data following the expenses scandal showed a two-point rise, from 3% to 5%, in the number of respondents reporting having donated or paid membership fees to a political party. Though the rise was marginal, this was the first occasion in which there was a year-on-year increase since the second *Audit* in 2005.

A comparative look at scandals and impact

The bulk of research into political scandal and its effects has focused on the US and Britain. However, available evidence from several other countries – constituting a variety of political contexts – reveals striking similarities in the electoral consequences of scandal: as in Britain and the US, they are consistently limited by other factors. In Europe, mayors convicted of corruption in both Spain and France have also enjoyed high re-election rates (Lafay and Servais 2000; Jimenez and Cainzos 2006). Similarly, in Japan, 60% of legislators convicted of corruption in the post-war period were subsequently re-elected (Reed 1999).

Furthermore, legislators who were indicted on charges and ran for re-election suffered only minor losses in vote share, while those convicted went on to *increase* their vote share in subsequent elections (Reed 2005).

Ferraz and Finan (2008) have studied the electoral effects of media coverage of corruption in Brazil and find that among municipalities with the same levels of reported corruption, those which released audits of their expenditures which were then reported by the local radio saw a significant effect on incumbents' electoral performance. Chang *et al.* (2010) note similar changes in the electoral consequences of scandal in Italy over the post-war period, specifically following operation *mani pulite* or 'clean hands' of the 1990s in reponse to the Tangentopoli scandal that rocked Italian politics. Tangentopoli was the name given to revelations that a number of political parties were being illegally financed by business and industry. Until this point Italy had constituted a particularly extreme case in which charges of corruption were not associated with loss of vote share. However, this shifted following increased public awareness of the extent of the issue and resulted in a dramatic increase in the electoral effects of scandal, rendering the country a unique example in which 'voters turned on a whole class of allegedly corrupt national political leaders and ejected them from public office' (Chang *et al.* 2010: 178). Despite these post-war shifts, a series of financial scandals, many associated with former Prime Minister Silvio Berlusconi in the run up to Italy's 2012 general election, has led to concerns from some quarters that the Tangentopoli of the 1990s may have re-surfaced.[15]

Cross-national similarities in the electoral consequences of scandal and the impact of media dissemination of information regarding corruption stand in contrast to differences in the types of scandal which capture media and public attention across different countries. These differences have been discussed previously in relation to the contrast between the UK and the US, but Thompson (2000: 10) notes similar differences elsewhere: 'sex scandals typically play a much less significant role in French or Italian political life than they do in Britain, for example, while political scandals in France and Italy have been concerned primarily with corruption and abuse of power'. While the focus on financial matters in Italian political scandals is explained by high levels of corruption in the country, the British and American focus on sex suggests the degree to which national media and the public in both countries continue to be scandalized by the infidelities of their political leaders.

While Italy and Sweden represent two extremes in terms of financial corruption in politics, mediated political scandal in both countries has focused on financial dealings. This is explained by the features of Nordic political culture, 'in which legislation and official regulation play a central role, [therefore] political scandals often involve violations of decisions, rules or statutes concerning economic affairs' (Allern and Pollack 2012: 15). So in Italy, the prevalence of financial scandal results from high levels of corruption, while in Sweden corruption levels are low and the focus on financial scandal is instead motivated by the severity with which even minor financial wrongdoing is judged. However, while economic affairs continue to dominate Nordic political scandal, those involving politicians' private lives have risen in prominence over the past few decades (Allern *et al.* 2012). This may perhaps point to a degree of convergence as global media trends continue to shape the way in which political scandal is mediated.

A modern, mediated scandal

The British MPs' expenses scandal cannot be understood in isolation from the modern, mass media which played an integral part in its revelation, dominance and persistence in May 2009. It was a *mediated* scandal. In other words, it was a scandal played out first and foremost in the media: public knowledge and experience of MPs' malfeasance was made possible via the mass media, which gave life to and sustained the scandal in the weeks following the initial revelations. Lull and Hinerman (1997: 11–13) provide a list of criteria that serve to systematically identify characteristics of mediated scandal:

> (1) social norms reflecting the dominant morality must be transgressed [...] The transgressions must be performed by (2) specific persons who carry out (3) actions that reflect an exercise of their desires or interests [...] Further, individual persons must be (4) identified as perpetrators of the act(s). The must be shown to have acted (5) intentionally or recklessly and must be (6) held responsible for their actions. The actions and events must have (7) differential consequences for those involved. [...] revelations must be (8) widely circulated via communications media where they are (9) effectively narrativized into a story which (10) inspires widespread interest and discussion.

Lull and Hinerman's definition sets out the necessary components of a mediated scandal, but it retains a degree of separation between the acts which constitute a scandal and their mediation. Conversely,

Thompson (2010) conceives of mediated political scandal as a unified *process* in which the scandal is itself constituted by its mediation and more accurately captures the expenses scandal under investigation here. Thompson (2000: 61) notes that 'disclosure through the media, and commentary in the media, are not secondary or incidental features of these forms of scandal: they are partly constitutive of them'. Therefore, he argues, 'a mediated scandal does not begin with the transgression itself, but rather with the act of disclosure and/or allegation which turns the original transgression into an object of public knowledge' (2000: 73).

Allern and Pollack (2012: 22) build on Thompson's conception, employing the metaphor of a drive hunt to describe the process:

> There must be a pack of hunters and numerous editors evaluating the situation's nature and news value in the same way. The media's dramatic focus requires the hunt to be undertaken over a certain period of time and-in order to increase the level of suspense and public attention, uncertainty regarding the consequences and outcome.
>
> (Nord 2001)

Thus, in the case of the British MPs' expenses scandal, *The Telegraph* maximized suspense by drip-feeding details of misdoing over several days, and meanwhile the news value of the story was consistent across other news publications and platforms, remaining at the top of the headlines wherever the reader turned.

Both Thompson and Allern and Pollack conceive of mediated political scandal as a collective event which includes several stages comprising a sequence of moves by all of the relevant actors. This conception of mediated scandal is useful in considering the distinctions between institutional and individual scandal discussed previously, given that to some degree this distinction rests not simply on the behaviour of those accused, but the way in which that behaviour is framed, and responses and counter-responses by the subjects, press and public are subsequently collectivized. Additionally, the similarities in Thompson's and Allern and Pollack's conceptions of mediated scandal, who consider US and Scandinavian contexts respectively, suggests an interesting degree of cross-cultural similarity in the way in which mediated scandals are manifested in each region, despite significant differences in their media and political landscapes.

Lull and Hinerman (1997: 1) suggest that the rising prevalence of mediated scandal in general may be viewed both as 'a distinctive sign of the "Murdochization" of modern media' and, in the US as, 'part of the ultra-conservative overall trend in popular culture' (1997: 5). In addition to sweeping changes to the make-up of the media industries and the role of journalists, Thompson (2000: 8–9) also argues that the weakening of ideological, class-based politics and belief systems in favour of more candidate-centred politics has contributed to the positioning of mediated political scandal in a 'a newly potent and self-reinforcing role as a "credibility test"'.

This aspect of mediated political scandal is perhaps most significant in the context of high-profile, closely fought and candidate-centred electoral contests. For example, Gronbeck (1997: 125) argues that during presidential campaigns, 'the line between political and entertainment reporting all but disappears [and] issues like character (political morality) and celebrity (popularity, likability) are melded'. In this context, Gronbeck argues, voters turn to character over issues as a guide to voting, and therefore scandal can make or break a campaign. 'Such an amalgamation of character and celebrity by the press has made meta-politics and meta-ethics, rather than actual political action and concrete morally relevant activity, the pivots upon which electoral decisions turn' (Gronbeck 1997: 125). Furthermore, Welch and Hibbing (1997: 228) note that 'the continued lack of policy awareness of many voters and the continued decline of political parties as voting cues mean that image-based variables have become more central'. Scandal can also be perceived as easier to judge than policy success or failure. For example, Jacobson and Dimock (1994: 622) point out that scandal can sometimes be measured in a way that responsibility for economic crises may not be. Thus in the context of elections following the US House Bank scandal 'voters had no way to measure their representative's personal contribution to the savings and loan fiasco or the budget deficits, but they did know who wrote overdrafts – particularly where challengers mounted vigorous campaigns to remind them'.

The suggested melding of political actors with celebrity, combined with a lack of policy awareness among voters as factors contributing to the central position of mediated political scandal in high-profile campaigns, points to the possibility of a self-reinforcing cycle in which issues slide down the agenda, while the hunt for scandalizing personal details increases in force. However, the issue agendas of particular campaigns may not always lose in the tug of war over column inches and, even if they do, voters may continue to prioritize other concerns. For example, Jacobson and Dimock (1994: 621) note that during the 1992 US presidential campaign, 'the economy, taxes, and the future direction of the country [...] may have reduced the importance of overdrafts compared to the candidates' basic partisan differences on these national issues'. Furthermore, despite 'a series of colourful stories about the sexual proclivities of certain Conservative candidates' (Farrell *et al.* 1998: 82), sleaze only accounted for 12% of all policy coverage during the UK 1997 general election campaign (Norris 1997, cited in Farrell *et al.* 1998: 83).

Examples from the US House Bank scandal and the UK 1997 general election, discussed previously, suggest that scandalous behaviour itself (as distinct from mediated political scandal) has limited electoral consequences and voters themselves report (though with debatable reliability) that other issues take precedence when weighing up their choices. However, Herrick (2000) finds that during the period 1977–1995, the more media coverage a member of the US Congress received relating to an allegation, the more likely their departure. This confirms the power of mediated political scandal to excerbate the electoral effects of scandalous behaviour by individual members.

This may have particularly troubling consequences for candidates and legislators from under-represented groups. Niven (2004) investigates racial, gendered and partisan bias in newspaper coverage of the US House Bank scandal, comparing the degree of criticism received by check-bouncing House members of different groups. He notes:

by utilizing a baseline of known political behavior, (the number of overdrawn checks) as a basis for studying media coverage, we can eliminate the vast number of complicating realities that otherwise preclude us from reasonably concluding that a difference in coverage is the result of bias, and the lack of difference in coverage is evidence of fairness.

(Niven 2004: 649–650)

While no partisan differences were found, women and ethnic minority members were penalized more severely than white males by longer, more prominent and more negative coverage. If an increase in the frequency of coverage of a political scandal increases the likelihood of departure of the individual concerned, and women and minorities receive disproportionately high levels of news coverage when embroiled in a political scandal, they are therefore likely to face consequences unequal to those of their white, male counterparts.

Furthermore, Hammarlin and Jarlbro (2012) argue that gendered comments and criticisms were rife in coverage of the then Swedish Deputy Prime Minister Mona Sahlin during the so-called Toblerone Affair, a high-profile financial scandal surrounding Sahlin's use of an official credit card for personal purchases which included, to the delight of the Swedish press, several Toblerone bars. Therefore, mediated political scandal may at times constitute a platform for the manifestation of gendered or other biases cloaked beneath scandalized indignation.

Mediated political scandals also remain in collective memory with possible effects long after the period in which they occur. For example, Lull and Hinerman (1997: 18) argue that 'Watergate and Richard Nixon have become synonymous with scandal. Any scandalous misdeeds attributed to a politician today will necessarily be read against this generalized reputation of party politics.' Thompson (2000: 265) also identifies the tendency of scandals to appear in cycles or waves in which 'each scandal raises the political stakes still further and increases the symbolic and political value that might be derived – both for political opponents and for media organizations and personnel – from further revelations'. However, while mediated scandals may damage the collective reputation of political actors over time, they do not necessarily have negative consequences for specific individuals in the longer term.

The expenses scandal: Evidence of a revolution?

The aim of this book is to understand the expenses scandal: its origins, evolution and consequences for political life; and where appropriate, we consider the generalizability of the MPs' expenses scandal to scandals elsewhere. In the chapters that follow, we take an in-depth look at the scandal, from its origins in the FOI Act, to the political response to the scandal, the creation of the IPSA, and everything in between. Five years on, and drawing on the best data available, the authors here consider the impact of the 2009 MPs' expenses scandal on British political life.

In Chapter 2, Ben Worthy examines the origins of the expenses scandal in the FOI Act and the efforts by campaigners, led by Heather Brooke, over a period of years to gain access to the expense claims made by MPs. Worthy provides an in-depth analysis of the workings of FOI, showing how it both constrained and facilitated the release of the data. The chapter draws on interview data with key actors, considering the role of FOI legislation in making government more transparent and accountable to the public. Worthy then provides a comparative look at how other countries with similar FOI legislation, including Ireland, New Zealand, Australia and Canada, and devolved institutions within the UK, have navigated expenses scandals/enquiries.

Chapter 3 looks at the expenses scandal from the inside. Tony Wright, who sat in the Commons from 1992 until 2010 explores the expenses system that MPs designed and administered in a culture of self-regulation. Wright explores the context of the scandal, showing how the pay and expenses system for MPs developed over time and the confusions and behaviours that this gave rise to. He gives considerable attention to the ACA scheme, the core of the expenses regime that allowed MPs to claim for expenses incurred from staying away from their primary residence and the focal point of much of the abuse. In conclusion, Wright explores the consequences of the scandal including reforms that have enabled the House of Commons to seek to restore its reputation by demonstrating its relevance.

The next three chapters consider the electoral impact of the scandal. In Chapter 4, Jennifer vanHeerde-Hudson asks to what extent the expenses scandal was a factor in MPs' decisions to stand down or voluntarily exit the House of Commons. The evidence here suggests that it was: it did not, however, have the impact many suspected given the intense media scrutiny and public outrage following the *Telegraph's* initial revelations. In fact, it was more mundane and less controversial factors such as age and seniority which played a bigger role in MPs' decisions to stand down before the 2010 general election.

In Chapter 5, Charles Pattie and Ron Johnston ask to what extent public anger over the expenses scandal had any measureable impact on the 2010 election outcome with respect to turnout and vote choice. Their analysis shows that despite worrisome predictions, voters didn't take the scandal as a reason to abandon electoral politics. At the constituency level, indignation over MPs' expenses was a mild discouragement to participation, no more. Moreover, the decision to vote or not was influenced by the same factors as in previous elections: what people thought of the scandal had no independent influence once these well-established factors were taken into account. Pattie and Johnston show that voters were undoubtedly disturbed by the expenses scandal, but few MPs who stood for re-election had their prospects damaged by their involvement in the scandal. Valence issues, such as concern over the state of the national and international economies, trumped concerns over the scandal.

In Chapter 6, Nick Vivyan, Markus Wagner and Jessica Tarlov examine voter knowledge of MPs' misconduct in the expenses scandal. Given the institutional make-up of the UK, which encourages voters to see their electoral choice as one between parties and not between candidates, we would not expect many voters to know whether their MP was involved in the scandal or not. They show that, in general, voters' perceptions of their MP's behaviour do correspond, at least somewhat, to their actual involvement in the scandal, and that voters' perceptions were biased by their political predispositions. However, voters did not punish their MPs for their perceived misconduct: the link between perceptions and vote choice was weak compared to that between publicly available information and perceptions.

In Chapter 7, Nicholas Allen and Sarah Birch shift focus and consider the impact of the scandal on public attitudes towards politicians and politics. They argue there is a structural gap between citizens' expectations of politicians on the one hand and their perceptions of politicians' conduct, on the other, that stems from differing understandings of the ethical norms governing politics. Their findings show that, contrary to expectations, the scandal's impact was surprisingly limited. If anything, respondents were less critical of politicians six months after the scandal than immediately before the media frenzy first broke. Allen and Birch discuss various psychological and structural factors that account for this finding and locate the public response to the scandal within the broader mood of disenchantment that currently pervades British politics.

In Chapter 8, Valentino Larcinese and Indraneel Sircar examine whether there is evidence of partisan media bias in coverage of the UK expenses scandal, since certain newspapers have traditional and fairly well-known right- or left-leaning preferences. Drawing on data from widely read UK papers, as well as biographical and electoral data, their results do not show evidence of partisan media bias. However, they show that MPs received higher levels of coverage across all newspapers if they were on the front bench, misappropriated higher sums of money or received more media coverage before the scandal. Their evidence also points to gender differences in media coverage of the scandal.

The regulatory consequences of the scandal are considered in the final two chapters. In Chapter 9, Oonagh Gay traces parliamentary reaction to the Members' expenses crisis, which led to the creation of IPSA. The chapter considers the evolution of IPSA, its role, remit and, importantly, the perceptions of both the public and MPs in regulating the new expenses regime. Gay argues that in its dual role as both regulator and administrator, IPSA has caused tension with its customers, and there are continuing questions about its long-term viability, given the administrative overheads.

In the concluding chapter, Justin Fisher and Jennifer vanHeerde-Hudson consider the impact of the MPs' expenses scandal on British politics and in light of scandals elsewhere. The chapter highlights some of the dangers of political reform in direct response to institutional scandals, in particular how reform efforts can often produce unintended consequences or encourage loophole-seeking behaviour elsewhere. Final consideration is given to the role of IPSA and its role in servicing its clients, restoring confidence in the parliamentary expenses regime and in parties and politicians themselves.

Notes

1. London-based MPs were not eligible for additional costs allowances, but instead received a London Supplement (less than £3,000 in 2007–2008).
2. See http://www.public-standards.gov.uk/Library/Background_Paper_No_2._ Timeline_of_ Events.pdf for a complete timeline to the expenses scandal.
3. The *Telegraph's* revelations were not the first to be brought to the public's attention. Leaks from the disk had emerged in February of 2009 including Jacqui Smith's claim for pornographic films published by the *Sunday Express* and Tony McNulty's parents' home as his second home, thereby qualifying for allowances under the ACA.
4. Katherine Viner, Interview with Gordon Brown, 20 June 2009, *The Guardian* Online.
5. Four MPs have been jailed for illegal expenses claims: Elliot Morley, Jim Devine, Eric Illsley and David Chaytor.
6. See for example, Robin Oakley, 'Anger at UK MPs' Expenses Could Change Politics, 11 May 2009.
7. *The Times*, 'Look at Our Expenses? No You Don't Say French MPs', 25 July 2012.
8. See BBC News Europe, 'French MPs Throw Out Proposal to Audit the Expenses', 26 July 2012.
9. *The Star*, 'Senators and MPs Likely Cheating on Expenses, Canadians Tell Pollsters', 14 June 2013.
10. *New York Times*, 'Corruption Rattles Already Shaky Italians' Trust in Politicians', 17 October 2012.
11. These figures exclude Scotland, where no Tory MPs had been subject to an allegation of sleaze.
12. Welch and Hibbing note: 'This is not consistent with the findings of Peters and Welch. It is consistent with the general pattern of results indicating that previous vote is less predictive for Republican candidates, leaving more clout to be exercised by national partisan swing, scandal, and presumably other, more idiosyncratic variables' (1997: 236).
13. See Chapter 4 for detailed analysis of the impact of the expenses scandal on MPs' decision to stand down.
14. See: http://www.bbc.co.uk/news/uk-politics-12934148, 19 August 2011.
15. *Financial Times*, 'Italy's Scandals Echo the "Tangentopoli"', 21 February 2013.

2
Freedom of Information and the MPs' Expenses Crisis

Ben Worthy

The Freedom of Information (FOI) Act played a key part in triggering the MPs' expenses crisis. Requests made under the Act led to the collation of all MPs' expenses into one record, while the drawn out process of appeal and counter-appeal drew attention to the issue. The number of FOI requests submitted and their impact were shaped by Parliament's unique governance arrangements, resistance to disclosure and the internal Commons culture. However, the crisis was not the result of a simple 'disclosure'; it was an old-fashioned leak that finally exposed information on MPs' expenses.

Introduction

In the wake of the expenses scandal David Cameron, the then Leader of the Opposition, spoke of how the simple provision of information had triggered the expenses crisis:

> 'What the *Daily Telegraph* did – the simple act of providing information to the public – has triggered the biggest shake up of our political system. It is information – not a new law, not some regulation – just the provision of information that has enabled people to take on the political class, demand answers and gets those answers'.
>
> (Cameron in Winnett and Rayner 2009: 348)

This statement, however, obscures a number of key points about the role that the FOI Act played in the expenses crisis.

The revelation of MPs' expenses was not obtained by simply 'providing information' but followed a four-year campaign by journalists using FOI laws. The FOI Act was a 'new law', which worked alongside a very old-fashioned form of information provision, a leak. The expenses crisis was also shaped by the interaction of FOI with the very particular environment and governance structure within Westminster. Far from being a 'simple' story of 'information disseminated', the expenses scandal represents FOI working within a complex chain of events in very particular circumstances.

FOI legislation allows access to information by requests, subject to certain areas being exempt or excluded, such as national security, personal information and certain parts of the policy-making process. The legislation is intended to bring a range of benefits both to the organizations subject to it and to the wider public. Its core aims are to increase transparency and accountability, and secondarily, to improve decision-making procedures, public participation and public trust while fostering a more open culture among secretive institutions (Hazell *et al.* 2010). The UK Act has been in force since 2005 and covers 100,000 public bodies including the House of Commons and House of Lords for their administrative work.

The UK Act, and others operating elsewhere, has an appeal system which comprises an Information Commissioner (ICO), which overturns around a third of government cases, and a second-level tribunal (formerly the Information Tribunal) that supports around 50% of the ICO's rulings (Hazell *et al.* 2010: 81–84). The High Court is the final, rarely used, recourse. FOI also commits public bodies to publish information proactively. While all bodies are protected by certain exemptions, both Houses of Parliament are protected by a unique clause, section 34, which allows information that threatens parliamentary privilege to be excluded. This is subject to the Speaker of either House signing a certificate (Hazell *et al.* 2012).

This chapter draws on a two-year project looking at the impact of FOI on Westminster. The project involved interviewing some 30 MPs and officials, and analysing newspaper articles and logs of requests made to Parliament.[1] The chapter begins by examining other FOI-driven scandals around the world. It then looks at why and how the UK Parliament was covered by FOI and traces the process of the requests relating to expenses. It then maps out the particular circumstance that created the crisis and the role the Act played.

FOI and scandal in comparative view

FOI is a relatively new area of research because most FOI laws have been passed within the last two decades (Ackerman and Ballesteros 2006; Roberts 2006; White 2007; Vleugels 2011). Darch and Underwood's

(2010) study is a first examination of FOI in the developing world, with increasing scholarly interest in India (Roberts 2010) and China with its new Openness in Government Affairs regulation (OGA) (Weibing 2010). These early studies offer a number of key insights into how FOI works. First, the impact of FOI varies as it is shaped by its environment, particularly the politics but also by wider factors of culture and society (White 2007; Darch and Underwood 2010: 7). Second, FOI is also shaped by the varied use to which it is put. In a number of countries the media and NGOs are key users of the law, employing it to highlight controversy or push issues; less visibly, the public use it for day-to-day issues, often to query local government (Roberts 2010; Worthy *et al*. 2011). Finally, FOI is a powerful accountability tool, from Mumbai to Manila to Westminster; however, it rarely works alone and often works in tandem with other mechanisms of accountability or transparency (Worthy 2010).

There has been little analysis of the impact of FOI on parliaments because few legislatures are covered.[2] Yet, despite a lack of coverage, FOI has been used to hold parliaments to account elsewhere. Using FOI to expose expenses or other abuse is not new and was pioneered in early FOI regimes in Australia, New Zealand and Canada in the 1980s. A study by Hazell (1989: 208) concluded that the Acts had led to greater accountability, but 'on a small scale with greater scrutiny of ministers expenses rather than of their management of economic policy'. In Canada, expenses disclosures led to one minister resigning and the 'personal wounding of the Prime Minister's reputation' (Gillis 1998: 152). More recently, Ian Paisley Jnr (Northern Ireland Assembly) was forced to step down when FOI revealed inappropriate lobbying (Hazell *et al*. 2010).

The case of Ireland has very similar parallels to the UK. The Irish Parliament has experienced a slow-burn crisis since 1999. A series of requests revealed dubious spending by Teachta Dálas (MPs), particularly Cabinet members. In 2006, in a further parallel, the Speaker of the lower house was forced to resign over his use of expenses and several Cabinet ministers were implicated (*Sunday Tribune* 2009). The controversy continued into the next decade (*Irish Times* 2012). However, this was part of a wider campaign by journalists and an independent politician to expose corruption and cases of patronage.

By contrast, the Scottish Parliament managed an expenses revelation very differently. In 2006, an FOI request under the separate Scottish FOI Act revealed taxi misuse by the leader of the Scottish Conservatives David McLetchie, who later resigned. In response, and in contrast to the actions of Westminster, MSPs quickly committed to publish expenses information proactively. As the Scottish Information Commissioner pointed out, 'rather than resist further disclosure, the presiding Officer of the Scottish Parliament agreed to the extensive publication of all expense claims, which occasioned no further scandal' (Dunion 2011: 440). Winetrobe (2008: 13) explicitly contrasted the Scottish Parliament at Holyrood with Westminster's behaviour:

> Holyrood's way is to operate both institutionally and parliamentary according to its key principles [and] a different culture and ethos [than Westminster]. Even if resistant at first, it did eventually seize the initiative [and] sought to produce more effective and coherent arrangements, which, by being derived from, its own principles, could maintain or raise public confidence and trust in them and in the Parliament itself.

Winetrobe concluded that 'the Holyrood response to the FOI/allowances challenge has been at much less immediate cost to public trust and confidence in parliamentary institutions' than if the response had been slower (2008: 13).

Why is the UK Parliament covered by the FOI Act?

Few Westminster-type legislatures are subject to FOI. Within Westminster, there were strong fears that Parliament's right to govern itself may be interfered with by rulings from an outside appeal body as well as that FOI may 'open' up privileged areas that need to be kept confidential – such as MP-constituent communications. Canada, Australia and New Zealand's legislatures are all exempt. One of the ironies of the expenses scandal in the UK is that the government did not originally intend FOI to include Parliament. Following practice elsewhere, Parliament was not included in the FOI White Paper and was only added following a suggestion by Public Administration Select Committee (PASC), during the pre-legislative stage. PASC argued: 'There are many administrative functions carried out within Parliament (and) the justification for the exclusion of Parliament has not been made out. The exclusion may well convey the wrong impression to the general public, given the purpose of this legislation' (PASC 1998). There was no objection to this and no mention was made as the FOI bill passed through Parliament. Amid claims that the government was seeking to 'water down' the proposals for FOI, and angry discussion over the strength of protections and power of the appeal bodies, the inclusion of Parliament passed unnoticed by MPs who failed to realize the possible implications.

The crisis unfolds: 2005–2009

The scandal that unfolded over MPs' expenses, first released in detail in May 2009, was not the first time expenses received media attention. In 2004, parliamentary authorities published topline figures of MPs' expenses resulting in some media attention. The *Daily Mail* ran stories about the 'Westminster Gravy Train', though with little follow up in the media (Belsey and Levaine 2005). However, in January 2005, a number of journalists – Heather Brooke, Jon Ungoed-Thomas and Ben Leapmen – and one MP, Norman Baker (Lewes), submitted similar requests for details of MPs' use of their expenses. Brooke's initial request started what would be a four-year battle between this group of journalists and the Commons authorities to reveal the details of expense claims.

It was, however, the publication of the headline expenses that actually motivated the first requests for detailed publication. Brooke spoke of how 'what came out in 2004 were bulk figures in various categories: travel, staff, second homes etc. I wanted the detail. I wanted actual receipts. That's where you find the truth.' (Brooke 2010: 229) Brooke's motivation had stemmed from previous work where she had investigated local politicians' expenses in the state of Washington in the US. She had also been told by journalist Michael Crick of possible abuse by MPs of staffing arrangements and expenses at Westminster (ibid).

This first series of requests constituted a set of false starts and dead ends; Brookes' initial request for the names of staff, to find out if MPs were employing family members, was blocked as was a later request about travel expenses. It was only in 2006 that she made a request about the Additional Cost Allowance (ACA) payments (Brooke 2010: 232–233). At the same time Ben Leapmen and Jon Ungoed-Thomas submitted similar requests. Initial refusals highlighted the difficulties. Two key questions dominated the next few years of appeal and counter-appeal: whether expenses were of legitimate public interest and whether some or all of this information represented an invasion of Members' privacy or even a threat to their safety. As the cases pursued by the journalists began to move through the appeals system they began to gather controversy and media attention. Although the Commons hoped to resolve in their favour, each appeal decision moved progressively more strongly against them. The ICO sought to balance privacy and transparency, but the Information Tribunal and the High Court ruled in favour of maximum openness (Table 2.1).

Table 2.1   The MPs' expenses scandal timeline

October 2004: Publication of limited expenses details.

January 2005: FOI Act comes into effect.

January 2005–2006: A series of FOI requests are made by three journalists (Heather Brooke, Jon Ungoed-Thomas and Ben Leapmen). Some are blocked and others go to appeal.

December 2006–June 2007: David Mclean attempts to pass a bill excluding Parliament from FOI.

June 2007: The ICO issues decision notice on ACA. The decision allows some access while protecting private and sensitive information.

February 2008: Information Tribunal hearing reveals existence of controversial 'John Lewis List' and rules allowances to be disclosed more fully than the ICO. It suggests only protecting Members where absolutely necessary.

May 2008: The High Court upholds the strong Tribunal ruling and orders the House of Commons to disclose all but the most sensitive personal information (bank details, exact address). Redaction begins.

May 2009: *Telegraph* begins detailing expenses abuse. Speaker Michael Martin resigns.

June 2009: Parliament publishes expenses belatedly.

July 2009: IPSA created to oversee the payment of expenses.

January–May 2011: A number of MPs are convicted and sentenced for expenses abuse.

May 2010–November 2012: A series of expenses revelations lead to individual resignations including David Laws MP and Denis MacShane MP.

Source: Adapted from Kelso 2011: 52–53 and CSPL 2009.

The then ICO, Richard Thomas, sought to resolve these issues when, in his judgement, the appeal over the requests, which were grouped together, was made:

> The Commissioner considers that there is a legitimate and general public interest in access to information in relation to the expenditure of the public funds falling within the Additional Cost Allowance. However, in this case there is greater potential than with travel expenses for intrusion into the private lives of MPs and their families [...] It is not necessary for fully itemised amounts to be disclosed in order meet the legitimate interest of members of the public in knowing how public money has been spent.
>
> (ICO 2007 FS50070469: 10)

The ICO sought to strike a balance: 'that conclusion, however, relates to the fully itemised details. The same conclusion does not apply to a more aggregated account of the requested information.' The Commissioner then outlined a set of 12 areas to be published, including mortgage costs, hotel expenses, food, service charges, utilities and furnishings (ICO 2007 FS50070469: 10).

Although the ICO ruled that only some details should be released, the House of Commons took the case to the next level of appeal, the Information Tribunal. Here the Commons argued that MPs were accountable for their spending at the ballot box and this was enough. In parallel, FOI pressure was building. It was claimed that by 2007 'the House had received approximately 167 requests for information about Members' allowances, since FOIA came into effect', most concerning MPs' travel (Information Tribunal EA/0006/0015 and 0016: 5–7).

The key Tribunal case took place in April 2008, when the body looked at a number of the FOI appeals at once from the journalists pursuing similar lines on ACA. It became clear during the hearing that there was a problem with the expenses system, outlined in the 'Green Book', the rulebook that detailed how expenses could be used. The system may, it appeared, be vague enough to hide abuse:

> The guidance on ACA in the Green Book is incomplete. No definitive statement of the rules for ACA is available to the public, or even to MPs themselves. It is administered by […] a confidential list indicating acceptable costs for certain classes of item based on prices derived from the John Lewis website. The list is kept secret from Members lest the maximum allowable prices become the going rate. Members are not trusted to have access to it.
>
> (Information Tribunal EA/2007/0060 and others,
> 26 February 2008)

Moreover, the list itself contained loopholes and gaps:

> The recent editions of the Green Book require receipts for hotel expenditure, but otherwise no receipts for any item up to £250, or for any amount in the case of food […] Mr Walker [representing Parliament] considered that Members were well aware of the limit on food, but was unable to say by what means they were made aware, except that those who claimed more than £400 per month would have been advised by individual letters.
>
> (Information Tribunal EA/2007/0060 and others, 26 February)

It was only at the Tribunal that many in the media were made aware of the issue of expenses when the so-called 'John Lewis list' was revealed. This detailed how 'middle England's favourite department store' was used as a 'suitable benchmark' for MPs' expenses claims (Winnett and Rayner 2009: 24).

The Tribunal had already ruled on travel expenses in 2007 but in its ruling on ACA the Tribunal made a very strong case for the information to be released: 'The ACA system is so deeply flawed, the shortfall in accountability is so substantial and the necessity of full disclosure so convincingly established, that only the most pressing privacy needs should in our view be permitted to prevail' (Information Tribunal, EA/2007/0060 and others, 26 February 2008). Around this time, it emerged that MP Derek Conway had been paying members of his family for work that had not been done (CSPL 2009). This added further impetuous to the story and the suspicion by journalists that FOI was on the verge of revealing a scandal. The case was then pushed to the High Court by the Commons authorities, a rarely used, highest stage of appeal. Any hope that it would 'protect' the Commons were soon dashed. Like the Tribunal, the court came down clearly on the side of public interest:

> We have no doubt that the public interest is at stake. We are not here dealing with idle gossip, or public curiosity about what in truth are trivialities. The expenditure of public money through the payment of MPs' salaries and allowances is a matter of direct and reasonable interest to taxpayers [...] In the end they bear on public confidence in the operation of our democratic system at its very pinnacle, the House of Commons itself. The nature of the legitimate public interest engaged by these applications is obvious.
>
> (High Court 2008 [2008] EWHC 1084 (Admin) Case No: CO2888/2008)

Following the High Court's ruling, the Commons committed to publishing details of ACA claims. According to the journalists who broke the story, as the information was being redacted to remove personal details, disgruntled soldiers working as security guards at the redaction location decided to leak the information having compared their lack of equipment in Iraq with the apparent abuse by MPs (Winnett and Rayner 2009: 357). Rumours circulated of the existence a 'disk' of the raw, unredacted expenses. It was offered to a number of papers and was bought by the *Daily Telegraph*, which began publishing them in May 2009 (Winnett and Rayner 2009: 75). Parliament released the redacted details a month later, but the damage had already been done.

The expenses scandal

When the scandal unfolded in 2009, it was characterized as an 'incendiary device thrown directly at the political establishment' (Kelso 2009: 334). Although the leaked information was given on the condition it be used to exposure the behaviour of all political parties equally, initial revelations began with the Cabinet, focusing on Gordon Brown's relatively minor claims. It then highlighted high-profile Members and MPs and only later moved on to the Conservatives, giving senior Conservatives a crucial three-day breathing space to defend themselves and seize the political initiative, including David Cameron who had claimed £80,000 over five years on his second home allowance (*The Guardian* 10 December 2009). Initial media and public attention on high-profile and unusual uses of parliamentary expenses, such as claims for a duck house or moat cleaning on expenses, hid a wide variety of claims – from the trivial to very serious allegations of tax avoidance.

The scandal also led to intense discussion of constitutional reform including suggestions for MPs' recall, changes to the voting system (which later played into the 2011 Alternative Vote (AV) referendum) and a reduction in the number of MPs. However, to date, the major change has been the introduction of the Independent Parliamentary Standards Authority (IPSA) (see Chapter 9), created to independently administer and monitor MPs' expenses (Hazell *et al.* 2012).

That the scandal came as a shock to the public, the media or MPs is somewhat surprising as FOI has long played a part in uncovering expenses misuse and other dubious activities in many other regimes and there were clear signs that FOI would be used for such issues here. Since 2005, FOI requests to Parliament had overwhelmingly focused on the House of Commons and, within this, on the activities of MPs (Worthy and Bourke 2011). Moreover, signals that the expenses system was, at the very least, problematic could be seen as early as 2002. A Commons official was quoted as saying in 2002 that 'many of us are worried about the way [expenses are] administered, but when we raise queries we are told it's all above-board' (*Mail on Sunday* 2002). Tony Wright, then Chairman of PASC, issued an even clearer warning at the same time: 'My guess is that any future issues with Members of Parliament are far more likely to occur around issues to do with the allowances system [. . .] Unless you get hold of these issues now and think about them, they will come and hit us later on' (Wright in Rush and Giddings 2010).

The decision in 2004 to release some expenses details was indicative of an understanding by at least some in Parliament that the 'public' wished to know about the issue. Nick Harvey MP spoke in 2007 of his concerns when discussing reform to expenses:

> There are those who are upset that the report recommends that Members ought not in future to be allowed to purchase items with their additional costs allowance. I think that they will have the devil's own job if we continue with the existing system. In an era when freedom of information requires every receipt to be perused by the public, they would have a difficulty in justifying the purchase of televisions, fridges, three-piece suites, curtains, carpets and whatever else.
>
> (HC Debates, 3 July 2008, c1102)

Despite these warnings and premonitions, the scandal happened. The way in which it did was determined not just by the FOI requests but by how various institutional, cultural and contextual factors shaped the release of the information: the opaque expenses system, the unique way in which the Commons was governed and the resistance to openness.

The opaque system, particularly around ACA claims, was partially responsible for the resulting spectacle. The ACA system was based on an informal agreement between Margret Thatcher and Michael Foot made in the early 1980s, permitting maximum allowance claims to increase while salaries remained relatively static (see Chapter 3 for details). The Kelly Review spoke of how this was in part a political failure: 'It has been argued that this situation came about partly because of the unwillingness of successive governments to increase MPs' pay for fear of a political backlash – a reluctance which has led, at times quite explicitly, to greater generosity in setting the regime for expenses' (Kelly 2009: 27). A number of interviewees also spoke of how signals of varying degrees of subtlety also informed MPs that ACA could be regarded as a 'top up' to salary and that claiming the maximum was the norm, an example of the 'socialisation' process of Westminster which was stronger than codified rules (Allen and Birch 2009; Kelso 2009; Rush and Giddings 2010).

The Information Tribunal described a 'laxity of and lack of clarity in the rules of the ACA [. . .] redolent of a culture very different from that which exists in the commercial sphere or in most other public sector organisations today'. The system was further hampered by the lack of any checks: 'To add to the lack of transparency the system was not even audited properly [...] If an Honourable Member certified that an expense had been properly incurred, that was regarded as the end of the matter' (Information Tribunal EA/2007/0060 and others, 26 February 2008: 2). There was also 'a culture of deference in the House, which made it difficult for members of staff to challenge claims submitted by MPs in the way which might be expected of finance staff in other organisations' (2008: 27). The lack of checks or an overview also meant that there was no one with a clear picture of what was happening within the system as a whole. When the FOI requests arrived few were sure of what, if the information was released, it would reveal.

The unique expenses system existed within a wider unique system that exacerbated the problem: the way in which the Commons is governed. Parliament is governed by its Members, a situation further complicated by the pressures of party competition and hierarchy. This meant that FOI was dealt with in a very different way. In a government department or local authority, a sensitive or 'difficult' request would eventually be considered by senior officials and politicians, in consultation with lawyers and the FOI officer. However, the system in Parliament was different and perhaps more cumbersome, involving the Members Estimate Committee and others: 'The usual process is to consult with the Members Estimate Committee (MEC), which replaced the House of Commons Commission, on a request before replying. The chair would then consider the request in the light of the views of the MEC and any legal advice from the House's legal advisors' (Information Tribunal EA/0006/0015 and 0016: 5–7).

The figures from the MEC were subject to competing interests, as overseers, but also politicians, with the added complication of being, at least in part, reliant on legal advice. Moreover, the Speaker of the House, looked to as a figure who could take 'action' on the issue, does not have the same relationship to MPs as a 'Minister and a ministry'. The Commons itself has no single dominant 'corporate identity' or, as one interviewee put it 'Parliament as an institution has a vacuum at the heart of it.' Tony Wright argues that this means 'there is no Parliament in collective sense at all [...] there is no voice of Parliament that can be collectively orchestrated' (2004: 871). Parliament thus did not have a figure or a body to 'take charge'. It was unclear within the institution who could or should take action. This was further complicated by a human factor: 'a number of those who ought to have shown leadership in maintaining high standards failed at key points to do so' (Kelly 2009: 2).

As the FOI requests moved through the appeal system a number of MPs and officials spoke of a 'sense of drift' as Members hoped someone would find a solution but were unsure who would or could do so and a pervading 'state of paralysis' (Winnett and Rayner 2009: 339). The internal discussions were influenced by a reliance, or indeed an over-reliance, on legal advice. It was alleged that the Speaker swapped legal teams when one team failed to give him the answers he wanted (Winnett and Rayner 2009: 25). The same phenomenon had been seen before with Parliament. Following the 1994 cash-for-questions scandal, the 'impotence of the Commons in the face of a threat' was shown as political division and partisanship led to 'total disarray' (Gay 2004: 104).

The difficulties were further compounded by a blind spot both over how open or secret the Commons was and, as later investigation showed, the scale of expenses abuse. Parliament was already a very open institution. New outreach work and the rise of websites such as theyworkforyou.com, which lists MPs voting records and activities, had made it more open still. Many MPs thus felt they were 'open'. Here the notion that Parliament was 'transparent' led to failure to appreciate the consequences of FOI exposing those areas that were not. The sense of 'drift' may have been reinforced by the Commons culture, bound up in its own uniqueness, a political equivalent of the 'too big to fail' thesis. Interviewees were divided on the extent to which the Commons had changed. Some felt it was driving a new openness, championed by an energetic leader of the Commons, but others expressed concerns that it could lead to 'superficial compliance' with a mechanistic openness but a continuing secretive culture (Hazell *et al.* 2012).

The only certainty in the response was resistance to the FOI requests. At each stage press attention and interest was engaged as the 'battle' went on. The persistence of the press, and the sense that something was being 'hidden', heightened the determination of those pursuing the information and, ultimately, made the leak more likely. The information would have been damaging at any point, but the drawn out process worsened it. Kelly (2009: 2) highlighted this: 'One of the more shameful aspects of the whole episode is the way in which the House of Commons fought for so long against the notion that the Freedom of Information Act should apply to them in the same way as it does to everyone else in public life.'

The first way in which resistance manifested itself was by fighting the appeal, with the Commons authorities appealing the decision to the ICO, the Tribunal and the High Court. At each stage legal advice may have driven the view that the next stage would be the one where the requests would finally be blocked. While the appeal process was reactive, in other ways resistance was more overt and active. In 2007 David Mclean's Private Members' Bill proposed taking the Commons outside of the ambit of FOI, citing the need to protect the privacy of MPs. The bill was alleged to have the tacit support of both the Labour front bench and David Cameron and did survive unusually long for a Private Members' Bill (Brooke 2009). Many MPs and peers opposed the bill, though some agreed with the ostensible justification for the bill to protect privacy. However, any tacit or apparent consensus broke down under the pressure of a strong media campaign against the bill, which led to it being dropped in the Lords. Numerous officials and peers interviewed felt that the justification for the bill concealed more personal motives and peers labelled it a 'cynical' move.

Despite the bill's failure, then Justice Minister Jack Straw later used provisions in the Act to exempt certain security and travel information in 2008. In 2009, just five months before the leak, Leader of the House Harriet Harman again proposed removing both Houses from FOI but the beginnings of media storm and opposition attacks caused it to be dropped (Kelly 2009a). The effect of the resistance was to continually stoke media interest and to cast Parliament in a poor light, which would be worsened when the information was released.

Not all Members resisted FOI, again reflecting the fragmented nature of Parliament. A group of MPs strongly opposed the resistance and some had already published details of their expenses voluntarily (Allington and Peele 2010). Many Members were unaware of the pressure for transparency around their expenses or, more likely, did not give it much attention.

FOI: Trigger and impact

Although the media and public came to learn of MPs' expenses via a leak, it was ultimately FOI requests that led to the collation expenses data that became the disk bought by the *Daily Telegraph*. But the requests did not work alone in exposing expenses claims; the preceding leak of unredacted information was crucial. When the Commons finally released its own version in June 2009, it was described as a 'sea of black ink' with much essential information censored or redacted. According to Winnett and Rayner, 'none of the scams uncovered by the Telegraph would have ever come to light if there had not been a leak of the uncensored version' (2009: 347). They claim that the changes of address that exposed the 'flipping' of first or second homes or possible tax avoidance would not have been uncovered had it only been released 'officially' by FOI (2009: 347). Without the requests there would have been no reason for such information to be collated; furthermore, access to the documents provided evidence of wrongdoing, rather than allegations that had been circulating.

In some ways the expenses crisis is an atypical use of FOI. More generally, it is used as part of a wider campaign by NGOs or journalists over, for example, less high-profile issues such as library closures. FOI requests are frequently part of a patient building up of evidence rather than finding a 'smoking gun' (Worthy *et al.* 2011) as demonstrated by Chris Ames' painstaking process of filing requests, compiling information around the construction of the Weapons of Mass Destruction [WMD] dossier, the so-called 'dodgy dossier'. Over the course of more than five years, Ames slowly unearthed emails and successively earlier drafts of the paper that challenged the official version of events (Hazell *et al.* 2010). Similarly, the All Party Group on Extraordinary Rendition patiently used FOI requests to the US and UK governments over many years to help piece together the record of so-called rendition flights involved in the alleged torture of terrorist suspects (Worthy and Hazell 2010).

The requests and resulting scandal have had an indelible effect on Parliament. The scandal has led to changes in the House of Commons with the creation of IPSA that, for the first time, has taken expenses and salaries outside of Parliament's control. IPSA remains a controversial creation with MPs' discontent fed occasionally by leadership attacks upon it (for a detailed discussion, see Chapter 9). The expenses issue has also bled over into the Lords, where allowances have been reformed and, indirectly due to other requests, changes have been made to peers' tax status (Hazell *et al.* 2012). It also fed into the debates on AV and reducing the size of the Commons (Kelso 2011).

The crisis also triggered a wave of media interest in Parliament. Since 2009 expenses revelations have led to several high-profile resignations, including one serving and one former Minister, as well as damage to politicians and the Speaker. In 2010, David Laws MP, seen as a key player in the new Coalition government, resigned as Chief Secretary to the Treasury when it was revealed that his rent payments went to his partner (*The Guardian* 29 May 2010). In October 2012, Speaker John Bercow wrote to IPSA to ask to keep secret, for data protection reasons, details of MPs' landlords. The media alleged this would cover up the fact that some MPs rented to each other. *The Telegraph* saw this as evidence that parliamentary authorities had failed to absorb the lessons of the scandal or adapt to the new circumstances. An editorial argued that John Bercow had 'not kept his word on MPs' expenses':

> Mr Bercow's attitude sits oddly with his avowed determination to ensure that Parliament is seen to have cleaned up its act [...] if there was one lesson that the parliamentary authorities should have learnt from the expenses scandal three years ago, it was surely the need to be open and transparent. After all, it was their efforts to suppress information about the abuse of MPs' allowances that precipitated the crisis [...] History appears to be repeating itself.
>
> (*Telegraph* 18 October 2012)

In the same week Chancellor George Osborne's use of first-class seats while travelling on a standard class ticket (which included allegations he refused to pay for an upgrade or move) led to claims that MPs were exploiting loopholes in the new expenses system (*The Guardian* 21 October 2012).

The following month, in November 2012, after an aborted police investigation, the House of Commons Standards and Privileges Committee ruled on former Minister Denis MacShane's expenses abuse case that included the submission of false invoices. The Committee argued that as 'this is so far from what would be acceptable in any walk of life that we recommend that Mr MacShane be suspended from the service of the House for twelve months' (Standards and Privileges 2012: 24). Denis MacShane subsequently resigned (*Telegraph* 3 November 2012).

The 'expenses' effect continues to spread outwards across other public bodies. The scandal has also initiated FOI requests to other public bodies for details of salaries and expense accounts, from local authorities to police forces and universities. Local authorities in England reported a wave of FOI requests related to the allowances and salaries of local politicians and officials, as well as a rise in requests generally (Worthy *et al.* 2011). In April 2012, for example, FOI requests to the Northern Irish Assembly revealed details of Members' trips (BBC 19 April 2012) while *The Guardian* revealed details of gifts and donations given to MP and peers (*The Guardian* 10 April 2012).

Conclusion

The FOI Act was crucial in triggering the MPs' expenses scandal. Parallel FOI requests by a group of journalists set in motion forces that ultimately provided evidence for the widespread abuse of parliamentary expenses for the first time. The appeal system and the slow drip of revelations increased pressure and attention. Although its long-term effects are not yet known, the crisis has led to a new body with independent oversight of Parliament, spun a variety of attempted reforms and profoundly influenced public attitudes.

FOI also worked in a very particular context. Although the scandal would have been damaging in any circumstances, it was exacerbated by a number of institutional and cultural factors. The governance structure of Parliament paralysed the process and led to inactivity and uncertainty, compounded by faulty leadership. The Commons secrecy culture led to efforts to thwart transparency, although within the House may MPs were supportive of efforts to reform the expenses regime. FOI requests also worked alongside other, more old-fashioned accountability instruments; investigative journalists doggedly pursuing an issue. The idea that the expenses crisis was a 'simple' provision of information is far from the truth.

Notes

1. The wider impact of FOI on Parliament can be seen in Worthy and Bourke (2011) and Hazell, Bourke and Worthy (2012).
2. See Snell and Upcher 2003; Mendel 2005; White 2007; Worthy and Hazell 2010 for studies that looked at its use by parliamentarians.

3
Inside a Scandal

Tony Wright

This chapter provides an insider account of the expenses scandal. The background to the scandal is explained, in terms of a culture of self-regulation, along with a description of how MPs sought to respond to the scandal when it broke. The scandal is then given context by a brief history of how the pay and expenses system for MPs had developed over time; and the confusions and behaviours that this had given rise to. Finally some of the consequences of the scandal are explored, including reforms that have enabled the House of Commons to seek to restore its reputation by demonstrating its relevance.

Introduction

> We have been set up at a time when the House of Commons is going through a crisis of confidence not experienced in our lifetimes.
> (Rebuilding the House, House of Commons
> Reform Committee, 2009)

I was there when it happened. Being in the House of Commons in May 2009, and for many months afterwards, felt rather like finding yourself in the middle of a battlefield. The enemy, an assorted collection of freedom of information campaigners, *Daily Telegraph* journalists and retired civil servants, had landed a succession of heavy mortars right into the heart of the parliamentary compound. The effects were devastating. There were casualties on all sides, some fatal. Many were wandering around in a daze. Everyone was in fear for their political lives. Further strikes were expected. An angry mob was at the gate. Leaders were in panic. Paralysis prevailed. Nobody could see how it would all end, except that it would end badly. Some even wondered if the compound could ever be rebuilt.

What was remarkable was that it was not some great issue of policy or principle that had shaken Parliament to its foundations, but a pathetic scandal about expenses. Yet this was also what made it so toxic for the whole political class, because it touched a raw nerve in the public and provided daily ammunition for the media on something that everyone could understand. Policy issues might be complicated, but fiddled expenses were not. The expenses scandal cut through rhetoric and reputation and exposed the individual ethical behaviour of politicians to public view. It also revealed the extent to which MPs had been keen to impose scrutiny and regulation on the activities of everyone but themselves.

The defensces offered by some MPs only served to make matters worse: that a malevolent media was out to get them; that they were only doing what was allowed by the rules; that they had been encouraged by the system to claim as much as possible; and that exploiting allowances was an accepted means of compensating for an inadequate salary. In other words, the offenders were in fact victims. Not surprisingly, none of this cut much ice with press or public, although it undoubtedly helped to keep spirits up in the beleaguered solidarity of the parliamentary bunker.

For MPs and Parliament, it was not a scandal that arrived like a bolt from the blue. It had been long in gestation. Everyone involved in the system of parliamentary expenses and allowances, whether as claimant or administrator, could not have failed to be aware that it was a system wide open to abuse. When I arrived in the Commons in 1992, I was provided with a sheaf of differently coloured forms on which I would make claims for the various expenses and allowances. This involved inserting a figure, signing a declaration (as an Honourable Member) to say that I had incurred the expense for a proper parliamentary purpose, and submitting it for payment. No supporting evidence was required, no inquiries made and no audit undertaken. It soon became pretty clear to me (and I suspect to everyone else) that here was a scandal waiting to happen.

At that time, though, I did not know the half of it. I could see that there were MPs claiming the maximum accommodation allowance (often by just dividing the allowable total by 12 monthly amounts) irrespective of actual housing costs, or claiming the maximum allowable mileage figure irrespective of actual travel costs, or having salaries paid to family members without checks on what they were doing for the money, or the practice of 'flipping' homes that came to represent some of the worst excesses of the scandal, but had no idea about the esoteric and extravagant items (duck houses!) that some were claiming for. It was only years later, when disquiet had started to grow and questions had begun to be asked, that evidence of actual housing costs and receipts for goods began to be required, providing the evidence that the inquiries prompted by the scandal could subsequently draw upon.

The view of expenses from inside the Commons

However what I did come to learn early on was that this whole matter of expenses and allowances was Parliament's dirty secret. It was part of the culture of the place, private and closely guarded, with resolute protectors against prying inquirers. This was the self-regulation of a sovereign Parliament composed of Honourable Members. New Members were soon inducted into this culture. It was in this spirit that I had it explained to me by a senior colleague how I could maximize my travel expenses by having a diesel car with the largest engine, thereby getting both the highest (and very generous) mileage allowance and the best mileage. He even identified the precise model of vehicle, which he described as being the 'MPs' car'. When I later recounted this story in a Commons debate on mileage allowances, intended as an amusing anecdote, I was accosted afterwards by an angry colleague (someone who was to preside over the expenses system), who told me that I would 'never be forgiven' for what I had said. A small incident, but an indication that this whole territory of expenses was a parliamentary no-go area. Perhaps this sense that the club would be unforgiving to anyone who dared to lift the veil helps to explain why the issue remained buried for so long.[1]

It would have remained so, had it not eventually been for the Freedom of Information (FOI) Act and those who used it, already well detailed in Chapter 2. I can add one ingredient to that story. In 1999 I became chair of the Public Administration Select Committee and one of our first tasks was to examine the proposed FOI legislation in draft. It was pointed out to us in evidence that the draft bill did not include Parliament among the public bodies that it applied to. We therefore recommended that Parliament should be included. This was accepted by Jack Straw, the minister in charge of the bill, and approved by the Commons without demur. At that time none of us, certainly not me, had any idea what the momentous implications of this inclusion would be.

Had I been asked at this period where any scandal about expenses was most likely to arise, I would have identified the consequences of the decision taken back in 1985 that allowed MPs to have mortgage interest on property paid, and not just rent as under the previous rules. The logic of this decision was impeccable: it gave MPs more housing choice and the maximum allowance remained the same. Yet it also meant that from this moment MPs became interested in property deals, as well as in the expenditure needed to maintain and improve properties. The whole second homes issue had been born. This was to be the source of many later problems. In the 1960s a group of reform-minded Labour MPs had floated the radical idea of one day having 'hostel accommodation' for Members; but this distant nirvana had instead become the second home. In an inflationary property market, especially in London, this also meant that MPs were able to make significant capital gains from property where the mortgage interest had been paid by the taxpayer.

A missed opportunity?

It was this that I had in mind when I gave oral evidence to the Committee on Standards in Public Life (CSPL) in 2002, having been invited as a select committee chairman with an interest in standards issues. The Committee was examining general issues about the parliamentary code of conduct, but at the end of my evidence I offered the Committee this further thought:

> My guess is that any future difficulties with Members of Parliament are far more likely to occur around issues to do with the allowances that they now get [...] If you have lax rules, I'm afraid that you will have lax use of money [...] Unless you get hold of these issues now and think about them, they will come and hit us later on.[2]

This was intended to be a signal to the Committee that here was an issue that it should turn its attention to; it was the only independent watchdog that had the ability to do this. There was no chance of the Commons undertaking serious reform of the expenses system for itself, which meant that any push had to come from elsewhere. A body that had been set up by John Major, in response to allegations of sleaze, to safeguard standards of conduct in public life was the obvious, and only, body to provide this.

Its failure to do so is part of the expenses story. It suffered from the disability that it could only investigate matters that it had agreed with the government (or so it evidently believed). There was certainly no official desire to have the parliamentary expenses system examined, as that would only bring both parliamentary and public trouble. I was told privately by Sir Alistair Graham, who had become chair of CSPL, that he had been warned off by Downing Street from doing any inquiry on the matter. It was only when the scandal had exploded into public view that the CSPL was finally called into action. One of the scandal's lessons is that watchdogs need to be able to bite, and in good time.

Even at the beginning of 2008, when the case of Conservative MP Derek Conway brought the first real indication of the scandal to come, the CSPL was unwilling to get involved. What the Conway case revealed was that it was possible to have public money paid to a relative (in his case, a son) for work that had not been done. It exposed the capacity of the system to enable glaring abuse to take place. Other cases on different fronts made the same point. Journalists like Peter Oborne had started to dig into the expenses issue. When the Conway case broke, I was away from the Commons recovering from medical treatment but fired off a letter from my sick bed (on 5 February 2008) to Sir Christopher Kelly, who had become chair of CSPL. I reproduce this letter here as it gives a flavour of the moment, and of my frustration:

Dear Sir Christopher,

I write because I am concerned that you have not already announced that the Committee on Standards in Public Life will be conducting an immediate inquiry into the whole system of MPs' allowances.

When we met, on your appointment, you will recall that I suggested the need for such an inquiry. I also said this in evidence to your Committee back in 2002. In view of current events, this has now become a matter of trust at the heart of our public life. If this is not something for your Committee to respond to, in view of the reasons for its existence, I do not know what is.

It is simply not acceptable, in terms of public trust, for an internal Commons committee to be the only body to examine this issue. Nor is it only a question of transparency and better reporting. The whole allowance system needs examining, and justifying, along with arrangements for audit and scrutiny.

The fact is that the current system is wide open to abuse on a number of fronts. If there are opportunities to use public money for private gain, that is corruption and corrodes public trust more than anything else.

You told me that you had only accepted the chairmanship of the Committee on the basis that it would not be prevented from examining any area of concern. I suspect that there is pressure on you currently not to get involved. I urge you to resist such pressure and to insist on an immediate inquiry being launched by the Committee. This is precisely what it was set up for. In my view you would be fully entitled to say that you were unable to continue in your role if you were prevented from undertaking this inquiry now.

We urgently need an inquiry that is independent and authoritative. Only your committee can undertake this, and the restoration of public trust demands it.

In his reply, Sir Christopher said that the Committee was 'currently considering its future work programme'. It had 'certainly not ruled out the possibility of such an inquiry' but wanted to see the outcome of the various parliamentary and political initiatives before making a decision. Back in 2002 there was perhaps some excuse for the CSPL not wanting to get involved, but in the circumstances of early 2008, it seemed to me both inexplicable and indefensible. It was a major missed opportunity. By the time the Committee did undertake its inquiry in 2009, the scandal had already happened.

A plague on the house: A scandal unfolds

The explosion came in the form of the *Daily Telegraph* disclosures of expenses claims, obtained from a stolen disk, and delivered daily over an extended period to deadly effect. MPs braced themselves for their turn, having witnessed the lethal impact on colleagues. Talk in the Commons was of nothing else and animosity against the *Telegraph* was intense. The day prior to publication the MP would receive a message from the newspaper with details of what was to be published about them, thus allowing a pre-publication response, producing much nervous checking of telephones and emails. I was in my constituency when I got mine. I was alarmed at its contents, until I realized they had confused me with another MP of the same name (a confusion that played a recurrent part in 'my' scandal). It was with particular satisfaction that I was able to point this out to them in my reply.

There was much protesting from MPs that some of the information was misleading and unfair, that it did not give a true picture of where the money went (e.g. that most went on staff salaries not into their own pockets) and that it failed to understand just what MPs did. None of this impressed the press or public, nor could it detract from the scale of abuse that had been revealed. MPs had to devote themselves to a fire-fighting operation in a desperate bid to save reputations and their seats. For much of the final year of the Parliament, this was their dominating preoccupation.

When the media storm was at its height, MPs would return from their constituencies with stories of the venomous abuse that was being directed at them and their families. Their bulging mailbags told the same story. Usually a political storm, however intense at the time, passes fairly quickly as interest wanes and attention turns elsewhere. This was different. It was a scandal that refused to go away. Each response to the scandal gave it renewed life. This was certainly true of the Legg inquiry into past expenses claims, the results of which MPs awaited with dread. Then there was the period when the findings were open to challenge and review, before finally being confirmed. All this kept the scandal on the boil and MPs began to despair that it would ever go away.

It was in the constituency, and in their constituency party, that the front line in the battle was being conducted for most MPs. That is where their fate would be determined (except in those cases where it had already been determined by their party leaderships). They either had to provide reassurance that they were not among the miscreants or plausible explanation if they were. Some decided that it was a good moment to announce an intention to retire. The press storm was intense and relentless, but for MPs themselves their local newspapers played a particularly important role. They carried the details of the expenses claims of local MPs, chased them for comments and conveyed public reaction. In turn, MPs needed to supply the local press with regular self-justificatory statements. I produced a statement setting out all the expenses details about myself, so that I could reassure constituents about my own position. However it was not always easy for some local newspapers to understand the intricacies of the expenses system that they were reporting, amid all the figures and claims that were circulating, and this could (certainly in my experience) produce errors that required regular correction and apology.[3]

I had never found it particularly difficult to operate the expenses system as it was intended. Nor did it seem difficult to work out what an appropriate expenses system for MPs would look like. There were certain expenses that were necessary for doing the job of an MP and these were paid for under the various headings. Representing a Midlands constituency, I needed somewhere to live in London on three nights a week. So I rented a one-bedroom flat, for which the rent was reimbursed. I authorized direct payment for staff I employed and the cost of office equipment and supplies. My train fares (first class) to London were paid for, along with constituency car mileage. The only area I found troubling was furnishing my flat (and replacing items when they wore out). On the one hand, I only bought this stuff because I needed to live there to do the job; but on the other hand, the public purse was paying for items that would belong to me. I only discovered that there was something called a 'John Lewis list' as a benchmark for claims when the scandal erupted, as I think did many MPs. Its existence had never been advertised and it had clearly not prevented some very extravagant claims being paid. As time went on, I solved this dilemma for myself by putting in claims for only half the cost of items I bought. This seemed to me to be a reasonable way of reconciling the competing considerations. However, there was no guidance or rules about this, and it did not seem satisfactory that I had to devise these for myself.

What I did not realize was that some MPs were operating the expenses system in a quite different way. When I became an MP I could have claimed the maximum accommodation allowance for living in London while making other arrangements; I could have authorized salaries to be paid to my wife or other relatives; I could have claimed for hundreds of miles I had not driven; and could have claimed for home and garden maintenance that was not done. All this would have been possible because of the lax way in which the system operated; but even this did not exhaust the list of possible abuses, as the eventual scandal was to reveal.

This did not mean that those MPs who did abuse the system were uniquely venal, however dishonourable they might have been. The system was so poorly regulated that it offered a standing invitation to abuse, which was too easy to accept. Those in other occupations, faced with an equally lax system, might well have responded in a similar way. Yet, there is one fundamental difference: this is that MPs controlled the system for themselves. They devised the rules and protected them zealously against external scrutiny and regulation. They invented and inflated their own allowances. Right up to the end, they tried to fight off disclosure, including a last-ditch attempt to disapply the FOI Act to Parliament. The rules they said they had followed were ones they had made up for themselves.

MPs' expenses: A substitute for pay?

At this point it may be useful to say something briefly about the history of parliamentary pay and allowances, as this provides the indispensable context for the scandal when it came. Over the previous century a number of recurrent questions had been asked whenever the matter was discussed. How much was it appropriate to pay an MP? What was the balance between salary and expenses? Should being an MP be seen as a full-time or part-time job? Should MPs set their own pay and allowances or should this task be given to a separate body? Should their pay be linked to that of other groups in the public sector? These and other questions were endlessly revisited over the years; and when the scandal came they were asked all over again.

The starting point is 1911, when – following the Osborne Judgement in the House of Lords against the political levy that had enabled trade unions to support MPs – the Liberal government introduced a payment of £400 for Members. This was denounced by Unionists on the grounds that it would corrupt politics and create a class of professional politicians. Lloyd George responded by claiming that the payment was not really a salary but 'just an allowance' and declared that: 'The only principle of payment in the public service is that you should make an allowance to a man to enable him to maintain himself comfortably and honourably, but not luxuriously, during the time he is rendering service to the State.'[4] When the Inland Revenue decided to treat a quarter of this payment as tax-free expenses, the confusion between salary and expenses in the payment was early established.

A select committee returned to the issue in 1920, with many of the same arguments about whether MPs should be paid at all and whether any payment should be regarded as a salary being rehearsed again. The committee said that it recognized 'the difficult financial position of certain Members at the present time' and, although not recommending a salary increase, proposed free travel and postage and raised the question of whether more of the salary should be treated as tax-free expenses. In the event the House voted against all these proposals, although in 1924 the Labour government introduced free railway passes for Members (only in 1961 was a car allowance also introduced).

It was not until 1937 that Members' pay was raised, to £600, with Baldwin declaring that: 'Once you admit that everybody has a right to be elected to this House if he can, you cannot logically create or leave a financial bar.' A change in mood on the issue was evident by this time. It was further evident when the Labour government elected in 1945 set up a new committee to examine the matter. This noted the financial pressure on many Members and recommended a salary increase to £1,000, with half of that to be regarded as tax-free expenses. The salary increase was accepted, but not the proposal on expenses. It is also interesting that this committee still rejected the idea of a 'professional salary' on the grounds that:

> though a Member may be called upon to devote a great deal of time to the business of the House, he has complete freedom to allot his time between his parliamentary duties, either at Westminster or in

his constituency, and his personal affairs. It would be most unwise to take this freedom from him by paying such a figure as would unequivocally demand his full time in return.

In the 1950s another committee, also recording the financial difficulties being experienced by some Members, recommended a further salary increase and a pension scheme, but this was resisted by the government at the time in favour of a daily allowance. In 1957 this allowance was replaced by a salary addition of £750. The committee had also suggested that in future it might be sensible to have a broader inquiry that would examine the whole issue of 'the status and degree of financial independence appropriate to Members of Parliament in relation to their duties as these have developed in the modern world'.

A step in this direction was represented by the Lawrence committee report in 1964, the first time that the issue of MPs' pay had been given to an outside body. Noting the continuing disagreement about whether being an MP was a full-time or part-time activity, and the widely different circumstances and expectations of Members, the report concluded that the only practical solution would be to set a salary level that enabled all Members to perform their duties 'without undue financial worry and to live and maintain themselves and their families at a modest but honourable level'. Its recommendation of a salary increase to £3,250 was accepted, along with a pension scheme. There were no recommendations about allowances; and rejection of any idea of linking MPs' pay to a civil service (or any other) comparator as this would have suggested it was a 'normal' job, which it was not.

As inflation eroded the value of the salary, there were soon demands for a further review. A secretarial allowance was introduced in 1969, designed to allow one full-time secretary for each MP. Then came the decisive break with ad-hocery on MPs' pay and expenses when, in 1970, the new Top Salaries Review Body (TSRB) was established and the remuneration of MPs was referred to it. Its 1971 report on the matter announced as a basic principle that there should henceforth be a 'clear separation [...] between salary, on the one hand, and provision for expenses on the other'. There should be no automatic uprating or civil service comparator, but a Review Body examination in each Parliament.

As a result of this 1971 report, salary was raised to £4,500 a year and a new system of allowances introduced. There were more generous secretarial and travel allowances, but most significant of all a new additional costs allowance to meet the accommodation cost of staying in

London or the constituency. The structure of the allowance system was now in place, along with a review mechanism for salaries. However this did not mean that the issue became less contentious or more easily settled. Instead, for the next four decades there was a constant interplay between government, Parliament and the TSRB (later the Senior Salaries Review Body (SSRB)) over recommendations and responses, with both the press and public looking on and weighing in. The typical pattern was that the Review Body would recommend, governments (with an eye on public opinion or pay policies) would resist, Parliament would press – and compromises would be confected.

One sort of government response, made explicit in 1974 when the TSRB was invited to review allowances only, was to increase allowances instead of salary. This produced significant increases, but at the expense of salary. When the Review Body did recommend a 78% salary increase (to £8,000) later in 1974, with further allowance increases, the government responded with only staged salary increases in line with pay policy. A review after the 1979 election produced a recommendation of a £12,000 salary, which was accepted but with another staged increase; and now with a government commitment to find 'professional analogues' to which the pay of MPs could be linked between reviews, seen as necessary in inflationary times. In 1981 the TSRB review made no new recommendations on the grounds that 'we see no point in putting forward new figures which would add to the existing shortfall' while its previous recommendation was not yet fully implemented.

However the TSRB undertook a comprehensive review in 1983, for the first time using external consultants to advise on comparative pay and other legislatures. It concluded that 'an appropriate level of salary for Members of Parliament is in the end a matter of judgement'; and judged that a salary of £19,000 was currently appropriate. The government wanted less, but the House voted for a salary in 1987 of £18,500 to be reached in five instalments; and with a direct linkage to a point on the civil service pay scale from 1988. The effect of this linkage was that MPs' pay increased automatically until 1995, and that the TSRB was not required to review it between 1983 and 1996.

In 1996 a new review, again using external consultants, produced a SSRB recommendation that MPs' salaries should be £43,000, with increases linked to the senior civil service. This was accepted, although another review in 2001 added a further salary increase. Then came the 2007 review, which produced a salary recommendation of £61,820, with a new uprating formula and extra salary increments of £650 for three years. The government accepted the salary figure, but not the other rec-ommendations, and asked Sir John Baker, the retiring chairman of the SSRB, to devise an uprating formula that would avoid MPs having to set their own salary increases. In 2008 the House agreed to a government proposal that pay increases should be linked to a basket of public sector workers.

What does this brief history of pay say about the issue of expenses? It provides a reminder that pay and expenses have been confused from the start, reflecting a continuing uncertainty about what MPs were being paid for and whether what they did was to be seen as a full-time occupa-tion or one activity among others. It provides some support to the view that, for a long period, MPs were not paid enough for many of them to avoid real hardship. 'It is all wrong when Members go about scratch-ing a meal here and there', Churchill told Lord Moran in 1954, adding: 'Do you know [...] that a large number, perhaps as many as a hundred and twenty of the Members of the House, have less to live on than a coal-miner?'[5] Even into the 1970s they were being paid less than the inflated value of the original 1911 figure; and expenses were a way of taking up the slack. Yet pay rose sharply from the 1990s, rising to almost dou-ble the inflated value of the original £400 payment by the early 2000s. A salary of £34,000 in January 1996 had become one of over £61,000 by April 2007, almost doubling in a decade, on the basis of Review Body recommendations. The fact is that, in the decade before the expenses scandal broke, both salary and expenses were expanding sharply. The expenses scandal did not correspond with a period when salaries were being squeezed; but with a period when salaries were rising steadily and substantially. Those MPs (and some commentators) who sought to argue that the expenses scandal was a consequence of depressed salaries are not supported by the evidence.

What is true is that it had proved much easier for MPs to increase and expand expenses and allowances than to hike their salaries. This received much less attention, met less opposition from governments and was easier to bring about through their own actions and internal House machinery. It could be done under the radar. The structure of allowances that had been established by the 1971 review – for travel costs, staff and office costs, and accommodation and living costs – could be inflated in value and extended in scope. This is what happened to the Additional Costs Allowances (ACA), which covered accommodation and living costs, and which was to become central to the expenses scandal. In 1985 MPs were allowed to claim mortgage interest payments against this allowance, so that they could buy property and not just rent. The allowance steadily increased and it was in the direct interest of MPs that it should. When, in 2001, the SSRB made no recommendations about the allowance, MPs voted on a backbench amendment to increase it by a whopping 46%. An allowance that had begun in 1972 at £750 had thereby jumped in one year from £13,322 to £19,469 (and by 2009 was over £24,000). A generation of MPs who had lived in cheap hotels or rented modest rooms had been replaced by one which expected to have all the trappings of a second home.

An allowance of this size (which, as the SSRB acknowledged in its 2007 report, many Members had come to regard as a supplement to pay) offered plenty of scope for creative accounting on the property front. More generally, it had become too easy for MPs to beef up their allowances and it was only late in the day that MPs were required to provide evidence that money claimed had actually been spent (e.g. by providing rental contracts and mortgage agreements). A 'resettlement' grant that had been introduced in 1971 to give transitional help to those MPs defeated at general elections had subsequently been extended to cover all departing MPs. It was, perhaps, appropriate that one of the last acts of the pre-scandal Commons was a vote by MPs in 2007 (based on a report from their own Members Estimate Committee) for a new Communications Allowance of £10,000 a year. Even as the scandal was preparing to break, MPs were still voting themselves a new allowance.

Like many other MPs, I tried to absent myself when there were votes on pay and allowances, as I did not feel comfortable about voting on my own remuneration. It seemed to me, and to others, that these matters should be decided independently by somebody else. When invited to give evidence to review bodies, I did so; but without believing that there was a 'scientific' way of determining MPs' pay and being sceptical about the methodology involved. Above all, it did not seem sensible to determine the remuneration of MPs without having a realistic understanding of what MPs actually do, how they perform their various roles and what proper expectations of them there might be (matters which the Independent Parliamentary Standards Authority (IPSA) has rightly begun to explore).[6]

The crisis and its consequences

A crisis brings consequences (though not always of the expected kind) and a scandal frequently opens up opportunities for reform. Thus, phone-hacking produced the Leveson inquiry, that then produced proposals for a new regulatory system for the press. So it was with the parliamentary crisis occasioned by the expenses scandal. Some of the expected consequences did not happen though. Although a large number of MPs decided not to face the electorate again, the 2010 general election did not produce the breakthrough for independent candidates standing on an anti-corruption ticket that might have been expected. It was largely politics as usual. This might well have been different if an effective recall mechanism for errant MPs had been in place at the time of the scandal, instead of emerging as one of the hastily invented policy proposals for the future. Once the scandal had abated, this proposal began to look less appealing to MPs and seemed likely to survive (if at all) only in diluted form.

An important factor in drawing the political teeth of the scandal was the fact that legislation had been rushed through, supported on all sides, to establish an independent regulator for MPs' expenses, enforcing tighter rules arising out of a report from the CSPL. This enabled politicians to claim by the time of the 2010 general election that the issue had been dealt with, the system reformed and the matter taken out of the hands of MPs themselves. There is still debate about whether a new regulatory structure of the kind established was in fact required, but at the time it seemed to be a political necessity as a visible symbol of reform.

It is not unusual for there to be regulatory over-reaction to a scandal or crisis, with new machinery being quickly established but poorly examined, because something has to be seen to be done. In the case of the expenses scandal, there is evidence that enforced transparency was already doing the trick (claims dropped sharply as soon as MPs knew these would be published) and, with tighter rules and proper audit, the system could certainly have been improved. Yet the political demands of the moment required something more than this, in the shape of the IPSA (see Chapter 9). Its function was political detoxification and public reassurance.

It also represented the end of parliamentary self-regulation, which had failed miserably to ensure that proper standards were adhered to. The failure of self-regulation in many other areas had been attended to; but in the House of Commons it had clung on. It was not just that MPs set their own allowances and voted on their own salary, but that they had sought resolutely to protect the system against external scrutiny or audit. This was evident in their fight to resist freedom of information disclosures about their expenses claims. It was also evident in the rejection, in July 2008, of modest proposals from the Members Estimate Committee for a more effective audit system for claims. The House committees which ran the system were not elected; it was not clear to most MPs how they worked; and some of the Members who sat on them seemed to see their role as that of parliamentary shop stewards with the task of extracting more money for Members while preventing any disclosure of information. The then Speaker saw his role as but-tressing this system rather than challenging it. Behind all this was a belief that what MPs got up to was nobody's business but their own. This was a club culture sheltering behind a doctrine of parliamentary sovereignty.

It was this belief that produced an expenses system that enabled abuse to take place. It was not so much the allowances themselves, but the fact that for a long time there was no effective scrutiny of how they were being used. This allowed a culture to develop in which the manipulation of the expenses system for private gain came to seem quite normal and, because not scrutinized or challenged, acceptable. For this reason it is not surprising that the prospect of disclosure of claims provoked such desperate resistance in some quarters, because there was a realization that once the window was opened it would be revealed that there was something very nasty in the parliamentary wood shed.

It is often said that one major consequence of the expenses scandal was a collapse of trust in the political class. Survey evidence at the time seemed to confirm this. Yet we have to be a little careful here. Political trust had been in decline for a long time, particularly since the poli-tics of 'sleaze' in the 1990s, and the expenses scandal certainly added significantly to it. But it did not cause the decline.[7] Rather, it seemed to validate (and reinforce) a feeling against politics and politicians that was already well entrenched. For a variety of reasons (not least the existence of an independent civil service), government in Britain was relatively free of serious corruption, certainly compared with many other coun-tries (something pointed out by the very first report of the CSPL in the mid-1990s), but the perception was rather different.[8]

In his autobiography, John Major records how he was irked by the allegations of ministerial misconduct in relation to the 'scandal' of arms sales to Iraq and why he knew the allegations were untrue:

> The main reason was that government simply does not work like that. The symbiotic relationship between ministers and civil servants, working along parallel lines of authority and accountability, does not permit such things to occur. If ministers had conspired to let inno-cent men go to prison the Whitehall machinery would have sounded the alarm, the Cabinet secretary would have been alerted, and he would have been in to see me immediately.[9]

It is not necessary to be quite so sanguine about how the system works to recognize the important element of truth in this description. Yet what the expenses crisis did was to make it much harder to convince people, in a climate where political distrust was already strong, that the political system was not corrupt.

In the case of parliamentary expenses, there was of course no 'Whitehall machinery' to safeguard propriety or sound the alarm. That was precisely the problem. MPs controlled their own internal affairs, including their own financial affairs, and defended this self-governing arrangement (in the name of parliamentary sovereignty) against external incursions. Those officials who administered the expenses system seemed to believe that their primary duty was to assist MPs to make claims. The role of officers of the House in ensuring that parliamentary proceedings were conducted in proper order clearly did not extend to those officials who administered the system of expenses and allowances. Parliament was to pay a high price for this laxity.

Opportunity for reform

Not only did the expenses scandal produce a regulator, which would determine pay and pensions as well as allowances, but also promises of assorted reforms to the conduct of politics from political leaders anxious to demonstrate that they had learned the lessons of the crisis. A competitive bidding war was opened up between the party leaders on reform proposals, most of which had little or no connection with the expenses issue or with the misconduct that it had revealed. It was in this context that an opportunity arose to make some reforms to the Commons itself. I had proposed the establishment of a parliamentary reform committee in a letter to Gordon Brown in June 2009, when the crisis was at its height, which produced a Select Committee on the Reform of the House of Commons with me in the chair. The work of this committee was to prove one of the enduring and positive consequences of the scandal for the House of Commons.

The story of this reform package has been told elsewhere,[10] so I shall confine myself to its connection with the expenses scandal. The simple fact is that without the scandal there would have been no reform. The parliamentary 'modernization' committee that had been established after Labour came to power in 1997 had produced a number of changes to the working of the Commons, but it had not addressed (and not been allowed to address) the central issue of the relationship between Parliament and the executive. This was not something that governments or party machines wanted to see disturbed, for perfectly understandable reasons, as Robin Cook had discovered to his cost when, as Leader of the

House, he had proposed some modest reforms to this relationship. It was this issue that the reform initiative prompted by the expenses crisis focused its attention on, with its proposals for the election of select committees and for the Commons to control more of its own business.

The Reform Committee was frank about the circumstances in which it had come into existence: 'Without the shock of recent events, it is unlikely that this Committee would have been established.'[11] It went on to talk about there being 'a rare window of opportunity' for reform. In normal times a committee of this kind would not have been set up; it would not have worked at such a frenetic pace to produce a report; and its proposals would not have been so readily accepted. It was only because the Commons was so destabilized, the usual forces of resistance so weakened, and MPs so anxious to have something positive to cling on to, that a coherent and committed group of reformers was able to achieve the success it did.

It was essential not to lose the reform opportunity presented by the expenses crisis before normalcy returned; and to get reforms agreed before Parliament was dissolved for the fast-approaching 2010 general election, after which the political environment was likely to be very different. The aim was to get reforms in place so that they would ready and waiting for a new Parliament to implement. If the momentum had been lost, then there was no guarantee that the reforms would have been returned to. In a direct sense then, reform depended for its success upon the abnormal parliamentary circumstances produced by the expenses crisis, a fact that those of us involved in the process were acutely aware of.

The expenses crisis had produced major reforms in two significant directions. On one side, a new regulator had been established that would replace parliamentary self-regulation across the whole field of expenses, pay and pensions. Without the expenses crisis, this would not have happened. On the other side, there were reforms that significantly shifted the balance between Parliament and the executive and offered the prospect of a more robust and vigorous House of Commons, already now in evidence. The Commons now controls more of its own business, producing debates and votes that would not otherwise have taken place; and the elected select committees have brought a new vitality to scrutiny. This too would not have happened without the expenses crisis. Added to this, in 2010 the Commons saw an exceptionally large influx of new Members following the post-expenses exit of equally large numbers of MPs, which provided the institution with a refreshing (and uncontaminated) tonic. The expenses scandal may have been a catastrophe for Parliament, politics and the political class; but it had nevertheless produced a set of changes that would not have happened without it and which together put Parliament in a much better place.

This prompts one final reflection. For much of the second half of the twentieth century the dominant narrative about Parliament was that of decline. It was said to be drifting into a supine irrelevance. With the expenses scandal the decline seemed to have reached its terminal stage, from which no recovery was possible. The fact that the decline narrative was flawed in a number of respects did not diminish its potency.[12] What is remarkable is that, within a few years of the 2009 scandal, the narrative has become one of parliamentary renewal and vigour. Instead of the decline of Parliament, the story is now of an institution on the rise. There is more to be done (not least in the scrutiny of legislation), but it has become interesting again; and what it does matters more. Of all the outcomes of the expenses crisis this is the most astonishing and the most welcome.

Notes

1. For more on this episode, and on the wider issue, see my 'Palace of Low-grade Corruptions', *New Statesman*, 9 August 1996; republished in my *Doing Politics*, Biteback, 2012.
2. Committee on Standards in Public Life, Oral Evidence, 11 June 2002.
3. For example, on one occasion a local newspaper produced a list of my mortgage payments despite the fact that I did not have a mortgage. Getting apologies and corrections was tiresome, but necessary. When the *Sunday Times* included my name in a front-page expenses story, confusing me (again) with someone else, I had to go to the Press Complaints Commission in order to get an apology with due prominence.
4. In this section I have drawn heavily on a paper by Paul Seaward, 'A Summary of Members' Pay and Expenses', published in the report of the Members' Expenses Committee, *The Operation of the Parliamentary Standards Act 2009*, First Report of session 2010–2012, HC 1484-ii, Ev. 112–123; and a series of standard notes produced by Richard Kelly in the House of Commons Library, especially 'Members' Pay and Allowances', May 2009. The factual information, and almost all the quotations here, comes from these sources.
5. Lord Moran Diary, 21 May 1954; in *Winston Churchill: The Struggle for Survival 1940–1965*, Constable, 1966.
6. I explore this theme in 'What are MPs for?', *Political Quarterly*, July 2010, republished in *Doing Politics* (2012). See also Independent Parliamentary Standards Authority, *Reviewing MPs' Pay and Pensions: A Consultation*, October 2012.
7. Recent evidence on this is provided by the chapter on 'Constitutional Reform' by John Curtice and Ben Seyd in *British Social Attitudes 29*, 2012, Nat Cen Social Research.

8. For an interesting comparative perspective on the modesty of the wrong-doing revealed by the expenses scandal in relation to political corruption elsewhere, see Peter Mair, 'The Parliamentary Peloton', *London Review of Books*, 25 February, 2010.
9. John Major, *The Autobiography*, London, HarperCollins, 2000, p.559.
10. In particular, Meg Russell, ' "Never Allow a Crisis Go to Waste": The Wright Committee Reforms to Strengthen the House of Commons', *Parliamentary Affairs*, 64, 4, 2011, pp.612–633.
11. House of Commons Reform Committee, *Rebuilding the House*, HC 1117, November 2009, p.7.
12. An interesting discussion of the 'decline' argument is to be found in Matthew Flinders and Alexandra Kelso, 'Mind the Gap: Political Analysis, Public Expectations and the Parliamentary Decline Thesis', *British Journal of Politics and International Relations*, 13, 2011, pp.249–268.

4
Should I Stay or Should I Go? The Impact of the Expenses Scandal on MPs' Decisions to Stand Down

Jennifer vanHeerde-Hudson

In total, 149 MPs stood down before the 2010 general election, but to what extent was the expenses scandal a factor in MPs' decisions to retire or voluntarily exit the House of Commons? This chapter adopts Jacobson and Kernell's (1983) strategic politicians hypothesis, arguing that, similar to the US banking scandal, British MPs acted strategically, taking advantage of available information in decisions relating to their electoral prospects. The evidence here suggests that the expenses scandal was a factor in MPs' decisions to stand down. It did not, however, have the impact many suspected given the intense media scrutiny and public outrage following the *Daily Telegraph's* initial revelations: more mundane and less controversial factors such as age and seniority played a bigger role.

Introduction

This chapter examines the impact of the 2009 expenses scandal on MPs' decisions to stand down prior to the 2010 general election. In total, 149 MPs stood down, including Cabinet and ministerial resignations, and Speaker Michael Martin, the first speaker to resign in some 300 years. Anecdotal evidence points to the record number of MPs standing down as the biggest consequence of the expenses scandal; however, the impact of the scandal on MPs' decisions to voluntarily exit the House of Commons has not yet been systematically tested. In Chapter 5, Pattie and Johnston examine the impact of the scandal on turnout and vote share; here, I test whether those implicated in the scandal took the decision to stand down, thereby removing the worst offenders prior to the election and, consequently, attenuating the electoral effects of scandal in terms of turnout and vote choice.

As the 'biggest scandal to hit Parliament in two centuries'[1] unfolded, public opinion polls revealed a British public outraged at MPs' profligate spending, lack of accountability and, more generally, the perception that Westminster politicians were not subject to the same rules as 'ordinary' British citizens. Public opinion surveys following the revelations showed that 95% of the public had heard of the scandal, nearly everyone (91%) was angered by it and 82% felt that MPs who abused the expenses system should resign immediately (vanHeerde-Hudson 2011). Moreover, blame for the scandal was not limited to a few 'bad apples', but to the wider Westminster culture or, in short, the 'parliamentary system' itself.[2] A year on, surveys showed that while public anger had marginally dissipated, the scandal had shamed Parliament (YouGov 2010).

In this chapter, I adopt Jacobson and Kernell's (1983) strategic politicians proposition to test the impact of the scandal on MPs' decisions to stand down. Under the strategic politicians assumption, incumbents weigh the electoral landscape before deciding to seek another term: those that are most vulnerable – whether vulnerability stems from exposure to scandal, redistricting or changes in macroeconomic conditions that no longer favour the party – are most likely to call it a day. The evidence here suggests that while the scandal did play a role in Members' decision-making, it was not the primary motivation. More 'ordinary' and far less controversial factors such as age, status and partisan change (a consequence of constituency boundary changes) had a greater impact.

Plus ca change?

The British MPs' expenses scandal bears a remarkable resemblance to the 'cheque-kiting' scandal that engulfed members of the US House of Representatives in the autumn of 1991 when the General Accounting Office revealed that members of the House had written over 8,000 bad cheques on personal cheque accounts held with the House bank (vanHeerde-Hudson 2011). Because the bank had covered cheques members wrote on overdrawn accounts, members had effectively benefited from interest-free loans (Jacobson and Dimock 1994). Following increasing scrutiny of members' financial arrangements with the House bank and growing media interest, the House announced that it would no longer honour 'interest free overdraft protection' to its members and the House Ethics Committee launched an investigation into the scandal (Banducci and Karp 1994: 6).

The subsequent investigation revealed that from July 1988 to October 1992 members of the House had written over 20,000 bad cheques, and while not every member was implicated, the banking scandal was institutional in scale: 60% of members were named as having benefited from the arrangements. Even after the Ethics Committee announced its investigation, the House resisted disclosing the full list of offenders, but eventually succumbed to media pressure and public interest, and published the full list of members with overdrafts and the number of cheques they had kited. Unsurprisingly, public reaction to the scandal was similar to expenses scandal here: anger and disgust and more generally the sense that politicians were not subject to the same rules as 'ordinary' citizens.

The banking scandal occurred alongside a number of important events and decisions that, taken together, suggested the 1992 congressional elections would be difficult at best for incumbents.[3] The scandal followed the decennial reapportionment of seats creating uncertainty for many members whose districts were redrawn. Second, large budget deficits and economic downturn made fighting the 1992 election an uncomfortable prospect for many an incumbent. Third, Congress's reputation had suffered in recent months under allegations of misconduct relating to campaign finance and for voting itself pay rises and the use of perquisites. Finally, a law passed three years earlier in 1989, allowed those members who had entered the House prior to 1980 a one-time opportunity to convert remaining campaign funds for personal use. For members surveying the political landscape in the run up to the 1992 elections, many had to ask themselves 'should I stay or should I go'?

Despite events that would make even the most seasoned politicians flinch, public fury and some of the lowest approval ratings seen in years, the impact of the cheque-kiting scandal, among other factors, was not as catastrophic as some feared and others predicted. Like the expenses scandal in Britain, the events leading up to the 1992 elections were influential in creating the largest turnover in the US House of Representatives since 1948, but for incumbents who stayed the course, 88% were successfully re-elected (Alford *et al.* 1994). In sum, the evidence suggests that while both the scandal and redistricting were significant predictors of members' decision to retire, and to a lesser degree, of their electoral fortunes, the impact of the scandal on voters in November 1992 has been shown to be muted (Dimock and Jacobson 1995). The next section briefly reviews the literature on the political/electoral impact of scandal, showing why, despite significant media and public attention, scandals often have limited electoral impact.

The limited impact of scandal

The political and electoral impact of institution-wide scandals varies considerably. Scholarly work has demonstrated the effects of scandal on politicians' decisions to retire or stand down (Hibbing 1982; Banducci and Karp 1994; Jacobson and Dimock 1994; Clarke *et al.* 1999), on vote choice and on vote share (Dimock and Jacobson 1995; Lafay and Servais 2002; Pattie and Johnston 2012). However, the evidence does not suggest there are consistent, sizeable and significant effects of scandals on electoral outcomes. The general consensus seems to be that electoral effects of scandal are, relatively muted, despite their predicted impact – often based on public anger and outrage in the immediate aftermath of a scandal.[4] Generally speaking, studies have split along three lines in addressing the impact of scandal: (1) explanations that focus on the attributes/attitudes of voters (2) explanations that focus on institutional/structural characteristics; and (3) explanations that focus on decisions of parties/politicians. Regarding the former, a number of factors serve to limit the electoral impact of scandal for citizens.

First, and more generally, scandal-related information isn't always taken as given by the public. As Rundquist *et al.* (1977) have shown, citizens are sceptical of information they receive about parties and politicians during scandals, often discounting such information as 'partisan tricks' by the media or their opponents. Citizens may block information inconsistent with their beliefs or partisan predispositions or simply weigh other considerations in the voting calculus more heavily (Blais *et al.* 2005).

Second, and related, scandal-related information is also mediated by citizens' prior levels of information and their partisan/ideological predispositions. Moreover, Zaller (1992) has shown that the influence of new information has differential effects for the more and less politically well-informed: more politically informed voters can incorporate more complex and competing information in their knowledge structures, and therefore may use different criteria in evaluating candidates. This is corroborated by Regner and Le Floch (2005) who show that the more prominent an issue is in the media, the more likely it will impact political judgements; however, voters with higher information levels about the target (politician) are less likely to be influenced by other considerations.

Third, while most citizens adopt a 'throw the rascals out' mentality following allegations of corruption or scandal, their attitudes and behaviour show less consistency (Peters and Welch 1980). For example, citizens may receive material benefits as the result of politicians' corrupt behaviour and therefore are less likely to punish; or they 'trade' negative for positive behaviours – essentially they care more about good policy than bad deeds (Stoker 1983). The disconnect between attitudes and behaviour may also help to explain voters' perceptions of candidates' competence and why some candidates are more insulated from scandal and maintain high-levels of support (Funk 1996), and why incumbents implicated in scandals are frequently returned to office (Brown 2006; Hirano and Snyder 2012).

Scholarly work has identified two factors, associated with institutions or features of the scandal itself, which serve to limit the electoral impact of scandal. Clarke *et al.* (2010) note the role of 'pulse-decay' or the time lapsed between the start of a scandal and time to election. In short, the longer the time between the two events, the less impact the scandal is shown to have on electoral outcomes. This is due, in part, because voters are confronted with changing political information over the course of an election cycle. Information received early in the cycle may matter less than information received later or simply may hold less weight. Exogenous shocks like the scandal usually have only short-term effects particularly as the 'further removed a scandal is from the election, the less impact it will have on the incumbent' (Alford *et al.* 1994: 790).

Finally, as shown by Alford *et al.* (1994), politicians can take advantage of institutional-wide scandals by shifting the 'locus of blame'. In explaining their behaviour members can invoke diffusion of responsibility rather than shouldering personal responsibility. With vertical diffusion, members shift blame to a higher authority (e.g. 'I was just following the rules') versus horizontal diffusion, where members seek comfort in others also implicated (e.g. 'everyone was doing it') (McGraw 1991 in Alford *et al.* 1994). Consequently, if a scandal is perceived to be institutional in scope as in the case of the expenses scandal, voters may discount individual responsibility of their own Member.

Strategic decision-making: When is it time to go?

A final factor explaining the impact of scandal on electoral outcomes looks at the strategic behaviour of politicians. One aspect of electoral politics where scandal has been shown to have consistent effects is in members' decisions to voluntarily stand down or retire following a scandal. Here, it is argued that research demonstrating more limited effects of scandal on vote share/vote choice is precisely because the real effect of scandal is to remove the most serious offenders from the electoral arena (Banducci and Karp 1994; Pattie and Johnston 2012). In other words, vulnerable incumbents get out before they are forced out.

Early work on members' decisions to stand down were largely US based and focused on a variety of variables including age, seniority, percentage of vote share received in the previous election, redistricting, party, economic conditions, the rigours of campaigning and disaffection with service in the US House of Representatives (Frantzich 1978; Cooper and West 1982; Hibbing 1982; Moore and Hibbing 1998). Later work by Jacobson and Kernell (1983) argued that the decision to stand down or retire is a strategic one based on a rational, cost-benefit analysis of the various factors that influence electoral outcomes (see also Brace 1985). Under this conceptualization, while incumbents are generally regarded as 'single-minded seekers of re-election' (Mayhew 1984), they do not seek re-election at any price (Hall and vanHouweling 1995).

Studies of members' decisions to stand down received a second wave of attention following the 1992 House banking scandal (Banducci and Karp 1994; Groseclose and Krehbiel 1994; Jacobson and Dimock 1994; Clarke *et al.* 1999). Groseclose and Krehbiel (1994: 94) demonstrate that while strategic retirements occur, 'there is significant variation in the causes and their magnitude'. But the story with respect to the banking scandal is one of relative consistency. Adopting the strategic politicians hypothesis (Jacobson and Kernell 1983), these studies employ similar models and find effects of the banking scandal on decisions to retire. They also show that with respect to the 102nd Congress, the opportunity to cash in unused campaign funds, redistricting, age and seniority were also factors. Importantly, despite the threat the scandal posed for those implicated, other factors played more heavily in members' decisions to retire: the opportunity to take unused campaign funds 'caused nearly twice as many retirements as redistricting and nearly four times as many as the House bank scandal' (Groseclose and Krehbiel 1994: 95).

One consequence of scandal then is the expectation of turnover, more specifically, that the real impact of scandals is to drive out vulnerable incumbents before the general election. The limited effects of the scandal on turnout and vote choice, as shown in Chapter 5, may be precisely because the most serious offenders got out before they were pushed. With a record 149 MPs standing down prior to the 2010 general election, the next section tests the general hypothesis that MPs who were implicated in the expenses scandal were more likely to stand down. Following Jacobson and Kernell (1983), I assume the decision to stand down is a rational one: where costs are greater than benefits and render MPs more vulnerable, they are more likely to stand down than face a difficult election and possible defeat.

Measures and methodology

The impact of the expenses scandal and boundary review on MPs' decisions to stand down from Parliament is tested via a multivariate probit model drawing on a variety of data sources detailed below. Given the similarity of the expenses scandal and the timing of boundary changes to that of the US cheque-kiting scandal, I follow Banducci and Karp (1994) and Jacobson and Dimock (1994) in modelling exit from the House of Commons. Standing down or retirement is defined as those MPs who announced they would not contest the 2010 general election but remained in office until Parliament was dissolved.[5] The explanatory variables[6] are grouped into three broad categories: the first associated with the chapter's key variables of interest – the expenses scandal and boundary review, the second associated with the MP's institutional and electoral position, and the third with personal characteristics of the MP themselves.

To measure the impact of the expenses scandal, I rely on two indicators, both of which aim to tap the extent to which MPs are thought to have *abused* the expenses system. Capturing the notion of abuse of the expenses regime is important as the vast majority of claims were well within the rules and very few involved illegal activity. The measures here attempt to capture the extent to which MPs misused the system and the degree to which they were implicated. The first measure is the number of times an MP was *named* in one of the major broadsheets or popular newspapers in the two weeks following the *Telegraph's* initial revelations. This measure is similar to the one employed by Pattie and Johnston (see Chapter 5; the measures are strongly correlated $r = 0.67$, $p = 0.001$).

The second measure results from the Legg Review of past ACA claims. On 19 May, party leaders and members of the Members Estimate Committee agreed to a review of ACA payments to be headed by retired civil servant Sir Thomas Legg. Legg was charged with investigating the validity of ACA claims and, where deemed inappropriate, and requesting repayment by MPs. I test the general hypothesis that MPs named in the media and asked to repay expenses are more likely to stand down rather than face a potentially hostile electorate.

A third variable related to the expenses scandal, an MP's ACA claims, is also tested. To the extent that an MP abused their ACA allowance, they are likely to be picked up in one of the two previous scandal measures. However, this variable simply measures how much MPs claimed, on average, from 2007 to 2009. The argument here is that average ACA claims is tapping something different[7] to the two variables outlined above and that, all else being equal, the more an MP claims in living costs, the more likely they are to stand down.

To measure the impact of boundary changes on MPs' exit from Parliament I again use two measures, both drawing on Rallings and Thrasher's (2007) 'Index of Change'. The first – *boundary change* – captures the number of deletions and additions to a baseline constituency boundary. This measure provides an indication of the extent of change or disruption to previous constituency boundary lines. It does not tell us how changes affect the partisan composition of the new constituency. This is captured via the second variable – *partisan change* – that measures the degree to which the new constituency boundaries (and its new electorate) moved in favour or against the incumbent candidate/party. Partisan change is calculated by subtracting the 2010 actual vote from the 2005 notional vote (how the constituency would have voted if it existed in 2005).[8] For example, in the constituency of Wellingborough, the incumbent candidate/party (Bone, Conservative) received 42.6% of the notional vote. In 2010, Bone received 48.1% of the vote. Subtracting the 2005 vote from the 2010 vote, the partisan impact of changes to constituency boundaries was +5.5% in favour of the incumbent. All else being equal, as partisan change in favour of the incumbent MP's party increases, they are less likely to stand down.

The second group of explanatory variables capture the impact of MPs' institutional or electoral circumstances. I include a modified measure of vote share, calculated as the difference between the first and second place candidate/party in the 2005 general election. This variable takes into account performance in the previous election – where the margin between the first and second place parties was smaller and hence a hard-fought race. Under Jacobson and Kernell's (1983) strategic politicians hypothesis, we expect those MPs who experienced hard-fought races in 2005 to be more likely to stand down. I also examine the extent to which MPs from different parties were more likely to stand down. Using a dummy variable for Labour MPs, I test whether two factors contributed to Labour MPs being more likely to stand down. First, after 13 years in government and as the party in power at the onset of the global financial crisis, Labour MPs may have been judged to be more responsible for Britain's poor macroeconomic conditions. Second, voters may have seen Labour and its MPs as responsible for failing to reform the expenses regime. MPs may, therefore, have been more likely to stand down the longer they had served in the Commons. A variable measuring an MP's *seniority*, measured as the number of years served in the House is included in the model. Finally, I consider the *status* of an MP in the chamber. Here, I expect senior Members who hold powerful positions within the House – serving as minister, opposition minister, chair of select committee, or (Deputy) Speaker – to be less likely to stand down.

The final set of explanatory variables tap personal characteristics of the MP, whether male or female, and their age. Although age is correlated with seniority, Hibbing (1982) has shown 'that each has a significant and separate effect on the probability of retiring' (in Banducci and Karp 1994: 13–14). *A priori* there is no expectation that male or female MPs are more or less strategic in their retirement decisions; however, the nature of press coverage in the weeks that followed expenses revelations was differentiated for male and female MPs (see Chapter 8 for analysis) and therefore I test here to see if there are gender effects.

A preliminary look at the evidence

This section examines preliminary evidence of the impact of the scandal and boundary changes on MPs' decisions to stand down before considering the role of these and other factors in multivariate analyses. I begin by examining requests for repayments from the Legg review of Additional Costs Allowances (ACA) claims. Requests for repayment were demanded in cases of a clear breach of rules governing the expense regime and where irregularities or errors (i.e. double claiming) had been made. In this regard, Legg's request for repayments provides a useful measure of where (actual) abuse of the expenses system occurred, as opposed to more general public condemnation of MPs for creating and sustaining an elaborate system of expenses in the first place, and for some of the more egregious individual claims. Although the general tenor of media coverage and subsequent public response suggested that all MPs were implicated in the scandal, the review provided a more balanced assessment of the degree of wrongdoing. Repayments ranged from

£0 to £42,458, with an average repayment of £1,803 (median £294). Of the MPs investigated, 42% were found to be in the clear, having been asked to repay none of their previous claims; of those asked to repay, 65% were asked to pay less than £1,000 (Table 4.1).

Table 4.1 shows the amount of ACA expenses MPs were required to repay by party. In short, 53% Labour MPs were not asked to repay, compared to 29% of Conservative MPs and 12% of Liberal Democrats. Of those MPs asked to repay, Labour MPs were asked to repay more than their counterparts in other parties. The exception here is the highest category – MPs asked to repay more than £10,000 – where Conservatives accounted for 56%, Labour 41% and Liberal Democrats 4%. However, there is no evidence to suggest one party abused ACA expenses more than another as differences in repayment requests across the parties is not statistically significant, falling outside of traditional levels of significance ($X^2 = 19.71$; $p = 0.07$).

In Table 4.2, I cross-tabulate the two measures of the extent to which MPs abused expenses – ACA repayments and whether an MP was named in the media – on standing down before the 2010 general election, a first test of whether the expenses scandal played a role in MPs' decisions to stand down. The content analysis of newspapers in the weeks following the expenses scandal showed that of the MPs who stood down, only 20% were named in the media; and here the media's attention appears to be rather focused on 15% who were named three or more

Table 4.1 Additional Costs Allowance (ACA) expenses repaid by party

Amount repaid	Conservative	Labour	Liberal Democrat	Other	Total
No repayments	29%	53%	12%	6%	100%
	(72)	(132)	(29)	(16)	(249)
£1–1,000	33%	58%	8%	2%	101%
	(44)	(77)	(10)	(3)	(134)
£ 1,001–2,500	37%	50%	6%	7%	100%
	(36)	(49)	(6)	(7)	(98)
£ 2,501–10,000	23%	62%	9%	6%	100%
	(18)	(48)	(7)	(5)	(78)
> £ 10,000	56%	41%	4%	0%	101%
	(15)	(11)	(1)	(0)	(27)
Total	(185)	(317)	(53)	(31)	(586)

Source: House of Commons, Members Estimate Committee. $X^2 = 19.71$; $p = 0.07^+$. Row totals may exceed 100% due to rounding.

Table 4.2 Turnover in the House of Commons: Effects of the expenses scandal

Stood down	Named in media				Legg repayment			
	Not named	1–2 mentions	3+ mentions	Total	No repayment	Repaid ≤ £1,803	Repaid ≥ £1,804	Total
No	86%	8%	7%	100%	42%	36%	22%	100%
	(421)	(37)	(32)	(490)	(183)	(159)	(99)	(441)
Yes	81%	5%	15%	100%	46%	27%	27%	100%
	(120)	(7)	(22)	(149)	(66)	(38)	(39)	(143)
Total	85%	7%	8%	100%	43%	34%	24%	100%
	(541)	(44)	(54)	(639)	(249)	(197)	(138)	(584)
	$X^2 = 10.90; p < 0.01$				$X^2 = 4.49; p = 0.11$			

Note: Column totals may exceed 100% due to rounding.

times. Further indication of the media's focus on perhaps the more seri-ous/notorious/unpopular offenders was that only 15% of all MPs were named, despite the general view that all MPs were tried and prosecuted in the press. As shown in Table 4.2, the relationship is statistically significant ($X^2 = 10.90, p < 0.01$).

It is worth reiterating that being named doesn't imply criminal wrong-doing; only a handful of the some 600+ MPs actually engaged in illegal activity. Moreover, being named doesn't necessarily mean that an MP's claims were excessive. In fact, a good deal of press attention focused on the more eccentric and peculiar claims: Chris Huhne's trouser press; Hazel Blears' Kit Kat; and Andrew Rosindell's jellied eels. But being named did mean that MPs had to respond, *publicly,* and it is the very public nature of expenses that may have contributed to MPs' decisions to stand down (Table 4.2).

The Legg review of past ACA expenses was, however, *inter alia,* tasked with identifying MPs who had submitted excessive claims and conse-quently were asked to repay. The second scandal measure then provides a more explicit measure of abuse.[9] Of the 584 MPs in the sample, 58% were asked to repay some of their previously claimed ACA expenses. However, the differences between MPs who stood down and those who did not was not particularly striking: 27% of MPs who stood down were asked to repay £1,804 or more compared to 22% of MPs who did not stand down. Unsurprisingly, the differences here are not statistically significant ($X^2 = 4.49$, p $= 0.11$).

Thus, it would seem that there is only limited evidence that the expenses scandal influenced MPs' decisions to retire. However, the sam-ple used in Table 4.2 includes all MPs who stood down prior to the general election – regardless of when they announced their retirement or whether or not they were implicated in the scandal – and thus may provide weaker evidence of the scandal's impact. For example, Brian Iddon (Labour) and Ann Widdecombe (Conservative) announced they would stand down in October of 2006 and 2007 respectively, well before the scandal broke. While Iddon was cleared in the Legg review, Widdecombe was asked to pay back £230 for a claim over the limit for gardening allowances; however to link her retirement with the expenses scandal would be nonsensical. However, subsequent anal-ysis coding those MPs who announced they would stand down from 1 January 2009 as '1' provided similar results to the data shown in Table 4.2: being in the media is a statistically significant predictor of standing down ($X^2 = 5.98$, p $= 0.05$); repayments are not ($X^2 = 0.185$, p $= 0.91$).

Turning our attention to other important features of the 2010 general election, with respect to the impact of boundary review on MPs' decisions to stand down, there is no evidence that the degree of change to constituency boundaries was influential. Table 4.3a shows that boundaries changed in 77% of constituencies prior to the 2010 general election. However, among those MPs with boundary changes the differences were not substantively or statistically different, with 24% of those experiencing boundary changes standing down compared to 19% standing down with no boundary changes ($X^2 = 2.07$, p = 0.15).[10]

Table 4.3b shows the relationship between partisan change for and against the incumbent MP/party and standing down. Partisan change

Table 4.3   Turnover in the House of Commons: Effects of boundary and partisan change

Table 4.3a   Boundary change

Stood down		No change	Boundary change	Total
	No	81%	76%	77%
		(118)	(376)	(494)
	Yes	19%	24%	23%
		(27)	(121)	(148)
	Total	100%	100%	100%
		(145)	(497)	(642)

Source: $X^2 = 2.07$; p = 0.15; column totals may exceed 100% due to rounding.

Table 4.3b   Partisan change

Stood down	Change against incumbent			Change in favor of incumbent			Total
	≥ 10.0	5.0–9.99	0–4.99	0–4.99	5.0–9.99	≥ 10.0	
No	12%	19%	19%	29%	17%	4%	100%
	(60)	(95)	(91)	(141)	(82)	(19)	(488)
Yes	23%	28%	14%	26%	9%	1%	100%
	(33)	(40)	(20)	(37)	(13)	(1)	(144)
Total	15%	21%	18%	28%	15%	3%	100%
	(93)	(135)	(111)	(178)	(95)	(20)	(632)

Source: $X^2 = 22.03$; p = 0.001; column totals may exceed 100% due to rounding.

measures the degree to which the new constituency boundaries, and consequently the new electorate, moved in favour or against the incumbent candidate/party. MPs facing significant (negative) changes to the partisan composition of their constituency may have given second thought to standing again. The evidence in Table 4.3b suggests this is the case. MPs who saw the partisan composition change in their favour won their race 95% of the time ($X^2 = 76.18$, $p < 0.001$).[11] At the more extreme end, for MPs who saw a 10% or greater point shift against their party, 23% stood down compared to 12% who did not. Similarly for MPs facing a 5–9.99% change against their party, 28% stood down versus 19% who did not. There is little difference between MPs standing down (1%) or not (4%) where partisan change was 10% or more in their favour. Differences in partisan change and standing down are statistically significant ($X^2 = 22.03$, p $= 0.001$).

The preliminary evidence shown above provides some evidence of the expenses scandal impacting MPs' decisions to stand down. This is true where MPs were named in the media, but not for the Legg repayment measure. Second, boundary changes in and of themselves are not related to MPs standing down, but changes in the partisan composition of the constituency as a result of boundary change are. In the next section, we subject these findings to multivariate analyses taking into account the range of factors that may influence MPs' decisions to voluntarily retire from the House of Commons.

In or out? Standing down in 2010

Following Jacobson and Kernell's (1983) strategic politicians hypothesis, it is expected that the most vulnerable MPs – those implicated in the expenses scandal and those whose electoral fortunes were made more uncertain as a result of the boundary review – were more likely to stand down prior to the general election. This section tests the robustness of the preliminary evidence shown above using a multivariate probit regression model. The model here follows that of Jacobson and Dimock (1994), Banducci and Karp (1994) and Clarke *et al.* (1999) who estimate the probability of retiring following a similar scandal, the US House banking scandal. Table 4.4 shows the results of the model (main effects) estimating the impact of the three sets of explanatory variables on MPs' decisions to stand down.

Model 1 shows the parameter estimates for the scandal and electoral explanatory variables correspond to the hypotheses set out above. The

Table 4.4 The effects of scandal and boundary changes on MP's decisions to stand down

Variable	Model 1 β	Effect on probability
Media named	.15*	.04
	(.074)	
Legg repaid	.000006	.0000016
	(.000013)	
Partisan change	−.028*	−.08
	(.012)	
Boundary change	.005	.001
	(.003)	
ACA claims	.00003*	.000007
	(.000013)	
Notional 05 majority	−.009+	.003
	(.005)	
Labour	.195	.05
	(.175)	
Status	−.434*	.10
	(.201)	
Seniority	.031**	.008
	(.011)	
Age	.05***	.12
	(.01)	
Female	.12	.03
	(.169)	
Constant	−4.46	−
	(.632)	
Pseudo LL	−254.47	
Pseudo R²	.19	
N= 570		

Source: Dependent variable is whether incumbent MP stood down = 1; robust standard errors in parentheses; $p < 0.10^+$, $p < 0.05^*$, $p < 0.01^{**}$, $p < 0.001^{***}$.

multivariate analysis also confirms what is shown in the descriptive analyses: named in the media and partisan change are statistically significant predictors of MPs' decisions to stand down, repaid and boundary change are not. As hypothesized, average ACA claims have a statistically significant effect; as the size of claims increases, MPs are more likely to stand down. Furthermore, the greater the difference between the first and second place parties – based on the 2005 notional vote – the less likely an MP is to stand down. A similar finding for status is observed; MPs holding high-status positions in the Commons (e.g. ministers, whips, committee chairs, etc.) are less likely to stand down, controlling for all other factors (Table 4.4).

Similar to other findings, seniority plays a significant role in Members' decision-making. The greater number of years served, the more likely an MP is to stand down. Finally, despite their long tenure in government and the poor economic conditions, for which Labour were largely deemed responsible, Labour MPs were no more likely to stand down than their Conservative or Lib Dem colleagues. The final two variables look at attributes of the MPs themselves. Despite differential press coverage for male and female MPs (see Chapter 8) there are no significant gender differences to speak of with respect to the decision to stand down. However, like most other occupations, age plays a significant role in MPs' decisions to retire. Older Members were more likely to stand down, perhaps deciding to get out while ahead, rather than face another election campaign.

So what does this mean in substantive terms? Was the expenses scandal a major factor in MPs' strategic decision-making? If so, relative to what? Table 4.5 shows the predicted probabilities of standing down for the seven significant explanatory variables in the model. Probabilities are calculated for each of the variables at the minimum and maximum values while others are held at the mean (model). The third column notes the absolute value of the difference between the minimum and maximum values and provides a useful substantive interpretation of the variables (Table 4.5).

As shown in the table, the change in the predicted probability of standing down for those MPs not named in the media to those named three or more times is 0.09. This is certainly not insignificant, but it

Table 4.5 Predicted probabilities

Variable	Min	Max	Difference
Media named	.17	.26	.09
Partisan change	.40	.08	.32
Seniority	.10	.54	.44
ACA claims	.08	.23	.15
Status	.21	.11	.10
Age	.02	.65	.63

Note: Predicted probability of standing down for minimum and maximum values of each variable; all other variables held at mean/mode.

pales in comparison (from the lowest to highest values) of the impact of boundary change, the partisan change in the MP's constituency, and whether that change is to their advantage or disadvantage. In short, the expenses scandal did play a role but less so than more 'ordinary' and less controversial factors: age, status and partisan change. Simply put, the longer an MP has served, the degree of partisan change and the higher status within the chamber appear to have bigger effects on MPs' decision-making. We can also see the sizeable effect of status, partisan change and age in Table 4.4 in the third column showing the effect on the probability of standing down (all others held at mean/mode). By a long margin, the biggest predictor of standing down is an MP's age; being implicated in the expenses scandal ranks a distant fourth. Important, but far from a revolution. These probabilities, along with the 95% confidence interval, are shown graphically in Figure 4.1.

Conclusion

The aim of this chapter has been to assess whether the expenses scandal was a factor in MPs' decisions to stand down. The evidence presented here shows that the expenses scandal was indeed a significant predictor of MPs' decisions to stand down, but it was not as decisive as might have been expected given public anger following the release of parliamentary expenses. Of the two measures, being named in the media and asked to repay as a result of the Legg review, only the former had a consistent and significant impact; no relationship is observed for those MPs asked to repay expenses by the Legg review. With regard to the latter, the public may not have paid (as) much attention to the Legg report compared to media reporting and therefore MPs didn't view being asked to repay as particularly damaging. Or, because the average repayment was so small, MPs could explain their inclusion in the report as accounting errors rather than evidence of abuse. It is important to keep in mind, however, that the substantive impact of the scandal is relatively minor, especially in comparison to age – the biggest predictor of MPs' decisions to stand down. The findings for scandal here echo those of Pattie and Johnston's in Chapter 4 with respect to turnout and the vote, and in the wider literature that finds limited effects of scandal.

The chapter also demonstrates that, similar to the US banking scandal, British MPs act strategically, taking advantage of available information

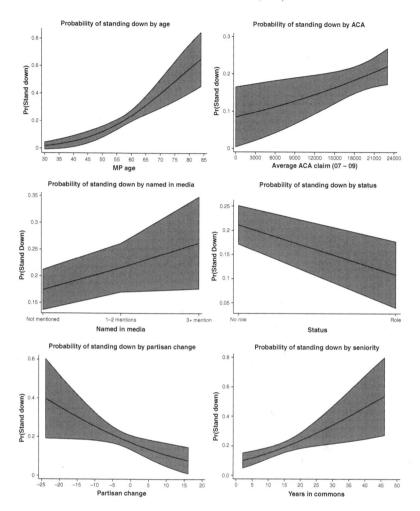

Figure 4.1   Predicted probabilities for significant variables

in decisions relating to their electoral prospects. The expenses scandal was one of many factors MPs weighed up in attempting to answer the question, should I stay or should I go? Thus, despite extensive media coverage and significant public anger, it appears that voters need not adopt a 'throw the rascals out' mentality: the evidence here suggests that MPs are happy to go when the time comes.

Appendix

Variable coding

Variable	Measure	Mean/distribution	Source
Dependent			
Stood down	Candidate stood down in 2010 = 1; sought re-election = 0	1 = 24% 0 = 76%	Electoral Commission (2010)
Independent			
Repay	ACA an MP was requested to repay	mean £1,803 sd = £4,419	House of Commons (2010)
Media named	Mentions in press in two weeks following the *Telegraph*'s revelation of expense claims (no mention = 0; 1–2 mentions = 1; 3 or more mentions = 2)	0 = 85% 1 = 7% 2 = 8%	Content analysis: author
ACA claims	Average amount of ACA claims made (2007–2009)	mean £17,146	House of Commons (2010)
Notional vote 05	Difference between vote share received between first and second place candidate/party in 2005 general election	mean = 19.1 sd = 12.5 (0.05–58.4)	Rallings & Thrasher (2007); Electoral Commission (2010)
Boundary change	Extent to which a constituency is changed by boundary reviews (total deletions from base constituency + total additions to base)/electorate of	mean = 17.6 sd = 25.5 (0–135.9)	Rallings and Thrasher (2007)

	base constituency (may exceed 100% where relationship between a new constituency and its base is tenuous)		
Partisan change	Degree to which the new constituency boundaries moved in favour or against the incumbent (2005 notionals – 2010 actual results)	mean = – 1.8 sd = 7.09 (–23.9–16.8)	Rallings and Thrasher (2007); Electoral Commission (2010)
Labour	Party (1 = Labour; 0 = other)	1 = 54% 0 = 46%	Electoral Commission (2010)
Age	MP age	mean = 56 sd = 9.3 (30–84)	They Work for You (2010)
Seniority	Number of years served in House of Commons (all)	mean = 14.4 sd = 8.3 (2–46)	They Work for You (2010)
Status	If MP was minister, opposition minister, chair of select committee, (deputy) speaker = 1; otherwise = 0	1 = 18% 0 = 82%	Various (available from author)
Sex	Female = 1; male = 0	1 = 19% 0 = 81%	Electoral Commission (2010)

Table 4A MPs standing down at the 2010 general election[12]

	MP name	Constituency	Announced		MP name	Constituency	Announced
Con	Ancram, Michael	Devizes	11/08/09	Lab	Fisher, Mark	Stoke on Trent Central	10/03/10
Con	Ainsworth, Peter	East Surrey	05/01/10	Con	Fraser, Christopher	Norfolk South West	28/05/09
Lab	Armstrong, Hilary	North West Durham	04/07/09	Lab	Follett, Barbara	Stevenage	01/10/09
Con	Atkinson, Peter	Hexham	19/06/08	Lab	George, Bruce	Walsall South	18/02/10
Lab	Austin, John	Erith and Thamesmead	31/07/08	Lab	Gerrard, Neil	Walthamstow	23/02/07
Lib	Barrett	Edinburgh West	25/07/09	Lab	Griffiths, Nigel	Edinburgh South	31/01/10
Lab	Battle, John	Leeds West	20/10/06	Con	Goodman, Paul	Wycombe	05/06/09
Lab	Blackman, Liz	Erewash	09/01/10	Con	Greenway, John	Ryedale	28/11/06
Con	Boswell, Tim	Daventry	31/03/06	Lab	Grogan, John	Selby	10/10/06
Lib	Breed, Colin	South East Cornwall	09/10/07	Con	Gummer, John	Suffolk Coastal	30/12/09
Lab	Browne, Des	Kilmarnock and Loudoun	27/11/09	Lab	Hall, Mike	Weaver Vale	02/02/10
Con	Browning, Angela	Tiverton and Honiton	17/11/06	Lab	Heal, Sylvia	Halesowen and Rowley Regis	09/03/10
Lab	Burgon, Colin	Elmet	23/04/09	Lab	Henderson, Doug	Newcastle upon Tyne North	04/07/09
Con	Butterfill, John	Bournemouth West	17/03/08	Lab	Heppell, John	Nottingham East	26/03/10
Lab	Byers, Stephen	North Tyneside	14/11/09	Lab	Hesford, Stephen	Wirral West	23/01/10
Lab	Caborn, Richard	Sheffield Central	13/09/07	Lab	Hewitt, Patricia	Leicester West	02/06/09
Lab	Challen, Colin	Morley and Rothwell	30/01/07	Lab	Hill, Keith	Streatham	23/05/07
Lab	Chapman, Ben	Wirral South	21/05/09	Con	Hogg, Douglas	Sleaford and North Hykeham	19/05/09

Name	Party	Constituency	Date
Chaytor, David	Lab	Bury North	02/06/09
Clapham, Michael	Lab	Barnsley West and Penistone	14/11/06
Clelland, David	Lab	Tyne Bridge	26/01/10
Cohen, Harry	Lab	Leyton and Wanstead	30/06/09
Conway, Derek	IC[13]	Old Bexley and Sidcup	30/01/08
Cormack, Patrick	Con	South Staffordshire	01/12/09
Cousins, Jim	Lab	Newcastle upon Tyne Central	09/06/09
Cryer, Ann	Lab	Keighly	21/08/08
Cummings, John	Lab	Easington	09/10/06
Curry, David	Con	Skipton and Ripon	05/02/09
Curtis-Thomas, Claire	Lab	Crosby	07/10/09
Davies, Quentin	Lab	Grantham and Stamford	09/2006
Dean, Janet	Lab	Burton	20/06/07
Devine, Jim[14]	Lab	Livingston	15/06/09
Ennis, Jeff	Lab	Barnsley East and Mexborough	09/02/10

Name	Party	Constituency	Date
Hoon, Geoff	Lab	Ashfield	11/02/10
Horam, John	Con	Orpington	12/10/09
Howard, Michael	Con	Folkestone and Hythe	17/03/06
Howarth, David	Lib	Cambridge	05/11/06
Howells, Kim	Lab	Pontypridd	18/12/09
Hughes, Beverley	Lab	Stretford and Urmston	02/06/09
Humble, Joan	Lab	Blackpool North and Fleetwood	27/02/10
Hutton, John	Lab	Barrow and Furness	05/06/09
Iddon, Brian	Lab	Bolton South East	05/10/06
Ingram, Adam	Lab	E. Kilbride, Strathvn & Lesm'gow	27/03/09
Jack, Michael	Con	Fylde	14/03/08
Jones, Lynne	Lab	Birmingham Selly Oak	01/2007
Jones, Martyn	Lab	Clwyd South	07/05/09
Keetch, Paul	Lib	Hereford	16/11/06
Kelly, Ruth	Lab	Bolton West	02/10/08

Table 4A (Continued)

	MP name	Constituency	Announced		MP name	Constituency	Announced
Lab	Etherington, Bill	Sunderland North	09/12/06	Lab	Kemp, Fraser	Houghton and Washington East	06/09/08
Lab	Kennedy, Jane	Liverpool Wavertree	09/11/09	Lab	O'Hara, Edward[15]	Knowsley South	26/04/07
Con	Key, Robert	Salisbury	02/12/09	Lab	Olner, Bill	Nuneaton	25/03/07
Lab	Kilfoyle, Peter	Liverpool Walton	23/02/10	DUP	Paisley, Ian	North Antrim	02/03/10
Con	Kirkbride, Julie	Bromsgrove	18/12/09	Lab	Pearson, Ian	Dudley South	21/01/10
Con	Lait, Jacqui	Beckenham	21/09/09	Lab	Pope, Greg	Hyndburn	11/06/09
Lab	Laxton, Robert	Derby North	19/10/06	PC	Price, Adam	Carmarthen East and Dinefwr	18/09/09
Lab	Lepper, Davi	Brighton Pavilion	19/09/06	Lab	Prentice, Bridget	Lewisham East	06/04/09
Lab	Levitt, Tom	High Peak	12/11/09	Lab	Prescott, John	Hull East	27/08/07
Con	Lord, Michael	Central Suffolk & N. Ipswitch	12/09/09	Lab	Purnell, James	Stalybridge and Hyde	19/02/10
Con	MacKay, Andrew	Bracknell	23/05/09	Lab	Purchase, Ken	Wolverhampton North East	27/10/07
Lab	MacKinlay, Andrew	Thurrock	24/07/09	Lab	Reid, John	Airdire and Shotts	15/09/07
Con	Maclean, David	Penrith and The Border	26/06/09	SNP	Salmond, Alex	Banff and Buchan	15/01/06
Con	Malins, Humfrey	Woking	16/03/09	Lab	Salter, Martin	Reading West	10/02/09
Con	Maples, John	Stratford upon Avon	10/01/10	Lab	Sarwar, Mohammad	Glasgow Central	21/06/07
Lab	Marshall-Andrews, Bob	Medway	17/07/07	Ind	Short, Clare	Birmingham Ladywood	12/10/06

85

Party	Name	Constituency	Date
Lab	Martlew, Eric	Carlisle	01/05/09
Con	Mates, Michael	East Hampshire	24/11/06
Lab	McAvoy, Tommy	Rutherglen and Hamilton West	20/02/10
Lab	McCafferty, Chris	Calder Valley	07/03/07
Lab	McCartney, Ian	Makerfield	23/05/09
SDLP	McGrady, Eddie	South Down	25/02/10
Lab	McFall, John	West Dunbartonshire	29/01/10
Lab	McKenna, Rosemary	Cumber, Kilsyth & Kirkintilloch	03/08/07
Lab	Milburn, Alan	Darlington	27/06/09
Lab	Moffatt, Anne	East Lothian	15/03/10
Lab	Moffatt, Laura	Crawley	15/03/10
Lab	Moran, Margaret	Luton South	28/05/09
Lab	Morley, Elliot	Scunthorpe	29/05/09
Con	Moss, Malcolm	North East Cambridgeshire	06/09/07
Lab	Todd, Mark	South Derbyshire	21/09/07
Lab	Touhig, Don	Islwyn	29/01/10
Lab	Simon, Sion	Birmingham Erdington	03/02/10
Lab	Simpson, Alan	Nottingham South	18/02/07
Lab	Smith, John	Vale of Glamorgan	22/05/09
Lab	Southworth, Helen	Warrington South	16/06/09
Con	Spicer, Michael	West Worcestershire	24/03/06
Con	Spring, Richard	West Suffolk	23/11/09
Con	Steen, Anthony	Totnes	20/05/09
Lab	Stewart, Ian[16]	Eccles	19/01/08
Lab	Stoate, Howard	Dartford	28/07/09
Lab	Strang, Gavin	Edinburgh East	27/06/08
Con	Taylor, Ian	Esher and Walton	16/06/09
Lib	Taylor, Matthew	Truro and St Austell	17/01/07
Lab	Tipping, Paddy	Sherwood	23/10/09
Con	Williams, Alan	Swansea West	09/2006
Lab	Williams, Betty	Conwy	12/09/08
Lab	Truswell, Paul	Pudsey	08/07/09

Table 4A (Continued)

	MP name	Constituency	Announced		MP name	Constituency	Announced
Lab	Mountford, Kali	Colne Valley	16/01/09	Lab	Turner, Des	Brighton Kemptown	23/10/06
Lab	Mullin, Chris	Sunderland South	10/05/08	Lab	Turner, Neil	Wigan	31/07/09
Lab	Murphy, Denis	Wansbeck	05/11/09	Lab	Ussher, Kitty	Burnley	17/06/09
Lab	Naysmith, Doug	Bristol North West	26/01/07	Con	Viggers, Peter	Gosport	20/06/09
Lib	Oaten, Mark	Winchester	25/07/06	Lab	Vis, Rudy	Finchley and Golders Green	28/05/08
Ind	Wareing, Robert	Liverpool West Darby	04/03/10	Con	Winterton, Ann	Congleton	25/05/09
Con	Widdecombe, Ann	Maidstone and The Weald	07/10/07	Con	Winterton, Nicholas	Macclesfield	25/05/09
Lib	Willis, Phil	Harrogate and Knaresborough	18/05/07	Lab	Wright, Tony	Cannock Chase	21/07/08
Lab	Wills, Michael	North Swindon	14/09/09	Lab	Wyatt, Derek	Sittingbourne and Sheppey	01/07/09
Con	Wilshire, David	Spelthorne	15/10/09				

Source: UK polling report; politics.co.uk.

Notes

1. Katherine Viner, Interview with Gordon Brown. 20 June 2009. The Guardian Online. http://www.guardian.co.uk /politics/2009/jun/20/gordon-brown-interview/print (Accessed 18 August 2010).
2. BBC News, 'Voters Believe MPs Corrupt – Poll'. http://news.bbc.co.uk/1/hi_politics/8078159.stm (Accessed 25 February 2010).
3. The scandal prompted a number of academic studies. See Ahuja *et al.* (1994); Alford *et al.* (1994); Banducci and Karp (1994); Clarke *et al.* (1999); Jacobson and Dimock (1994); and Dimock and Jacobson (1995) for excellent analyses.
4. Elsewhere, Bowler and Karp (2004) and Kumlin and Esaiasson (2011) have shown a stronger relationship between scandal and trust and satisfaction with democracy respectively.
5. This excludes Members who resigned and consequently left office prior to the 2010 general election. The analysis also excludes former Speaker Michael Martin who resigned in disgrace following his handling of the expenses scandal and those MPs who died while in office.
6. Many thanks to Phil Cowley, Justin Fisher, Ron Johnston, Charles Pattie, Colin Rallings and Michael Thrasher for advice on data and measures.
7. The variables are correlated and statistically significant but the correlation is weak in both cases (ACA and repaid $r = 0.09$, $p = 0.02$; ACA and named $r = 0.11$, $p = 0.01$).
8. See appendix for details.
9. The two scandal measures are moderately and significantly correlated (Pearsons' $r = 0.30$; $p < 0.001$).
10. Boundary change here is a dummy variable (1= changes to boundaries, 0= no changes). However, this finding is robust across different (ordered measures) specifications of boundary change.
11. Analysis not shown.
12. Seats vacant at the time of the 2010 election have not been included here (Ashok Kumar, Middlesbrough South and East Cleveland; Iris Robinson, Strangford; David Taylor, North West Leicestershire).
13. Derek Conway's Conservative Party whip was withdrawn on 29 January 2008 in response to allegations that he misused expenses by paying his son for work that was not done. This effectively left him permanently suspended from the parliamentary party.
14. De-selected by Labour Party on 15 June 2009.
15. Defeated in selection for merged seat on 26 April.
16. Defeated in selection for merged seat on 19 January.

5
The Impact of the Scandal on the 2010 General Election Results

Charles Pattie and Ron Johnston

To what extent did public anger over the expenses scandal have any measureable impact on the 2010 election outcome? Our analysis shows that despite worrisome predictions, voters didn't take the scandal as a reason to abandon electoral politics. At the constituency level, indignation over MPs' expenses was a mild discouragement to participation, no more. Moreover, the decision to vote or not was influenced by the same factors as in previous elections: what people thought of the scandal had no independent influence once these well-established factors were taken into account. Voters were undoubtedly disturbed by the expenses scandal, but few MPs who stood for re-election had their prospects damaged by their involvement in the scandal. Given the parlous state of the economy, voters had bigger issues to worry about.

One of the most striking manifestations of the 2009 expenses scandal was the extent and ferocity of public hostility towards politicians that it unleashed. Newspaper letters pages, radio phone-in programmes, on-line comments sections on most major media net pages and the blogosphere were overrun with often vitriolic comment. Memorably, in an edition of the popular BBC television *Question Time* programme broadcast from Grimsby on 14 May 2009, shortly after the story broke in the *Daily Telegraph*, two senior politicians from different parties (Labour's former deputy leader and Foreign Secretary in the mid-2000s, Margaret Beckett MP and Sir Menzies Campbell MP, former leader of the Liberal Democrats) were subjected to repeated and vociferous heckling from the studio audience throughout an evening of discussion dominated by the scandal. The depth of public anger was already clear, though much of the detail of the story had yet to be revealed.

In the days immediately after the story broke, we took part in a meeting, on a quite different topic, with academics, journalists and

Conservative MPs in the Palace of Westminster. It is no exaggeration to say that the atmosphere at the meeting was exceptionally tense: almost no politician in the room knew what was coming next or whether they personally would be swept up into the developing story (some subsequently were), but all were fearful of how the story might evolve and of what it might result in, not just for individual careers but also for the wider public standing of politics and politicians in Britain.

Furthermore, the scandal was unusual not only for the depth of feeling it evoked, but also for how widespread it proved. Most previous parliamentary scandals in the UK have involved either a few individual MPs or members from one party only (often the incumbent government). As such, it was relatively straightforward for others to protect themselves from the scandal, or even to seek to benefit from it (for instance, by opposition parties not implicated in the scandal arguing that the fault lay with the government, and that voters' best means of expressing their anger would be to vote for an opposition committed to 'cleaning up' politics). But the 2009 expenses scandal was different. No one party was a particular focus for concern and none could argue that it was an exemplar of probity. MPs from all parties and at all levels within Parliament, from junior backbenchers to senior figures in the Cabinet and Shadow Cabinet, were found wanting. To an unusual extent, almost the entire political class was drawn into the mire. The party leaders, sensing the baleful public mood, quickly insisted that MPs should pay back excessive claims.

Even so, not all MPs were equally exposed. Some, such as Ann Widdecombe (Conservative), were not implicated at all. And of those who were, some found themselves in a considerably worse position than others. Some MPs, such as Chris Mullin (Labour), made very modest expenses claims. Luton's two (Labour) MPs provided a particularly striking contrast. Although they came from the same party and represented neighbouring constituencies within the same relatively short commuting distance from central London, Kelvin Hopkins (Luton North) did not claim expenses for a second home, preferring to commute home each night, while Margaret Moran (Luton South) not only claimed for a second home, but did so for one which was neither in central London nor in – or even near – her constituency. In addition, she 'flipped' her designated second home address between three different houses, an act alleged to maximize benefits (Table 5.1).

Nor did public anger over the scandal fade quickly. As data from the British Election Study monthly Continuous Monitoring Surveys

Table 5.1 Public attitudes to the expenses scandal, June 2009–April 2010

	Expenses scandal makes me very angry		Expenses scandal proves most MPs are corrupt		Expenses scandal not that important		Expenses scandal: Corrupt MPs should resign	
	June 2009	April 2010	June 2009	April 2010	June 2009	April 2010	June 2009	April 2010
	%	%	%	%	%	%	%	%
Strongly agree	63.3	57.8	28.6	19.4	1.7	1.5	51.4	51.9
Agree	28.3	32.9	30.7	34.4	5.3	6.8	31.7	30.2
Neither agree nor disagree	5.6	6.9	17.8	20.6	5.9	6.1	9.1	10.7
Disagree	1.9	2.0	19.0	21.3	28.1	31.6	6.4	6.6
Strongly disagree	1.0	0.4	4.0	4.3	59.0	54.1	1.5	0.6
N	1761	941	1747	935	1761	933	1749	937
Chi-square	11.497		26.830		7.713		5.865	
significance	0.022		0.000		0.103		0.209	

Source: BES CMS.

(CMS) show, it had abated only slightly by the time of the 2010 general election, a year later. In June 2009, immediately after the scandal broke, 63% of CMS respondents strongly agreed that the scandal made them very angry. By April 2010, on the eve of the general election, this had dropped, but only to 58%. But the proportion saying they agreed (though not strongly) with the statement rose with the effect that the combined percentage of those agreeing and strongly agreeing that they were very angry about the scandal remained almost unchanged at around 91% in both surveys. Over the same period, there was a significant drop in the percentages strongly agreeing with the proposition that the scandal showed all MPs to be corrupt (down from 29% in June 2009 to 19% in April 2010). Even so, over half of all respondents still agreed to some extent with this claim by April 2010. And opinions on the extent to which the scandals mattered (around 86% of respondents felt they did) and on whether MPs found to have acted corruptly should resign (around 83% agreed here) changed little over the course of the year.

A plausible hypothesis, therefore, would be that anger over the scandal would be reflected in the ballot box come the election. Given a clearly demarcated group of 'rascals' seeking re-election, voters might well be expected to put the cliché definition of an election into practice, and kick them out. But, continued fury notwithstanding, did the scandal have any measureable impact on the election outcome? In this chapter, we examine the evidence.

Scandals and votes: Lessons from the past?

The expenses affair was hardly the first, nor will it be the last, political scandal. Looking at the fallout from previous scandals, both in the UK and abroad, gives some indications of what we might have expected at the 2010 election. Some scandals have far-reaching electoral consequences. The Tangentopoli scandal which engulfed Italian politics in the early and mid-1990s provides a particularly dramatic example. A judicial investigation found such pervasive evidence of political corruption that the Christian Democrat and Socialist parties, which had dominated Italian government since the end of World War II, collapsed. A fundamentally new party system emerged from the ruins, launching media magnate Silvio Berlusconi on his way to the top of Italian politics (Agnew 1997; Giannetti and Laver 2001; Wellhofer 2007). Most scandals do not have quite such extreme consequences, but they can affect election outcomes. Analyses of the impact of scandal on US Congressional elections shows that candidates accused of involvement in scandals lose support as a result, especially where they involve a moral lapse or bribery (Peters and Welch 1980). Between 1982 and 1990, for instance, 25% of all incumbents who had been charged with corruption and then ran for re-election were defeated, compared to only 3% of incumbent candidates who were not implicated in corruption (Welch and Hibbing 1997: 233).

The most recent substantial comparison in the UK is with the wave of sleaze allegations which engulfed John Major's Conservative government in the early 1990s (Ridley and Doig 1995). The comparison is not perfect, for two reasons. First, while the 2009 expenses scandal involved MPs from all parties, the 1990s sleaze allegations were mainly focused on MPs from the governing Conservative party: the latter was an asymmetric scandal, and therefore adverse electoral consequences, if any, should have been disproportionately focused on the government. Second, while the expenses scandal focused on one, relatively straightforward, issue and the key allegations all became public at roughly the same time, the scandals of the early 1990s were much more diffuse, both in content (some involving money, some influence peddling, and others moral shortcomings and sexual tittle-tattle) and in duration. Even so, like the expenses scandal a decade and a half later, it was widely anticipated that sleaze would be an important factor in the 1997 general election, and that MPs found wanting would suffer at the ballot box.

But while the scandals almost certainly contributed to the erosion of the Major government's authority and to its landslide defeat in 1997 – though not so much as the Exchange Rate Mechanism debacle and its consequences for the Conservatives' reputation for economic competence (Sanders 1999) – there was surprisingly little evidence that support for individual MPs was affected. A careful study of the impact of involvement in sleaze allegations on individual MPs' vote shares at the 1997 election found only very modest effects: very few if any MPs who stood for re-election in 1997 lost their seats as a result of personal accusations of sleaze (Farrell *et al.* 1998). A closer comparison can be found in the House Bank scandal (detailed in Chapter 4) that shook the US House of Representatives in the early 1990s (Banducci and Karp 1994; Williams 1998). Many Representatives chose to retire rather than take their chances: those who did stand for re-election faced harder battles than normal, and other things being equal, the more they personally had benefited from the House Bank scandal, the fewer votes they received in 2010 (Banducci and Karp 1994).

Just because past scandals had electoral effects does not mean that the same should be true of the 2009 expenses scandal, however. Over time, the frequency with which political scandals emerge seems to have increased, thanks to less deferential media, changing social norms and the cumulative effect of previous scandals (Williams 1998; Thompson 2000). One consequence seems to be that voters are increasingly inured to scandal. A comparative and cross-temporal analysis of political scandals' impacts on European voters between 1977 and 2007 suggests that a sort of 'scandal fatigue' has increasingly set in: voters exposed to more and more scandals are becoming harder to shock, and the political fallout from scandals is generally weakening (Kumlin and Esaiasson 2012). It takes a major event to pierce public cynicism. Was the 2009 scandal such an event? Kumlin and Esaiasson's (2012) analysis suggests it might have been. They find that scandals which engulf several parties, rather than just one party or individual politicians, are the most likely to produce negative reactions from voters. And the 2009 expenses scandal was nothing if not multi-party. Therefore, we might well expect electoral consequences.

Assessing the electoral impact of the 2009 expenses scandal

Assessing whether the expenses scandal did affect the results of the 2010 election is not straightforward, however, as it was not necessarily clear how disgruntled voters should react in 2010. Several different scenarios were possible. Voters could vent their rage on the incumbent Labour government, for failing to regulate MPs' expenses with sufficient vigour. Or, recognizing that MPs from all parties were found wanting, they might focus on those MPs whose behaviour was most unacceptable, whatever the MP's party affiliation.

But how were voters to assess how unacceptable an MP's behaviour was? Only a very few MPs faced outright criminal charges (and these were only laid some months after the general election): most others caught up in the scandal were enmeshed in a rather greyer netherworld of apparently morally dubious but not illegal activity. And some voters may have taken the view that those named in the scandal were just the group who were unlucky enough to be caught; those MPs not implicated directly were probably up to no good in some other way. For voters who felt this, a further option would have been to reject any incumbent MP seeking re-election. If this was the case, then incumbency, normally seen as an electoral advantage, should have become a pronounced disadvantage in 2010. Where parties were defending a seat, they should have done better where their candidate was not the incumbent than where he or she was. And in seats which they did not control going into the election, but where they hoped to make gains, they should have done better where they faced the incumbent MP than where the incumbent was standing down.

Alternatively, voters might feel that the scandal had tainted the entire political class. If so, then why should they expect any better from MPs elected for the first time in 2010 than from the old guard? Voters who felt this might, not unreasonably, have decided to abstain entirely. Finally, it is quite possible that, without underplaying voters' deep anger regarding the scandal, they did not let it influence their voting choices in 2010. Two factors might point to this outcome. First, the scandal was far from the only, or even the most serious, problem facing the country in 2010. The most serious global economic crisis since the 1930s had engulfed the UK economy in 2007: the national economy was still extremely fragile in 2010 and voters were rightly nervous about future prosperity. At the same time, British troops were still engaged in violent conflict in Afghanistan. Voters might well have taken the view that there were bigger things to worry about in 2010 than MPs' financial rectitude.

So what happened? To find out, we look at evidence from two different scales: voting in parliamentary constituencies and the decisions made by individual voters. An immediate challenge is how to measure the scandal. This is not straightforward. As noted above, different MPs were implicated to different extents, and for a range of different activities. Some were the subject of considerable press attention, while others' involvement was buried in the small print. Some were entirely innocent of any questionable actions; a very few strayed into outright illegality. Some alleged misuses of the expenses system suggested carelessness, some thoughtlessness and a failure to understand how claims might be seen by constituents (e.g. the widely-publicized claim, by Douglas Hogg MP, for the cost of cleaning the moat around his country manor). Most attention focused on the practice of 'flipping' second homes in order to maximise the yields from the second homes allowance.

We therefore utilize four different indicators of involvement in the scandal. The first builds on press reporting of the supposed 'worst offenders' among MPs by combining two newspapers' (the *Daily Telegraph* and the *News of the World*) lists of MPs whose claims they highlighted as particularly egregious: 15% of MPs were named in one or other (or both) lists. But the scandal extended further than this group. A second measure therefore draws on the official Legg Report into MPs' expenses, set up in response to the scandal. As part of its work, Legg's committee reviewed MPs' expenses claims and identified those which it felt to be either over-stated or unjustified: MPs were then required to repay the excess identified. Around 300 current and former MPs were judged to have nothing to repay. For the remainder, the average repayment was £1,500 and the maximum was £40,000. The repayment required of each MP by Legg therefore gives another measure of exposure to the scandal.

Public anger was not focused simply on those MPs whose claims were found to be questionable; more generally, many voters felt that even legitimate claims were excessive and unwarranted. To capture those, we employ a third measure, the amount claimed by each MP in 2008 (the year before the scandal broke) to cover the costs of staying away from their main home. Finally, we assess how individual voters felt about the scandal by the time of the 2010 general election using responses to the four questions outlined in Table 5.1, taken from the British Election Study (BES) face-to-face survey's pre-election wave.[1] An individual who strongly disagreed with the claims that the scandal made them very angry, that most MPs were corrupt, that corrupt MPs should resign, and who strongly agreed that the scandal was 'not that important', would score 1 on our combined scale; someone holding the diametrically opposite views on each question would score 5. Just before the 2010 election, the average BES respondent scored 3.85 on our scale, indicating that they were still quite angry about the scandal. As this survey interviewed the same individuals immediately before and after the 2010 election, this allows us to connect what they thought about the scandal on the eve of the election with how they actually voted in 2010.

Getting out or being forced out?

As demonstrated in Chapter 4, one electoral impact of the scandal began to manifest itself well before the election was called.[2] In some seats, therefore, the fact that the sitting MP stood down in 2010 in record numbers (Criddle 2010) removed voters' opportunity to vent their feelings towards that MP directly. Some of the heat might therefore have been taken out of the scandal by the removal (voluntary or involuntary) of some of the worst offenders before the electorate had a chance to pass judgement on them. After all, as we have seen, most voters thought that MPs caught out by corruption should resign. Many if not most voters will not have been too concerned with the precise legal status of MPs' actions: whether legally actionable or not, the taint of corruption demanded that they go – and go many of them did. The expenses scandal, however, was not the only factor behind the very high levels of retirement among MPs prior to the 2010 election. The previous parliament had been a long one; the incumbent government was widely expected to lose badly and some Labour MPs would not relish a prolonged period on the opposition benches; and boundary changes in England, Wales and Northern Ireland (though not in Scotland) meant some MPs' seats had disappeared.

Don't vote, it only encourages them?

But did the resignations assuage public anger enough to remove the expenses scandal as an issue at the 2010 general election? To answer that question, we need to look at the election results themselves. Perhaps the most severe potential electoral consequence of the scandal is the last outlined above: voters deciding that the entire political class, both in and out of office, was tainted by corruption, and hence that there was no point in voting at all. This sentiment, well-captured in the famous graffito 'don't vote, it only encourages them', was a real concern, particularly given the anaemic levels of participation at other recent British elections. Turnout at general elections since 1997 has been well below the post-war average, and many have looked to a growing disconnection between voters and politicians and declining trust in politics as causes (Stoker 2006; Hay 2007). How much worse would things be now that the scandal seemed to have confirmed many voters' worst opinions of politicians?

Perhaps the most severe potential effect of the scandal on turnout would have been a substantial drop in participation at the 2010 election. On the face of things, this did not happen. The national turnout rate rose slightly compared to 2005, from 61% to 65%. Whatever else was happening, voters weren't taking the scandal as a reason to abandon electoral politics entirely. That said, there is a longstanding relationship between turnout and how close an election is (Pattie and Johnston 2001). Where one party is clearly well ahead of its rivals and the result is not in much doubt, turnout tends to be relatively low. But where the competition is closer and the result more uncertain, turnout tends to increase. The 2010 election falls very much into the latter category. While it was widely anticipated that Labour would lose its majority, it was by no means certain that the Conservatives would be able to win a majority in turn, and the potential still existed for Labour to emerge as the largest single party in the Commons and hence the core for a coalition government. As a consequence, therefore, a rise in turnout was to be expected in 2010. Given the circumstances, the actual rise was surprisingly modest. This raises an intriguing, though hard-to-test, counterfactual: would the increase in turnout have been greater had the scandal not occurred?

While we cannot directly assess this, we can get an indirect idea by comparing the change in turnout in seats where the sitting MP was caught up in the scandal with the change in seats where the MP was not. For instance, if the scandal discouraged participation, then turnout might fall more in seats defended by MPs who were implicated in the row than in seats where they were not. Alternatively, it is possible that turnout increased more in seats defended by offending MPs than elsewhere, as voters there used their ballot box leverage to pass judgement on the malefactor. Neither possibility gains much support from the evidence however (see Table 5.2). Whether we look at turnout in all seats at the 2010 election, or only at turnout in seats being defended by sitting MPs, how exposed to the scandal the MP representing the seat before 2010 had been made no real difference to the turnout at the subsequent election.

There is one exception to this: the amount claimed by the MP on second home expenses was related to turnout in 2010. Turnouts were highest in seats where the MP had claimed a relatively middling amount on their second home in 2008, and almost as high in seats where the MP had claimed a relatively large amount for their second home. But they were lowest in seats where the MP had claimed least (the relationship falls narrowly short of significance when we look just at those MPs standing again in 2010). But the effect was hardly substantial: on average, turnout was about one percentage point higher in seats where the MP had claimed a relatively large amount on housing allowance than in seats where less had been claimed.

Turnout in 2010 is only part of the story, however: if MPs who made higher claims on their housing expenses represented seats where turnout was generally higher than average at most elections, for instance, it would not be terribly revealing to point out that the same pattern held in 2010. What is really of interest, therefore, is how turnout changed over time: the relevant data are also shown in Table 5.2. On average, turnout rose across the board between 2005 and 2010, whether or not MPs had been embroiled in the scandal. As before, however, being named and shamed in the press had no impact on turnout change. But interesting things happen when we look at the other indicators. Where a sitting MP was defending their seat again in 2010, the increase in turnout was lower in seats where Legg had asked the MP

Table 5.2 The impact of the scandal on average constituency turnout in 2010

	All MPs			MPs standing again in 2010		
	Average % turnout, 2010	Change in % turnout, 2005–2010	N	Average % turnout, 2010	Change in % turnout, 2005–2010	N
MP named by *Daily Telegraph* and/or *News of the World*						
Named by neither	65.10	4.24	541	65.24	4.16	421
Named by one	64.93	3.66	64	65.95	3.44	50
Named by both	66.45	4.76	34	65.44	4.79	19
F	0.977	1.721		0.374	1.845	
Sig.	0.377	0.180		0.688	0.159	
Amount required to be repaid by Legg Commission						
Nothing to be repaid	65.17	4.43	322	65.50	4.44	250
£0.01–£746.45	64.78	4.43	100	65.03	4.28	81
£746.46–£2163.99	65.81	3.67	102	65.87	3.48	79
£2164.00–£42458.21	64.86	3.91	115	64.50	3.56	80
F	0.707	2.274		0.997	3.202	
Sig.	0.548	0.079		0.394	0.023	
Expenses claimed for second home, 2008						
£0.00–£9634.89	64.22	5.37	124	64.44	5.47	101
£9634.90–£16761.65	64.16	4.13	124	64.12	3.89	87
£16761.66–£20539.67	65.80	3.52	125	65.90	3.67	101
£20539.68–£23351.74	65.59	3.51	125	65.87	3.29	103
£23351.75–£24006.00	65.53	4.47	124	65.73	4.12	80
F	2.566	9.112		2.317	8.800	
Sig.	0.037	0.000		0.056	0.000	

to repay a relatively large amount than where only a small, or no, repayment had been requested (though there was no difference when looking at all MPs). Similarly, the more an MP claimed on their housing in 2008, the lower the increase in turnout between 2005 and 2010. But again, we should not overstate the effects here. The differences in change in turnout are in the order of one percentage point or so. At the constituency level, indignation over MPs' expenses was a mild discouragement to participation, no more.

So much for the constituency contests: what about individual voters? To find out we turn to the 2010 BES face-to-face survey. The survey used a panel design, interviewing the same individuals shortly before and again immediately after the election. We therefore know whether they voted and we also know what they thought of the expenses scandal just before the start of the election campaign. Consequently, we can assess how those views might have influenced their chances of voting without worrying that their views on the scandal might have been affected by the outcome of the election, as might have been the case had we been forced to use attitudes on the scandal gathered in a post-election survey.

To assess people's attitudes to the scandal we turn our scale of how angry people were about the scandal on the eve of the 2010 election. On the face of it, those who voted in 2010 were slightly less angry about the scandal than were those who reported abstaining.[3] However, there is a risk that both individuals' feelings about the scandal and whether they voted in 2010 might be related to something else. For instance, we know that turnout tends to be higher among older voters than among younger voters, among the highly partisan than among the non-partisan and among those with especially degree-level qualifications than among those with no formal educational qualifications (Pattie and Johnston 2001). The same might conceivably be true of attitudes towards the scandal. It is plausible, for instance, that older voters, more partisan voters and voters with more formal education might be less angry about the scandal than their younger, less partisan and less formally educated peers (for education and partisanship at least, this does indeed seem to be the case; see Pattie and Johnston 2012). If this is the case, then the apparent effect of views on the scandal on individual turnout might be spurious. To find out, we need to take into account the effects of other, potentially confounding, factors.

Table 5.3 shows the effect of controlling for age, education and partisanship.[4] Each line in the table looks at two otherwise equivalent voters, one of whom was at the angriest end of the 'expenses attitudes' scale, and the other was at the least angry level: the numbers are the

Table 5.3 Individual voters' attitudes on the scandal and the probability of voting in 2010

Attitudes to the expenses scandal	Probability of voting 2010		Significance
	Least angry	Most angry	
No controls	0.89	0.72	0.004
Controls, Scenario 1: 40 year old, no party ID, no formal educational qualifications	0.86	0.80	0.155
Controls, Scenario 2: 40 year old, very strong party ID, university degree	1.00	1.00	0.155

Source: BES 2010 face-to-face survey.

probabilities of such an individual actually voting in 2010. The first line looks at the raw effects of feelings about the scandal, with no attempt to control for other factors. This confirms that angrier voters were less likely to vote in 2010 than less angry ones. Those most incensed about the scandal had a probability of voting of 0.72, compared to a probability of 0.89 for the least angry (and the effect was significant).[5] To demonstrate the impact of adding our controls for age, education and partisanship, we have estimated the equivalent probabilities for two different hypothetical groups of voters.

The first group (Scenario 1) are 40-year olds who have no formal educational qualifications and who are non-partisan. The second (Scenario 2) are also aged 40, but are highly partisan and are university graduates. Hence, even if the scandal had not happened, we would expect individuals in the first group to be less likely to vote than their compatriots in the second, and this is indeed what we observe. But, more importantly for the story here, whichever hypothetical group of voters we look at, the impact of feelings about the scandal on propensity to vote are much smaller than had seemed to be the case when no controls were included. Not only that, but the impact of views on the scandal ceases to be a significant influence on participation in the election. The decision to vote or not was influenced by the same factors as in previous elections: what people thought of the scandal had no independent influence once these well-established factors were taken into account.

This does not quite resolve the matter, however. Even though individuals' attitudes regarding the scandal had no independent effect on their propensity to vote in 2010, once the strength of their partisanship was taken into account, it is still possible that the scandal had an indirect influence on individual turnout, by weakening partisanship. Anger regarding the scandal might have disproportionately weakened voters' attachments to parties. If this was the case, then controlling for strength of partisanship on the eve of the 2010 election might mean we inadvertently miss the effect of the scandal on turnout. To find out, however, we need information over a longer time-frame than just the period immediately before and after the 2010 campaign. We turn, therefore, to the BES 2005–2010 panel, which used an internet survey to follow the same group of 2,231 individuals from the 2005 to the 2010 election. Over the five years from just after the 2005 election until just before the 2010 campaign, 40% of this group changed how strongly they said they identified with a political party, 22% becoming less partisan, and 18% becoming more partisan – though most changed only a little (going from very to fairly strong partisanship, for instance). But the relationship between what people thought of the expenses scandal on the eve of the 2010 election, while significant, was not linear (see Figure 5.1).[6] Those whose level of partisanship did not change over

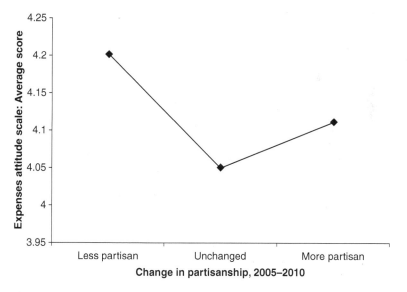

Figure 5.1 Changing strength of partisanship and attitudes to the expenses scandal
Source: 2005–2010 BES panel survey.

time were, on average, the least angry about the scandal. The angriest group were those who became less intensely partisan over time. But those who became more partisan over the course of the parliament were also angrier about the scandal than were those whose identification with one party or another did not shift. What is more, the actual variations in attitudes regarding the scandal between these three groups were small.

It seems as though the scandal had only a muted net effect on the decision to participate in the 2010 election. This does not mean, of course, that it had no effect on individuals' decisions. Some may have been discouraged from voting by the revelations. But others may have come to the opposite conclusion – get involved and get even! Overall, though, the two motivations seem to have cancelled each other out. Despite media anxieties, the scandal did not, in the end, prove to turn people away from electoral politics.

The partisan consequences

Even if the net effects on participation were only small, however, it is still possible that the scandal might have affected who individuals actually voted for. As noted above, there are several possibilities: voting against incumbents most implicated in the scandal, whatever their party; voting against all incumbents seeking re-election whether guilty or not (on the grounds that those not exposed by the scandal could well have been up to something too); or voting against the incumbent Labour government, on the grounds that it had not done enough to control MPs' questionable behaviour.

One possibility is easily dashed. There was no general anti-incumbent mood in 2010. Indeed, other things being equal, parties did better in the 2010 election when they were represented in a seat by an incumbent MP than where their incumbent had stood down, and a new candidate had stepped in (Denver 2010: 16). Among the three main parties, the incumbency effect was smallest for the Conservatives (the party's 2010 vote shares were on average 1.3 percentage points higher where they were represented by sitting MPs than where they had a non-incumbent candidate) and highest for the Liberal Democrats (whose average incumbent candidate advantage was worth 5.3 percentage points; the equivalent for Labour was a 2.3 percentage point incumbent advantage). But in every case, and as in previous elections, incumbent candidates were generally more of an advantage for parties than they were a disadvantage. Of course, as noted above, many of those MPs with the most problematic records on the expenses scandal had stepped down and were not seeking re-election. Even so, there was no blanket rejection of sitting MPs.

That said, even among those MPs seeking re-election, some had been more exposed to scandal than had others. So did the extent to which MPs were implicated in the expenses row make a difference to their party's vote share in 2010? There is some evidence that it did. Table 5.4 looks at the average change in each party's vote share in each constituency between 2005 and 2010, broken down by the three measures of the sitting MP's exposure to the scandal employed earlier. The first three columns of the table look at all seats. Perhaps the most noticeable thing here is that in almost every case, the extent to which MPs had been drawn into the scandal had no significant impact on how much their vote share changed between the two elections. The only exception is the relationship between Labour's changing vote share in a seat and the amount the sitting MP (of any party) had claimed on their housing expenses in 2008. Here, the story is a simple one: Labour's vote share fell least in those seats where the MP claimed least on housing expenses.

Looking at all constituency contests risks confusing the story, however, as it does not take into account the possibility that parties' candidates might be treated differently in seats the party had won at the previous election (and hence where any misdemeanours on the part of the MP would fall at the party's door) compared to seats where the party came second or worse in 2005 (and where its candidate could not really be held responsible, either directly or by association, for any dubious claims made by the MP). The next set of columns therefore looks only at those seats each party was defending in 2010: we concentrate just on Labour and Conservative seats here, as there were too few Liberal Democrat seats to allow for reliable analysis of the scandal's impact on that party's vote in its own constituencies. Here, there is rather stronger evidence of an impact on voting. In those seats they were defending in 2010, Labour and Conservatives both did worse, relatively speaking, in constituencies where the MP had been named by the press during the scandal than in seats where they had not, and in seats where the MP had claimed a relatively large amount on their second home than in seats where they had claimed only a little. How much an MP had been asked to repay by the Legg Commission did not have quite as consistent an effect, however. Only in the case of the changing Labour vote in Labour seats did repayments required by Legg seem to be related to changing support, and then not in a straightforward way. Relatively speaking Labour did best (or, more accurately, lost a smaller share of its vote) not in those seats where the MP had been asked to repay nothing,

Table 5.4 The impact of the scandal on average change in constituency vote shares between 2005 and 2010

	All MPs: average % change, 2005–2010			Seats defended by party: Average % change 2005–2010		Seats where party candidate in 2010 was an MP: Average % change, 2005–2010	
	Labour	Conservative	Liberal Democrat	Labour	Conservative	Labour	Conservative
MP named by *Daily Telegraph* and/or *News of the World*							
Named by neither	−6.41	3.79	0.85	−5.43	4.11	−4.89	4.57
Named by one	−6.15	4.21	0.88	−8.22	3.46	−7.48	3.19
Named by both	−7.55	3.00	1.79	−7.53	1.28	−6.38	1.93
F	0.60	1.42	0.68	3.31	5.11	1.92	3.58
Sig.	0.548	0.242	0.505	0.038	0.007	0.149	0.030
Amount required to be repaid by Legg Commission							
Nothing to be repaid	−6.23	3.85	0.91	−5.78	4.38	−4.39	4.66
£0.01–£746.45	−6.08	3.62	0.79	−4.77	3.46	−5.23	3.47
£746.46–£2163.99	−7.54	3.85	1.44	−7.85	3.09	−6.89	3.98
£2164.00–£42458.21	−6.42	3.73	0.50	−4.86	3.64	−5.76	4.35
F	1.26	0.14	0.79	2.88	1.74	1.71	1.07
Sig.	0.286	0.937	0.499	0.036	0.159	0.165	0.364
Expenses claimed for second home, 2008							
£0.00–£9634.89	−3.69	3.68	0.15	−2.47	5.29	−1.97	5.75
£9634.90–£16761.65	−7.13	3.82	1.20	−7.23	2.64	−6.13	3.68
£16761.66–£20539.67	−6.35	3.53	0.79	−6.19	3.54	−5.77	3.59
£20539.68–£23351.74	−6.89	3.98	1.00	−5.97	3.52	−6.08	4.04
£23351.75–£24006.00	−7.73	3.69	1.34	−6.42	3.85	−6.68	4.14
F	7.94	0.31	1.28	6.87	2.85	5.76	2.49
Sig.	0.00	0.87	0.278	0.000	0.025	0.000	0.046

but in its seats where Legg had asked either for a small or for a large repayment. And the party did worst in those of its seats where Legg had asked the MP to repay a middling amount.

The final two columns in Table 5.4 focus in even more, to look only at changes in Labour and Conservative vote shares in those seats they were defending and where the incumbent MP stood for re-election in 2010 (once again, there were too few Liberal Democrats to analyse separately). This allows us to get some idea of whether voters took their frustrations over the scandal out on those MPs with the temerity to face them, or whether the retirements of some of the worst offenders had largely contained the damage for the parties. The story is broadly similar to that for all seats defended by each party. Conservative incumbents seeking re-election who had been named in both the *Daily Telegraph* and *News of the World* lists of 'worst offenders' saw their party's vote rise by less, on average, than did their peers who had not been named (the effect for Labour incumbents was similar, but did not reach statistical significance). And both Labour and Conservative incumbents whose housing claims had been modest did somewhat better than other incumbents with more exorbitant claims.

That said, even though it did have some effect, the expenses scandal was not a major influence on each party's constituency vote share in 2010. One way of demonstrating this is to look at the amount of variation in each party's 2010 vote share which can be explained by our measures of exposure to the scandal, once we control for how well it did in the same seat at the previous election (recognizing that there is substantial long-term stability in where parties do well or badly). Once we do this, our measures of exposure to the expenses scandal add only about one percentage point on average onto our ability to explain Labour's 2010 vote share in its own seats, and almost exactly the same, on average, to our explanation of the Conservatives' 2010 vote share in the seats they were defending. Long-term trends continued to dominate Britain's electoral geography in 2010: the effects of the scandal were felt only at the margins.

What about individual voters' party choices? To keep things simple, we concentrate here too on voting for a party in seats it was defending in 2010, and that means we once again have to leave the Liberal Democrats out of the picture. We want to see whether attitudes to the scandal affected whether or not people living in Labour-defended seats went on to vote Labour in 2010, and whether those in Conservative-defended seats voted Conservative. But voting is a complex decision, reflecting many different influences, so we need to take some of these into account in order to get a fair impression of the net effect of attitudes regarding the scandal. We therefore build our analyses up in three steps, adding controls at each stage.[7]

The first step looks only at the impact of attitudes regarding the scandal on the likelihood of voting for each party. But attitudes to an MP's behaviour during the scandal might be shaped not only by what the MP did, but by which party the voters supports; people may well think better of MPs from 'their' party than of MPs from other parties. Furthermore, at the individual as at the constituency level, there is a considerable degree of long-term stability in which party people vote for: many voters vote for the same party in successive elections. The second stage therefore looks at the impact of attitudes to the scandal on the 2010 vote, controlling for how each individual voted in 2005. While long-term support can explain some of the variation in individual voting, it cannot explain it all. Individuals' decisions are also influenced by their assessments of how well or badly they think the government is performing, or the opposition might handle things if it were in power (so-called valence judgments, see Clarke *et al.* 2004, 2009). The third stage of our analysis therefore adds further controls for individuals' pre-election evaluations of how the Labour government was performing, and their assessments of how the Conservative opposition might have performed if it had been in office.[8] At each step, we compare the likelihoods that hypothetical individuals who were at either extreme of the scale of anger regarding the scandal would vote for each party in 2010. Table 5.5 shows the key results for voting Labour in Labour-defended seats, and Table 5.6 shows the equivalent results for voting Conservative in Conservative-defended seats.

Our first scenario looks just at the effects of attitudes to the scandal, with no attempt to control for other influences on the vote. The impact of attitudes to the scandal on the probability that individuals in Labour-defended seats would vote Labour in 2010 was significant and large: whereas there was a 0.72 probability that those who were least angry about the scandal would vote for the party, this fell steeply to a probability of just 0.31 for those who were angriest (see Table 5.5). Controlling for which party an individual had voted for in 2005 (Model 2) only slightly reduced the significance of attitudes to the scandal on voting Labour. We look at two different scenarios here: first of all, the impact of views on the scandal for those who either abstained or were too young to vote in 2005, and then their impact on those who voted Labour at the earlier election. In both cases, the angrier someone was about the scandal, the less likely they were to vote Labour in a Labour-defended seat. But adding controls for valence judgements (Model 3) renders the

Table 5.5 Individual voters' probabilities of voting Labour in Labour-defended seats, 2010

Attitudes on expenses scandal:	Probability of voting Labour		Significance
	Least angry	Most angry	
Model 1: No controls			
Scenario 1: No controls	0.72	0.31	0.000
Model 2: Control for 2005 vote			
Scenario 2: Abstained in 2005	0.38	0.06	0.002
Scenario 3: Voted Labour in 2005	0.72	0.22	0.002
Model 3: Control for 2005 vote and 2010 pre-election valence judgements on Labour and Conservatives			
Scenario 4: Abstained in 2005, indifferent on both valence measures	0.15	0.15	0.992
Scenario 4: Voted Labour in 2005, indifferent on both valence measures	0.46	0.47	0.992

Source: 2010 BES face-to-face survey.

effect of opinions on the scandal on voting Labour insignificant and insubstantial. In similar analyses for individuals in Conservative-held seats, views on the scandal had no significant effect on the likelihood of actually voting Conservative in 2010, even when no controls were used (see Table 5.6).

This suggests that deciding whether or not to vote Labour in Labour-defended seats or Conservative in Conservative-defended seats depended on two things: past support and how well or badly individuals felt the government was performing (or the opposition might perform on major policy issues of the day), none of which were linked to the scandal. By the time of the 2010 election, therefore, attitudes to the scandal, though still strongly held, were not a major independent influence on how individuals voted.

Conclusions

The above analyses point to an apparent paradox. Voters were undoubtedly very disturbed indeed by the expenses scandal. But, with only a few exceptions, such as Jacqui Smith and Hazel Blears, few MPs who stood for re-election could truly be said to have had their prospects

Table 5.6 Individual voters' probabilities of voting Conservative in Conservative-defended seats, 2010

Attitudes on expenses scandal	Probability of voting Conservative		Significance
	Least angry	Most angry	
Model 1: No controls			
Scenario 1: No controls	0.57	0.49	0.900
Model 2: Control for 2005 vote			
Scenario 2: Abstained in 2005	0.35	0.38	0.827
Scenario 3: Voted Conservative in 2005	0.94	0.95	0.827
Model 3: Control for 2005 vote and 2010 pre-election valence judgements on Labour and Conservatives			
Scenario 4: Abstained in 2005, indifferent on both valence measures	0.48	0.18	0.060
Scenario 4: Voted Conservative in 2005, indifferent on both valence measures	0.93	0.77	0.060

Source: 2010 BES face-to-face survey.

damaged by their involvement in the scandal. Not only that, but where explicitly anti-scandal candidates from outside the party system stood, they generally did not do well. The most notable example was the television consumer champion Esther Rantzen, who stood in Luton South, where the incumbent MP was, as discussed above, deeply implicated in the scandal: Ms Rantzen not only lost, but lost her deposit, taking only 4% of the vote in 2010. For all the furore (and fury) that surrounded it, the scandal's impact on the outcome of the 2010 election seems to have been muted.

So what happened? Clearly, voters were not in a forgiving mood. But, given the parlous state of the national and international economies, they had bigger issues to worry about. Furthermore, as many of the most serious malefactors had removed themselves (or had been removed by their party hierarchies) before the election and did not stand again, some of the more obvious targets for public ire, and with them the electoral sting of the scandal, were taken out of the frame before the vote. Valence concerns seem to have trumped public anger. Nor was this entirely novel. The sleaze scandals of the early 1990s had only a limited effect on the outcome of the 1997 British general election. Similarly – though not strictly a comparable type of scandal – many Australian voters were incensed when, in 1974, the Labor Prime Minister was dismissed by the Governor-General, prompting a constitutional crisis. But though they were deeply angered by the perceived constitutional impropriety, this did not translate into votes for Labour in the subsequent election, which was dominated by economic issues and resulted in Labor's defeat. Scandals might be terrible news for individuals' political careers, but there is no inevitable relationship between scandal and election outcomes, particularly when more pressing matters are at stake and when the wounds of the scandal are cauterized by removing the most egregious offenders from public judgement.

Notes

1. The scale was constructed by taking each question in Table 5.1 and coding the five possible answers to it from 1 to 5, where 1 represents the least angry response and 5 the angriest. Individuals' answers across all four answers were then added and divided by 4 to create a summary scale running from 1 (not terribly angry regarding the scandal) to 5 (very angry).
2. In fact, those who decided to retire in 2010 were, on average, asked by the Legg Commission to pay back twice as much in wrongly awarded expenses as were those who did not retire (£2,353 vs £1,247 respectively).
3. Although small (the averages for voters and non-voters on our scale of attitudes regarding the scandal were 3.82 and 3.99), the difference was statistically significant (t = 3.644, p = 0.000).
4. The table is based on the results of two binary logistic regressions, both with self-reported turnout in 2010 as the dependent variable. The first ('no controls') model has only one explanatory variable: individuals' scores on the 'attitudes to scandal' scale. The second ('controls added') model also includes individuals' age in years, educational qualifications (split into four groups: those with no formal qualifications; those whose highest qualification is a school qualification; those whose highest is a post-school qualification short of degree level; and those with a degree), and the strength of their partisanship (also split into four groups: those who say they support no party; those who generally support a particular party, but not very strongly; fairly strong partisans; and very strong partisans).
5. It should be noted that reported turnout tends to be higher in surveys than in reality, partly because some respondents wrongly report voting when they actually abstained, but mainly because non-voters tend also to be

disproportionately less likely to take part in surveys (Swaddle and Heath 1989).

6. An analysis of variance test for the averages displayed in Figure 5.1 produced an F-statistic of 11.71, significant at the 0.000 level.

7. As with the analysis of individual turnout, these analyses were conducted using binary logistic regressions.

8. The valence measures were constructed using answers to a series of questions in the pre-election wave of the 2010 BES. Respondents were asked 'how well (did they) think the present (Labour) government has handled/ a Conservative government would handle each of the following issues': crime: education; immigration; the National Health Services; terrorism; the economy generally; taxation; the war in Afghanistan; and the current financial crisis. Answers were given on a 1–5 scale, where 1 indicated that the respondent thought the Labour government or the Conservative opposition had handled/would handle the issue very well, and 5 indicated that they felt the issue had been/would be handled very badly. Each individual's responses across all nine issues were summed up separately for Labour and the Conservatives. The higher an individual's score on each valence scale, therefore, the less well they thought that party was performing or would perform in office.

6
Where Did Electoral Accountability Fail? MP Misconduct, Constituent Perceptions and Vote Choice

Nick Vivyan, Markus Wagner and Jessica Tarlov

Many voters know little about their MPs, so we would not expect many constituents to have known whether their MP was involved in the expenses scandal or not. Yet, we show evidence from the British Election Study (BES) internet panel that, in general, voters' perceptions of their MP's behaviour did correspond, at least somewhat, to their actual involvement in the scandal. Nevertheless, it is also the case that almost half of voters did not know whether their MP was involved in the scandal, and perceptions were also biased by political predispositions. Moreover, voters did not punish their MPs for their perceived misconduct: the link between perceptions and vote choice was weak compared to that between publicly available information and perceptions.

Introduction

A key puzzle arising from the expenses scandal was that voters largely failed to punish MPs who had been publicly implicated in the scandal. Among sitting MPs who stood for re-election in 2010, the electoral cost of implication in the scandal has so far been estimated at around a mere 1.5% (Curtice *et al.* 2010; Eggers and Fischer 2011; Pattie and Johnston 2012). This apparent lack of strong electoral accountability is surprising because voters told pollsters that they felt strongly about MPs over-claiming on expenses. According to the 2010 BES pre-election survey carried out nine months after the scandal first erupted, 93% of British voters had heard of the scandal, while over 90% agreed or strongly agreed with the statement that the scandal made them very angry. Moreover, 80% of voters agreed or strongly agreed that MPs implicated in the scandal should resign.[1]

Why was electoral accountability so limited? One potential explanation is that the MPs implicated in the scandal anticipated electoral punishment and therefore declined to re-stand for election at the 2010 general election. Yet even among those MPs most severely publicly implicated in the expenses scandal, over 50% chose to stand for re-election in 2010 (Pattie and Johnston 2012). Thus, strategic retirement cannot entirely explain the apparent lack of electoral accountability for expenses-related misconduct in 2010.

In this chapter, we explore why voters can fail to punish misbehaving representatives who decide to run again. Electoral accountability could have failed because constituents did not know whether their local MP had over-claimed or formed incorrect perceptions about their MP's behaviour. Yet, even if citizens did know about their MP's misconduct, accountability could have failed if voters chose not to sanction the MP by voting for an alternative candidate (Ferejohn 1986; Przeworski *et al.* 1999). Put simply, electoral accountability for misconduct can fail at either the *perceptions* or the *sanctions* step.

There are good reasons to believe that accountability fails at the perceptions step. Specifically, voters may either not know about their representative's behaviour (Delli Carpini and Keeter 1996; Holmberg 2009) or develop incorrect perceptions based on personal or partisan biases (Campbell *et al.* 1960; Fenno 1978; Peters and Welch 1980; Ferejohn 1990). Yet it is also plausible that voters fail to hold their representatives accountable at the sanctions step. They may often not be willing or able to punish representatives for wrongdoing, for example if they think the balance of power in Parliament is more important (Rundquist *et al.* 1977). This may be strongly influenced by the institutional features of a political system, most importantly the electoral system (Carey and Shugart 1995; Persson and Tabellini 2000; Persson *et al.* 2003; Chang and Golden 2006).

In this chapter, we primarily test whether electoral accountability following the 2009–2010 expenses scandal failed at the *perceptions* step. If we find evidence that the main problem was here, then electoral accountability was limited mainly due to the fact that constituents did not know about their MP's misbehaviour or had formed biased views based on partisan or MP-specific predispositions. If we find evidence that voters did tend to be well informed about their MP's behaviour, then to explain the lack of electoral accountability we have to look at causes other than voter information, for example institutional incentives.

The chapter is structured as follows. In the next section, we expand on the perception and sanction steps necessary for electoral accountability for misconduct and discuss factors that may aid or hinder their operation in practice. Then we describe our measure of whether or not each MP was publicly revealed to have made improper expenses claims. Following this, we empirically examine the influence of public information on perceptions of misconduct, before turning to the consequences of perceptions of misconduct for electoral choices. We conclude by summarizing our findings and considering their broader implications, also beyond the UK context.

Electoral accountability for misconduct: Perceptions and sanction

Before electoral accountability for misconduct can occur, the wrongdoing by representatives of course needs to be exposed. This is often done by a media outlet, such as the *Daily Telegraph* in the 2009–2010 expenses scandal. In many cases, further instances of misconduct may come to light due to a subsequent official investigation or inquiry. For instance, testimony given at the Leveson inquiry has revealed an unsavoury relationship between members of the government and the media as well as inappropriate conduct by members of the police force, resulting in arrests. The Nolan inquiry, set up to investigate MPs' outside interests after the 1994 cash-for-questions affair, released a report which publicly named and shamed representatives and led to the creation of the Committee on Standards and Privileges. In the case of the expenses scandal, the House of Commons commissioned Sir Thomas Legg to investigate all MPs' claims in detail. Legg's final report, published in February 2010 (House of Commons Members Estimate Committee 2010), focused on excessive claims made within the Additional Costs Allowance, a scheme that allowed MPs to claim money to pay for and maintain a second home, either in their constituency or in London.[2] Of course, voters did not need to read the *Telegraph* or download the Legg report to find out whether their MP implicated in the scandal. Rather, awareness of misconduct will often have spread via other national and local media, campaign groups, local competing candidates and the politicians themselves.

Perceptions of misconduct

Why might public perceptions of misconduct of MPs nevertheless have been limited? The literature suggests two main reasons. First, voters can simply be ignorant of their representative's wrongdoing. Gathering and processing such information is generally costly (Ferejohn 1990).

Moreover, institutional settings vary in the extent to which they provide voters with incentives to become informed (Holmberg 2009; Stevenson and Vonnahme 2009). In Britain, these incentives are weak: this is because the political system is characterized by strong party control of representatives in the legislature, so it makes sense for voters to choose their MP largely based on each candidate's party affiliation. Furthermore, the costs of becoming informed about local MP behaviour are high: information about individual MPs is relatively hard to come by due to the low levels of local campaign spending and local media coverage (Cain *et al.* 1987; Pattie *et al.* 1994; Pattie and Johnston 2004; Kam 2009).

In addition to a lack of knowledge, voters may also have biased perceptions. To reduce the costs associated with information-gathering, individuals make use of heuristics when forming an opinion about their representative (Ferejohn 1990). A simple decision rule allows voters to make judgments about their representative even while remaining relatively ignorant about the representative's actual behaviour. Two such rules of thumb may be particularly influential in the British context: affect towards an MP and affect towards the MP's party. Voters may be less likely to think that their MP misbehaved if they are positively predisposed towards them or to the MP's party. Recent findings from the UK (e.g. Marsh and Tilley 2010; Tilley and Hobolt 2011; Wagner *et al.* forthcoming) indicate that theories of partisan perceptual bias (Campbell *et al.* 1960) travel well.

Sanctioning of misconduct

Why might voters have failed to punish their MPs even when they knew they had been implicated in the expenses scandal? While some voters may decide that their MP's misconduct is worth punishing, for many voters other concerns will be more important than the misbehaviour of their representative (Rundquist *et al.* 1977). For example, they may think that re-electing such an MP is an acceptable price to pay in order to ensure that their party gains as many seats as possible in Parliament. They may also believe that the MP deserves to be re-elected despite their misconduct, for example if they have otherwise proven themselves to be a successful and effective representative. As a result, many voters may decide not to punish a representative who they believe has engaged in wrongdoing. The consequence of such decisions would be that electoral accountability for misconduct would only be limited.

Accordingly, research from the US has found that incumbents are moderately punished for their misbehaviour (Peters and Welch 1980;

Ahuja *et al.* 1994; Banducci and Karp 1994; Dimock and Jacobsen 1995; Welch and Hibbing 1997; Clarke *et al.* 1999). In the UK, Farrell *et al.* (1998) study the relationship between corruption and vote loss and find that candidates involved in a scandal lose upwards of five percentage points, a magnitude similar to that in the US. As noted above, the specific electoral effects of the 2009–2010 expenses scandal have previously been studied by Curtice *et al.* (2010), Eggers and Fischer (2011) and Pattie and Johnston (2012). In the following sections, we turn to our empirical test of the two possible ways in which electoral accountability can fail.

Coding MP involvement in the expenses scandal

Our measure of whether a British[3] MP who sat in the 2005–2010 Parliament was publicly implicated in the expenses scandal is constructed based on two sources: the Legg report together with the *Daily Telegraph* and *Sunday Telegraph*.[4] We coded an MP as being 'implicated' by Legg if they were formally asked to repay money in his report. We coded an MP as being 'implicated' by the *Telegraph* if the *specifics* of the MP's claim were discussed in a *Telegraph* article (MPs were not coded as 'implicated' by the *Telegraph* if their claims were only mentioned in a general article on the scandal).[5] We focus on the *Telegraph* as a media source because it had sole access to the expenses records and acted as a gatekeeper on public information; prior to the publication of the Legg report, any MP publicly implicated was therefore first mentioned by the *Telegraph*.

Our final *implicated* variable equals one if an MP was coded as being implicated by either the *Telegraph* or the Legg report, and zero otherwise. Both the Legg report and the *Telegraph* exposed misconduct, but who was implicated in each source differed. The Legg report did not encompass all potential types of expenses-related misconduct. For instance, Geoffrey Clifton Brown, who was the Conservative Shadow Minister for International Development, was accused of 'flipping' (i.e. changing) his second home designation from London to his Gloucestershire home and, at the same time, buying another countryside home for almost three million pounds. His case garnered tremendous media attention and ridicule, but he was not asked to repay any money by Legg because his claims were within the rules. In contrast, Alun Michael's claims were not detailed in the *Telegraph*, but he was ordered in the Legg report to repay over £19,000 for invalid mortgage claims. These types of cases illustrate the importance of using both sources to capture public implication in the scandal. Overall we have 587 MP-level observations on our *implicated* variable.[6] Of these, just over two thirds (418) are coded as implicated and just under a third (169) are not.

Constituent perceptions of misconduct: Data and analysis

To test the first step necessary for electoral accountability, we combine our measure of MP involvement in the expenses scandal with survey data from four waves of the BES 2005–2010 internet panel study:[7] the first wave, carried out in March and April 2005, before that year's general election; the third wave, from May 2005, after that year's election; the fifth wave, from June 2008; and the seventh wave, from late March/early April 2010, before the 2010 election.[8] Each survey respondent was matched to an MP from the 2005–2010 Parliament and assigned the corresponding *implicated* score for that MP.[9] Our sample consists of all survey respondents located in one of the 587 constituencies for which there is a non-missing value on our MP *implicated* variable. Our resulting data set contains observations on respondents from 579 of the 587 constituencies for which we measure our *implicated* variable, with an average of five respondents per constituency. Of the 3,218 respondents in this data, almost 70% (2,245) were represented in the 2005–2010 Parliament by an MP who was implicated in the scandal by the *Telegraph* or by Sir Thomas Legg. The remaining 30% (973) had an MP who was not implicated in the expenses scandal.

To measure respondent perceptions, we utilize responses to a question from the seventh wave (March/April 2010). Survey participants were asked whether they had heard or read about the expenses scandal. Those answering 'yes' were then presented with the following question: 'Now, thinking about the MP in your local constituency, has he or she claimed expense money to which they are not entitled?'[10] The item was fielded just before the 2010 election campaign got underway but after the February 2010 Legg report, so it measures constituent beliefs shortly after the last public revelations concerning the scandal.

Descriptive analysis

Table 6.1 breaks down respondents' perceptions of their MP's expenses claims according to whether or not the MP was publicly implicated in the scandal or not. The first notable feature of this table is that almost half of the 3,218 respondents (44.9%) 'don't know' whether or not their MP over-claimed. That such a high proportion of respondents feel unable to state a clear opinion on the claims of their MP places an immediate limit on the operation of the *perceptions* step necessary

Table 6.1 Voter perceptions of MP behaviour

MP involved in expenses scandal	Respondent perception of MP over claiming			
	Don't know	Did not overclaim	Overclaimed	Marginal N
Not implicated	46.6% (453)	40.8% (397)	12.6% (123)	973
Implicated	44.2% (993)	25.7% (577)	30.1% (675)	2245
All MPs	44.9% (1446)	30.3% (974)	24.8% (798)	3218

Note: Row percentages shown; data from BES 2005–2010 panel survey and own coding.

for accountability for misconduct. So, while almost all respondents had heard of the scandal, many could not say whether their own MP was implicated. This may partly have been due to the nature of the scandal, which involved many MPs at the same time, perhaps making it more difficult to know whether one's own MP was mentioned or not. Moreover, some voters may not know the name of their MP or even of their constituency, so even if they had heard about their MP's behaviour, this may not have led them to actually know whether they were implicated.

Table 6.1 also shows that voters who do state an opinion (i.e. do not answer 'don't know') have a tendency to attribute innocence to their own MP, a finding that echoes Fenno's (1978) well-known paradox that American voters tend to disapprove of Congress but trust their district's representative. The bottom row shows that of the 1,772 respondents who state an opinion, over half (55%) think their MP did not over-claim.

But despite this, there is also clear evidence of an association between public implication of an MP in the scandal and respondents' perceptions. Of respondents whose MP was not implicated, 40.8% think their MP did not over-claim, compared to 12.6% who think their MP did over-claim. In contrast, among those respondents whose MP was implicated, the corresponding proportions are 25.7% and 30.1%, respectively. This still means that many people whose MP was implicated still believed he or she was innocent, but respondents were nevertheless more likely, by a magnitude of 17.5 percentage points, to think that their MP had over-claimed when the MP was publicly implicated in the scandal.

Multivariate analysis

Regression analysis provides firmer evidence for the finding that constituent perceptions of MP conduct differ depending on whether the MP was publicly implicated in the scandal. We model our main dependent variable using multinomial logit since it has three response options ('over-claimed', 'did not over-claim' and 'don't know'). Standard errors are clustered by constituency to account for the fact that respondents are nested within parliamentary seats.

Our key explanatory variable is our measure of whether or not a respondent's MP was *implicated* in the expenses scandal. We also control for a number of other variables that might plausibly influence respondent perceptions. The most important control variables measure partisan and MP-related voter predispositions. We thus include a measure of a respondent's previous electoral support for their 2005–2010 incumbent MP, coded as one if the respondent reported voting for this MP at the 2005 general election and zero otherwise. Second, we control for whether, in the 2008 wave, the constituent identified with the party of the 2005–2010 incumbent MP. This variable equals one if a respondent identifies with the party of their MP, and zero otherwise. We also control for more general respondent attributes that may influence their responses: attention paid to politics, political knowledge, general trust and political efficacy (see Vivyan *et al.* 2012 for details on coding).

Further, we include two constituency-level variables: the party affiliation of a respondent's MP and the notional size of the majority the winning MP enjoyed in the respondent's constituency in 2005 (Norris 2010).[11] Finally, we also include a dummy variable that equals one when a respondent's 2005 constituency matches their 2010 constituency, and zero otherwise.[12] The variable controls for the possibility that the respondent moved between 2005 and 2010 or that they were assigned a new incumbent MP due to boundary changes. While our dependent variable is based on a survey question fielded before the 2010 election, and therefore refers to a respondent's incumbent under the 2005 electoral boundaries, a respondent whose constituency is due to change under the re-drawn 2010 boundaries might be less sure of their MP's identity and therefore more likely to answer 'don't know'.

Our key results are presented in Table 6.2. Model 1 includes only our main explanatory variable. Models 2 and 3 then add the series of controls described above, but vary in the measures of constituent predisposition toward an MP included: in Model 2, we control for whether the constituent voted for the MP in the 2005 election, whereas in Model 3 we also control for identification with the party of the MP.

Table 6.2 Predicting voter perceptions of MP behaviour

	Model 1		Model 2		Model 3	
	"did not overclaim" vs. "overclaimed"	"don't know" vs. "overclaimed"	"did not overclaim" vs. "overclaimed"	"don't know" vs. "overclaimed"	"did not overclaim" vs. "overclaimed"	"don't know" vs. "overclaimed"
Implicated	−1.33*** (0.14)	−.92*** (0.13)	−1.41*** (0.16)	−1.05*** (0.15)	−1.43*** (0.16)	−1.12*** (0.15)
Voted for incumbent			0.77*** (0.12)	−0.02 (0.12)	0.63*** (0.14)	0.04 (0.14)
Party identification					0.29* (0.14)	−0.06 (0.14)
General trust			0.09*** (0.03)	−0.01 (0.03)	0.09** (0.03)	−0.007 (0.03)
Political efficacy			0.07* (0.03)	0.04 (0.03)	0.06* (0.03)	0.03 (0.03)
Attention to politics			−0.07* (0.03)	−0.28** (0.03)	−0.07* (0.03)	0.03 (0.03)
Political knowledge			0.09* (0.05)	−0.10** (0.04)	0.09 (0.05)	−0.11** (0.04)
Seat change			−0.03 (0.16)	0.33* (0.14)	−0.08 (0.16)	0.30* (0.14)
Majority 2005			0.01 (0.01)	0.01 (0.01)	0.003 (0.01)	0.01 (0.01)
Conservative MP			−0.14 (0.15)	−0.16 (0.14)	−0.19 (0.16)	−0.22 (0.14)
Lib Dem MP			0.58* (0.25)	0.11 (0.24)	0.55* (0.26)	0.039 (0.24)
Other MP			0.56 (0.60)	0.69 (0.56)	0.31 (0.63)	0.24 (0.60)
Intercept	1.17*** (0.12)	1.30*** (0.11)	0.36 (0.32)	3.18*** (0.28)	0.38 (0.33)	3.31*** (0.28)
N	3218		2465		2305	
Pseudo-R[13]	0.02		0.1		0.10	
−2 Log Likelihood	−3361.72		−2379.24		−2220.01	
AIC	6731.43		4806.47		4492.03	

Note: ***: $p < 0.001$, **: $p < 0.01$, *: $p < 0.05$; cluster robust standard errors in parentheses; data from own coding and BES.

These results provide strong evidence that constituents' perceptions regarding the propriety of their MP's expenses claims do respond to publicly available information. The negative and significant coefficients on the *implicated* variable across Models 1–3 indicate that a constituent whose MP was publicly implicated in the expenses scandal is more likely to think that their MP over-claimed (relative to either the 'did not over-claim' and to 'don't know' response options), and that this result is robust to the inclusion of control variables.

The control variables also largely have the expected effects. For example, increasing general trust and political efficacy make a constituent more likely to think that their MP 'did not over-claim' (relative to thinking the MP did over-claim), while increasing self-reported attention to politics and political knowledge make a 'don't know' response less likely. Interestingly, the coefficients also indicate that an increase in self-reported political attention also significantly increases a constituent's probability of perceiving their MP to have 'over-claimed' relative to 'not over-claimed'. Finally, the coefficients on the MP party affiliation suggest that, all else equal, in 2010 Liberal Democrats were perceived as more honest with regard to their expenses claims than other MPs.

To interpret the magnitude of the effect of MP implication in the expenses scandal on constituent perceptions, in Figure 6.1 we plot predicted probabilities based on Model 3. We hold all continuous variables at their mean and categorical variables at their mode. The top panel presents predicted probabilities for a constituent who did not vote for their MP in 2005 and did not identify with the MP's party in 2008, and the bottom panel for a constituent who did both.

The effect of a constituent's MP being implicated in the scandal is surprisingly strong. For example, for voters in the top panel and whose MP is not implicated in the scandal, the probability of an 'MP did not over-claim' perception is around 0.33 and that of a 'MP did over-claim' perception is 0.14. In contrast, for such voters with an MP implicated in the scandal, the equivalent numbers are 0.20 and 0.35, respectively. This is a clear reversal of relative perceptions among those with an opinion on their MP's behaviour. The change in the predicted probabilities is very similar for voters who voted for their MP in 2005 and who identified with their MP's party in 2008 (bottom panel). Given the general belief that voters in Britain know little about their representatives, the effect of publicly available information is much stronger than we would have expected.[14] This suggests that voters are either more motivated to learn about the behaviour of their local MP than commonly assumed or, perhaps more likely, that voters become well informed about MP

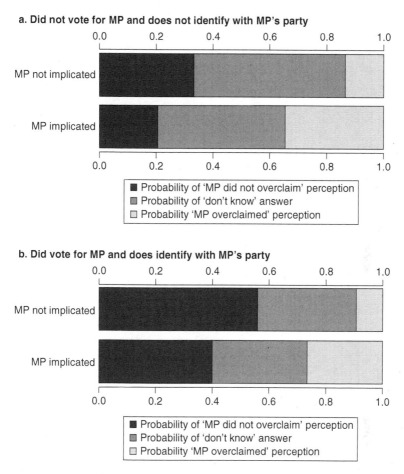

Figure 6.1 Voter perceptions of whether MPs claimed excessive expenses
Note: Based on Model 3, Table 6.2. Panel (a) holds 2005 vote for MP and party identification with MP's party at 'no', panel (b) at 'yes'. All other variables held at their means (continuous variables) or modes (indicator variables).

behaviour when extensive media coverage of this behaviour lowers the costs of becoming informed.

Further analyses show that voter perceptions of how much MPs over-claimed are related to the actual amount they were ordered to repay in the Legg report. BES respondents were also asked how much expense money they thought their MP had over-claimed, on a scale of 0–10. We use answers to this item to assess perceptions of the severity of an MP's wrongdoing. As a proxy for the publicly revealed severity of an MP's expenses misbehaviour, we code the *amount* of money, if any, they were asked to repay in the Legg report (if applicable using the figure after appeal by the MP). We then run a simple Ordinary Least Squares (OLS) regression where the main explanatory variable of interest is this *amount* variable, and the outcome variable is the 0–10 scale measuring respondent beliefs as to how much the MP had over-claimed. We also include as further controls whether the respondent voted for the MP in 2005 and whether they identify with the MP's party.

Model 1 in Table 6.3 presents the results for two sub-sets of respondents. First, all those who believed their MP to be guilty and, second, Model 2 includes all respondents who formed some definitive opinion on the original question as to whether or not their MP had over-claimed (i.e. are not recorded as a 'don't know' on our key measure of perceptions in the main text). We coded those who believed that their MP had not over-claimed as one on the dependent variable.

While the overall explained variance in these models is relatively low, it is nevertheless clear that the amount the MP had to repay is indeed significantly related to constituent perceptions. The magnitude of this effect is clearer if we calculate predicted values (here using Model 1, Table 6.3). If we take a respondent who does not identify with the MP's party and did not vote for their MP in 2005, then the predicted response if the MP did not have to repay any money is 4.73 on the 0–10 scale. If the MP had to repay the mean amount of money (£3,179), the predicted value is 4.94. For the MP with the maximum amount to repay (£42,458), the equivalent value is 7.50. In other words, perceptions of

Table 6.3   Amount asked to repay and perceptions of the extent of over-claiming

	Model 1 Respondents who think MP overclaimed	Model 2 Respondents who state a perception
Amount to repay	0.07*** (0.01)	0.14*** (0.03)
Voted for incumbent	−0.92** (0.30)	−1.04*** (0.23)
Party identification	−0.27 (0.30)	−0.44+ (0.23)
Intercept	4.73*** (0.18)	1.71*** (0.16)
n	549	1259
Adjusted R^{15}	0.07	0.12

Note: ***: $p < 0.001$, **: $p < 0.01$, *: $p < 0.05$, +: $p < 0.1$; cluster robust standard errors in parentheses; data from own coding and BES.

the amount to repay follow the actual severity of the scandal relatively closely.

While this provides further evidence that voter perceptions of MP misconduct do reflect publicly available information on the scandal, it is not the case that constituent perceptions of MP misconduct are overwhelmingly accurate. For one, Table 6.1 showed that a large proportion of voters simply do not know whether their MP was involved in the expenses scandal or not, or at the very least do not feel certain in their beliefs. Moreover, voter predispositions towards their MP are also very important in determining voter perceptions of MP misbehaviour. The two panels of Figure 6.1 help us to understand the predicted differences. For example, where an MP is not implicated in the scandal, a typical constituent who voted for that MP and identifies with the MP's party is estimated to think that the MP 'did not over-claim' with probability 0.56, whereas the equivalent estimate is 0.33 for a constituent who did not vote for the MP and does not identify with the MP's party.

The effect of voter predispositions toward their MP may also depend on whether or not there is negative public information about the MP's behaviour. To investigate this, in Models 1 and 2 in Table 6.4 we interact our measure of MP implication with our two measures of voter predispositions in turn. In both models the estimated interaction coefficients show that, when an MP has been implicated in a scandal, the gap in perceptions between voters who are predisposed towards an MP and voters who are not is significantly reduced (at the 0.1 significance level in Model 1 and 0.05 significance level in Model 2).

What this means is illustrated in Figure 6.2. On the left, we see the difference in perceptions of guilt for MPs not implicated in the scandal. Here, voter predispositions have a clear impact: voters who identify with the MP's party are less likely to think their MP was guilty of misconduct. On the right, we see the same comparison for those MPs who were implicated in the scandal. Here, partisan predispositions have little effect. It seems therefore that the effect of predispositions was stronger in situations where the MP was not implicated in the scandal. Perhaps this shows the power of negative information about one's representative to overcome pre-existing biases.

Perceptions of misconduct and constituent vote choice

We therefore have evidence that at least some constituents did base their beliefs about misconduct by their MP on existing information about that MP. But did constituents then *sanction* MPs they perceived

Table 6.4 Voter predispositions and perceptions of MP expenses-related behaviour

	Model 1		Model 2	
	"did not overclaim" vs. "overclaimed"	"don't know" vs. "overclaimed"	"did not overclaim" vs. "overclaimed"	"don't know" vs. "overclaimed"
Implicated	-1.21*** (0.19)	-1.08*** (0.17)	-1.23*** (0.19)	-1.07*** (0.17)
Voted for incumbent	1.08*** (0.29)	0.22 (0.32)	0.64*** (0.14)	0.04 (0.14)
Implicated X Voted for inc.	-0.61+ (0.31)	-0.18 (0.33)		
Party identification	0.30* (0.14)	-0.06 (0.14)	0.73* (0.26)	0.14 (0.28)
Implicated X Party id.			-0.60* (0.29)	-0.21 (0.30)
General trust	0.87** (0.28)	-0.07 (0.26)	0.87*** (0.28)	-0.07 (0.26)
Political efficacy	0.67* (0.03)	0.03 (0.03)	0.07* (0.03)	0.03 (0.03)
Attention to politics	-0.07* (0.03)	-0.28*** (0.03)	-0.07* (0.03)	0.28*** (0.03)
Political knowledge	0.09+ (0.05)	-0.11** (0.04)	0.09+ (0.04)	-0.11** (0.04)
Seat change	-0.08 (0.15)	0.30* (0.14)	-0.08 (0.16)	0.30* (0.14)
Majority 2005	0.003 (0.006)	0.01 (0.01)	0.004 (0.006)	0.008 (0.006)
Conservative MP	-0.20 (0.16)	-0.22 (0.14)	-0.19 (0.16)	-0.22 (0.14)
Lib Dem MP	0.56* (0.26)	0.04 (0.24)	0.56* (0.26)	0.04 (0.24)
Other MP	0.28 (0.63)	0.23 (0.59)	0.34 (0.63)	0.24 (0.59)
Intercept	0.32 (0.33)	3.26*** (0.29)	0.31 (0.33)	3.25*** (0.28)
N	2305		2305	
Pseudo-R²	0.10		0.10	
-2 Log Likelihood	-2217.27		-2217.62	
AIC	4490.54		4491.24	

Note: ***: p < 0.001, **: p < 0.01, *: p < 0.05, +: p < 0.1; cluster robust standard errors in parentheses; data from own coding and BES.

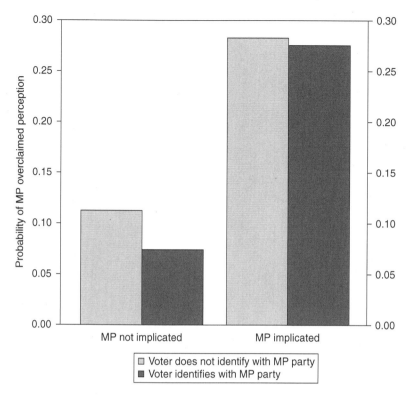

Figure 6.2 How MP implication conditions partisan biases in perceptions of MP over-claiming

Note: Based on Model 2, Table 6.4. The predicted probabilities are calculated for a constituent who voted for the MP in 2005. All other variables held at their means (continuous variables) or modes (indicator variables).

to have over-claimed? To answer this question, we test whether a constituent was less likely to vote for an incumbent MP at the 2010 general election if they believed that the MP over-claimed in the expenses scandal. Of course, not all 2005–2010 incumbent MPs stood for re-election in 2010, and boundary changes introduced at the 2010 election further complicate the picture. Because we are interested in whether constituents use their votes to hold their incumbent representatives electorally accountable for perceived misconduct, for this part of the analysis we restrict our sample to those respondents who were located in a 2010-defined constituency where a sitting MP ran for re-election in 2010, and who had been represented by that MP between 2005–2010.[14]

We ask whether voters who thought their MP over-claimed were more likely to vote for an opposing candidate. Our dependent variable here is a binary measure that equals one if the respondent voted for the incumbent MP at the 2010 general election, and zero if they voted for another candidate. This variable is coded based on a respondent's self-reported vote choice in the 2010 post-election wave of the BES panel. Since our dependent variable is dichotomous, we use binary logistic regression, again clustering standard errors by constituency. Our main explanatory variable of interest is the categorical measure of whether or not a respondent believed that their incumbent MP was guilty of over-claiming on expenses, or whether they did not know; we use the 'did not over-claim' perception as the baseline.

In the models, we control for whether, at the 2005 election, a respondent voted for their 2005–2010 incumbent MP. This is because respondents who were predisposed towards their incumbent MP (either for MP-specific or partisan reasons) are less likely to perceive that MP to have over-claimed on expenses, but these predispositions are also likely to influence vote choice. Furthermore, in Model 9 we include a further control for whether the respondent identified with the party of their incumbent MP when surveyed in 2008. In both models we also account for differential partisan swings at the 2010 election by including dummy variables indicating the party affiliation of a respondent's MP.

As the estimates for Models 1 and 2 in Table 6.5 show, our measures of respondent predisposition towards an MP are strongly positively associated with voting for an incumbent MP. Nevertheless, while the coefficient on the 'don't know' dummy variable is not significant, the coefficient on the 'over-claimed' dummy variable is both significant and negative. This provides strong evidence that when a constituent perceived their MP to have made improper expenses claims, they were less likely to support that MP at election time.

To gauge the magnitude of this effect, we present predicted probabilities based on Model 2 (Table 6.5) for two types of respondents in Figure 6.3. The left panel shows the probability of voting for the incumbent MP for a respondent who did not vote for that MP in 2005 and who does not identify with the MP's party. For such voters, a perception of guilt reduces the probability of voting for the incumbent by five points, from 0.14 to 0.09. The right panel shows the same probabilities for voters who identify with the MP's party and voted for the MP in 2005. The overall predicted probabilities are much higher, but the decline due to a perception of MP over-claiming is a similar seven points (from 0.84 to 0.77). Furthermore, 95% confidence intervals (not graphed

Table 6.5   Constituent perceptions and vote choice

	Model 1	Model 2
Perception of MP overclaiming		
(Reference: Did not overclaim)		
Don't know	−0.19 (0.18)	−0.20 (0.19)
Overclaimed	−0.50* (0.21)	−0.47* (0.24)
Voted for incumbent in 2005	2.65*** (0.16)	1.92*** (0.19)
Party identification		1.62*** (0.20)
Conservative MP	0.33* (0.16)	0.48** (0.18)
Liberal Democrat MP	0.27 (0.25)	0.65* (0.26)
Other MP	−0.15 (0.76)	−0.21 (0.88)
Intercept	−1.46*** (0.19)	−1.86*** (0.20)
N	1134	1076
Pseudo-R^2	0.41	0.471
−2 Log Likelihood	−1122.159	−987.9484
AIC	1136.159	1003.948

Note: ***: $p < 0.001$, **: $p < 0.01$, *: $p < 0.05$; cluster robust standard errors in parentheses; data from own coding and BES.

here) indicate that the marginal effects on vote choice of moving from a 'did not over-claim' to an 'over-claimed' perception are significant for both types of voters.[15] Further analyses show that perceptions of the severity of MP implication in the scandal are also significantly associated with vote choice (Vivyan *et al*. 2012).

In sum, there is evidence that at the 2010 general election British voters to some extent acted to sanction MPs electorally for perceived over-claiming on expenses by voting for an opponent. Considering that perceived MP implication in the scandal is just one of many possible considerations at a general election, a 5% reduction in the probability of voting for a candidate due to perceived wrongdoing is not trivial. Note that these findings for individuals' voting decisions are consistent with the 1–2% reduction in aggregate constituency vote share found in other research on the expenses scandal (Curtice *et al*. 2010; Eggers and Fischer 2011; Pattie and Johnston 2012; Vivyan *et al*. 2012). However, while there was an effect of MP misconduct, effects of this size do not suggest that voter perceptions were strong determinants of voting behaviour.

Conclusion

Why did electoral accountability for the expenses scandal function imperfectly? With regard to voter *perceptions* of their MP's conduct,

a. Did not vote for MP in 2005 and does not identify with MP's party

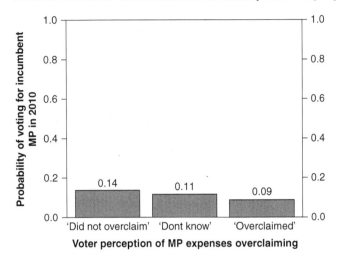

b. Did vote for MP in 2005 and does identify with MP's party

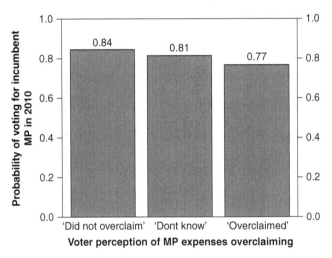

Figure 6.3 Perceptions of misconduct and vote choice

Note: Based on Model 2, Table 6.4. Panel (a) holds 2005 vote for MP and party identification with MP's party at 'no', panel (b) at 'yes'. All other variables held at their means (continuous variables) or modes (indicator variables).

almost half of voters did not know whether their MP was involved in the scandal and perceptions were biased by political predispositions. Nevertheless, our findings show that voter beliefs about their MP are clearly and strongly influenced by public revelations about them. Given past research and the institutional setting of the UK, we are surprised that the responsiveness of perceptions to publicly available information is as high as it is. Yet, turning to *sanctions*, we find that constituent perceptions did not translate strongly into electoral punishment. Thus, constituents to some extent held their MPs accountable for perceived misconduct, but the link between perceptions and vote choice was weak compared to that between publicly available information and perceptions.

What do these findings tell us beyond the context of the 2009 expenses scandal? First, we need to be careful to extend this pattern as it need not apply to other cases of scandal in the UK. For example, in situations where a politician's wrongdoing was more severely unethical or more clearly isolated in media reporting, British voters may be likely to overwhelmingly punish their representative. One example is the case of Neil Hamilton, a Conservative MP who lost his seat as a direct result of his involvement in the so-called cash-for-questions affair in 1997.

Second, these findings have important implications for representative accountability beyond the UK. The UK's political system is dominated by party – rather than candidate – competition (Cain *et al.* 1987; Carey and Shugart 1995; Pattie and Johnston 2004; Kam 2009), so we were sceptical about how much citizen perceptions about their representative would be affected by publicly available information. However, we found that information about representatives clearly influences constituent perceptions. While ignorance and bias about MP misconduct of course also play a role, they do not dominate voter perceptions. Interestingly, information that one's MP was involved in the scandal to some extent even seems to overcome existing predispositions. Given that the UK's system should limit the effectiveness of the perceptions step of accountability, our results are hopeful concerning the extent to which information can reach a representative's voters.

However, our findings also underline that electoral accountability can fail even in situations where a lack of information is not the main problem. To us, this finding implies that institutional arrangements can have a big impact on whether voters use information about their MP to determine their electoral choices. Carey and Shugart (1995) discuss how electoral systems vary in the extent to which they allow for a personal vote. The extent to which they allow voters to sanction their representatives should vary along similar lines.

Thus, if electoral accountability for misconduct is our goal, it is important to ensure that voters can use the information they have to sanction their representatives. The British-style party-centric political system works against voters conditioning their vote choice on MP behaviour. In contrast, other institutional arrangements allow voters to separate their vote for their MP from their vote for a party. For example, open lists and multi-member districts can enable voters to choose between different candidates from the same party, avoiding the trade-off between supporting a party and punishing a representative. Similarly, party primaries at the local level can allow constituents to remove a representative involved in misconduct; this would be a form of indirect electoral accountability. So, those who want voters to be able to punish misbehaving MPs should consider which institutional frameworks help or hinder voters in making use of that information to guide their vote choice.

Notes

1. BES 2010 pre-election internet cross-section survey of 15,660 British voters, weighted using the standard BES weight.
2. See Besley and Larcinese (2011) for a more detailed discussion of the different types of expenses allowances available to British MPs.
3. We exclude the 18 Northern Ireland MPs from our analysis, since the BES did not survey Northern Ireland residents.
4. We refer to the combined source of the *Daily Telegraph* and the *Sunday Telegraph* as 'the *Telegraph*' throughout the chapter.
5. We searched the *Daily Telegraph* and *Sunday Telegraph* articles published between 1 January 2009 and 26 March 2010, via NexisUK. A general article refers to those pieces wherein the *Telegraph* listed the claims of five or more MPs without specific details of, for example, the amount an MP claimed per year.
6. Though there were 628 sitting British MPs in the 2005–2010 Parliament, we exclude four groups of MPs when coding our implicated variable: MPs representing inner-London constituencies, as they were not allowed to claim expenses under the Additional Costs Allowance and were therefore never likely to be implicated in the scandal; the three MPs involved in criminal proceedings as a result of their expenses claims, as their misbehaviour was qualitatively far different from that of other MPs; the MPs elected in by-elections between 2005 and 2010, because the survey respondents did not vote for these MPs in 2005 and because they often had less chance to be involved in the scandal; and an MP who died in March 2010, so just before the period the survey was fielded.
7. The BES ran parallel internet and face-to-face surveys in 2005, and detailed inspection has shown that the samples are almost indistinguishable (Sanders

et al. 2007). Sanders *et al.* (2011) also report that the 2005–2010 panel continued to be representative of the population in terms of their reported vote and their vote intention.

8. For full details on the BES questions used, see Vivyan *et al.* (2012).

9. The BES matches respondents to seats using the postcodes provided by the participants.

10. We add to the 'don't knows' the very small number of respondents who in the previous question indicated they had not heard of the scandal at all.

11. We use the notional 2005 majority size based on the 2010 boundaries since this is more likely to reflect the competitiveness of the constituency in 2010 than the actual 2005 majority size using the old boundaries.

12. This variable ('seat change') was created by manually pairing up the 2005 and 2010 constituencies. In cases of boundary changes, 2005 constituencies were matched to successor constituencies. In most cases a successor constituency was identified when the incumbent ran again in a newly formed constituency that contained part of their old constituency. In the remaining cases, we tried to match 2010 to 2005 constituencies based on the similarity of electorate. The fifteen 2010-defined seats that we did not match a 2005 constituency to were either entirely new seats or correspond to 2005-defined seats where a by-election occurred between 2005 and 2010.

13. One concern with these results is that they may be an artefact of the particular way in which we measure public implication of an MP in the expenses scandal. We checked our findings using alternative measures of MP implication by breaking down our *implicated* measure into its two constituent parts and then either included these in separate regressions or together in the same regression. Both measures are significantly positively associated with the probability that a voter thinks their MP over-claimed.

14. We would be underestimating voter sanctioning of misconduct if the worst offenders had resigned before the election. However, as noted above even among the most consistently implicated MPs, more than half chose to run again (Pattie and Johnston 2012), so focusing on re-standing MPs should not make our estimates strongly unrepresentative.

15. We also checked whether the link between perceptions and vote choice depends on party identification or MP effect. To do so, we ran models with an interaction between respondent perceptions of misconduct, identification with MP's party in 2005, and respondent vote in 2005. None of the interaction term coefficients were significant. However, the direction of the moderating effect indicates that perceptions of wrongdoing may influence vote choice only among voters those who did not identify with their MP's party, which would mean that party identifiers are more resistant to changing their vote choice as a result of their beliefs regarding their MP's behaviour.

7
Tempests and Teacups: Politicians' Reputations in the Wake of the Expenses Scandal

Nicholas Allen and Sarah Birch

This chapter examines the impact of the 2009 MPs' expenses scandal on public attitudes towards politicians and politics. Drawing on data from a three-wave representative panel survey fielded between early 2009 and spring 2010, the chapter probes citizens' evaluations of MPs. It reports the immediate response to the scandal before exploring its impact over the medium term. The chapter finds that, contrary to expectations, the scandal's impact was surprisingly limited. If anything, respondents were less critical of politicians six months after the scandal than immediately before the media frenzy first broke. The chapter discusses various psychological and structural factors that may account for this finding and locates the public response to the scandal within the broader mood of disenchantment that currently pervades British politics.

Introduction

Claims of impropriety and wrongdoing involving politicians are an all-too-common feature of British politics. Almost every month, it seems, brings fresh allegations in the pages of newspapers. Every such allegation constitutes a scandal of sorts, insofar as the reported behaviour involves a violation of widely held ethical norms and prompts a public expression of disapproval (Thompson 2000). However, the extent and intensity of public disapproval can vary enormously. In this respect, some allegations of misconduct are clearly more scandalous than others, either because of their individual significance or because they are seen to be part of a broader pattern of misconduct. Occasionally, the violation of ethical norms can appear endemic to an entire institution and may prompt an especially vocal expression of public disapproval. Such institutional scandals can bring virtually the whole of the political class into disrepute. They might be expected to leave a pronounced footprint in the collective memory.

This chapter examines the long-term impact of the 2009 MPs' expenses scandal, an institutional scandal of tempestuous proportions, on public attitudes towards politicians and politics. In particular, it examines the impact of the scandal on popular perceptions of the honesty and integrity of Britain's political class.[1] It is not concerned with exploring how individuals responded to specific allegations about MPs' expenses on a day-to-day basis, nor is it concerned with the relative importance of different forms of media coverage and media effects. Instead, we treat the 2009 expenses scandal, in particular the media frenzy of May and June that surrounded the *Daily Telegraph*'s detailed revelations, as a discrete event. We examine the effect of the scandal on the attitudinal landscape of British politics and investigate whether it fundamentally altered citizens' perceptions of politicians, or whether it was a proverbial 'storm in a teacup'.

Exploring the long-term impact of the expenses scandal in this way is important for a number of reasons. Most obviously, of course, hindsight enables a fuller appreciation of the scandal's significance. If scandals are a function of time and place (King 1986: 176), so too are people's evaluation of them. Given the availability of data, contemporary judgements about the expenses scandal were necessarily tentative and provisional. They may even have been caught up in the immediate public response. Distance can foster detachment, and there are now more data available on which to base judgements. Moreover, a long-term perspective may serve as a window onto the broader 'anti-politics' mood that pervades the UK (Allen 2006; Hay 2006; Stoker 2007; Heath 2011). Reflecting similar trends in other Western democracies, large sections of the British public have become increasingly detached from formal political processes, and cynicism and mistrust have become deeply entrenched (Norris 2011). The responses to the expenses allegations were almost certainly a reflection of this mood, but they may also have served to reinforce it. At any rate, a clearer understanding of the public's responses to the expenses scandal can inform our understanding of citizens' broader orientations towards politics and politicians in the early twenty-first century, as well as of the long-term consequences of major institutional scandals.

Our analysis of the impact of the expenses scandal draws on existing survey data but also brings to bear new data from a panel study that spanned the scandal. This study comprised three online surveys that were conducted as part of the British Cooperative Campaign Analysis Project (BCCAP). The first survey was fielded in April 2009, just before the media frenzy broke; the second was fielded in September 2009; and the final survey was fielded in April 2010.[2] Each survey was administered by YouGov and included a range of questions about the significance of political misconduct, the prevalence of misconduct and the propriety or otherwise of different types of conduct.[3] Because the study followed a true panel design, the same respondents were tracked over time.

The resulting data provide a unique perspective on the scandal. In short, the data suggest that the scandal's long-term direct effects were much less than might have been supposed at the time. Doubts about politicians' probity had already been given a thorough public airing in the months before the scandal broke, and levels of popular cynicism were already high. To a large extent, the details published by the *Daily Telegraph* merely confirmed what people already suspected or thought they knew all along. The expenses scandal was not a storm in a teacup, but it was more of a reflection than a shaper of the public mood.

The remainder of the chapter proceeds as follows. The next section explores the immediate response to the expenses scandal. The third section describes the surprising improvements in our respondents' evaluations about politicians, and the fourth section examines a number of possible explanations for this effect. The final section considers the structural nature of contemporary popular dissatisfaction with politicians' ethics and conduct.

The immediate response

Exploring the public's response to a specific scandal requires a clear sense of its temporal parameters. Yet, identifying any scandal's beginning and end is not always straightforward (see Chapter 2). This point is especially true of the 2009 expenses scandal. For several years prior to the *Daily Telegraph*'s revelations, the House of Commons' ethical watchdog, the Parliamentary Commissioner for Standards, had been receiving and investigating complaints against MPs and the apparent misuse of official allowances (Allen 2011). In 2003, for example, the Conservative MP for Windsor, Michael Trend, was briefly suspended from the House for misusing the Additional Cost Allowance by claiming for the costs of staying in his main residence. In 2008, another Conservative MP, Derek Conway, was suspended for using his parliamentary allowances to pay members of his family for work that may not have been undertaken.

Such scandals served to arouse journalists' and campaigners' interests in what MPs were claiming for, and the growing interest led to yet more allegations of impropriety. In early 2009, two Labour ministers, the Home Secretary Jacqui Smith and the employment and welfare reform minister Tony McNulty, were accused of abusing Parliament's second-home allowance scheme. Partly as a result, in March 2009, the Committee on Standards in Public Life announced an inquiry into the operation of the expenses system. The issue of parliamentary expenses was already very much on the agenda.

Pinpointing the start of the media frenzy that surrounded the issue of parliamentary expenses is, however, a comparatively easy exercise. On 8 May 2009, the *Daily Telegraph* published previously undisclosed details of several Cabinet ministers' claims and began what became a daily routine of new revelations. This routine came to an end on 20 June, when the newspaper published its magazine supplement 'The Complete Expenses File' (Winnett and Rayner 2009). The controversy and discussion of the issue did not end there, of course, but the media frenzy was effectively over.

The duration of the frenzy is illustrated in Figure 7.1, which reports the number of articles per calendar month in national newspapers

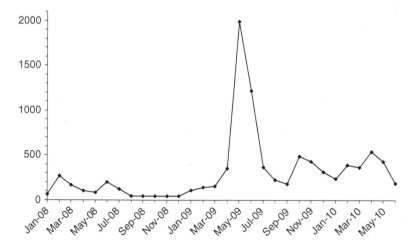

Figure 7.1   The salience of parliamentary expenses in the national print media, January 2008–June 2010

Source: Lexis Nexis. The figure reports the total number of articles per calendar month that contained the words 'expenses' and 'parliament' in national newspapers according to the Nexis database. The search used the 'high similarity function' that excludes most articles included more than once in the database.

(as covered by the Nexis UK database) that contained the words 'parliament' and 'expenses'.[4] As Figure 7.1 reveals, the months of May and June 2009 witnessed by far the most intensive media focus on the issue. Just 353 newspaper articles contained these key words in April, rising to 1,989 in May and 1,216 in June. Thereafter the frenzy died down. In July, the relevant articles numbered just 368. By January 2011, this figure had declined to just 192 (not shown), and a year later it had declined to just 128.

The precise impact of the various individual allegations could in theory be picked up in public opinion polls of the type commissioned by newspapers. In the case of the 2009 MPs' expenses scandal, the *Daily Telegraph* initially organized its revelations by political party, and it would be intriguing to ascertain how the revelations affected support for the different parties on a day-by-day basis. Unfortunately, the opinions polls published during this time were too irregular and infrequent to make sense of the public's response.[5] Moreover, since the expenses scandal engulfed an entire institution, it would be especially desirable to have access to daily data about voters' approval of or trust in Parliament and MPs. Unfortunately, again, there are no such data.

Some evidence of the public's immediate response to the *Daily Telegraph*'s revelations comes from the British Elections Study's (BES) Continuous Monitoring Survey (CMS), a series of monthly polls intended to capture long-term changes in public opinion. From March 2009 to August 2011, respondents to the CMS were asked the following question: 'Using a scale from 0 to 10 where 0 means "no trust" and 10 means "a great deal of trust", how much do you trust politicians'? Figure 7.2 shows the 'average' response to this question as it was asked each month. Three points are immediately apparent. First, the level of 'average' trust in politicians was generally poor. It never exceeded 3.5 on a 0–10 scale. Second, the nadir of reported trust in British politicians occurred in May 2009, when the mean score fell to 2.3. This was the first CMS poll fielded after the *Telegraph* began publishing details of MPs' expense claims (the first day of this survey was 21 May, a fortnight after the frenzied media coverage began), and it suggests that the flurry of allegations did indeed undermine trust in politicians. Third, reported trust recovered briefly before dipping again in October 2009, just after newspapers began reporting the results of Sir Thomas Legg's initial audit of past claims and the amounts of money that MPs were expected to repay. Thereafter, reported trust seemingly returned to pre-scandal levels.

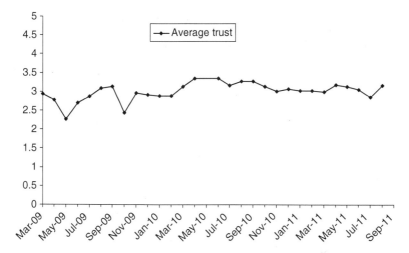

Figure 7.2 Average trust in politicians, March 2009–August 2011
Source: British Election Study Continuous Monitoring Survey.

There was, then, an apparent dip in people's perceptions of politicians as a whole. Further evidence about the immediate reaction is suggested by responses to other questions asked shortly after the media frenzy began. In June 2009, in the second CMS poll fielded after the *Telegraph* began printing details of the expenses claims, an overwhelming majority of respondents, some 91%, tended to agree that the way some MPs had claimed expenses made them 'very angry'. The allegations also seemed to confirm a large number of citizens' jaded views about the honesty and probity of their representatives. In our own survey fielded in September, four months after the initial media frenzy, respondents were asked whether they agreed that politicians 'were in it just for themselves'. In response, 59% tended to agree; a mere 13% tended to disagree.

In addition to the anger and heightened mistrust, an additional feature of the initial response is worth commenting on: how different political parties were perceived to have been affected. In an ICM poll for the *Sunday Telegraph* fielded in late May 2009, respondents were asked: 'Which one of the three main parties do you think has been most damaged by the recent scandal surrounding MPs and their expenses?'[6] Perhaps because there were more Labour MPs, or perhaps because the scandal occurred on a Labour government's watch, a clear majority of respondents, some 55%, said that Labour had been most damaged.

In contrast, just 13% said the Conservatives and a mere 2% the Liberal Democrats. Exactly a quarter of respondents answered that all parties had been damaged equally.

Curiously, this 'plague on all their houses' mindset appeared to grow by the time that the BCCAP asked a similar question in September 2009: 'Thinking about the expenses claimed by MPs, which political party do you think has been damaged the most in the eyes of ordinary voters, or have they all been damaged equally?' Although the results are not strictly comparable, they do suggest that the attribution of blame had shifted. As Figure 7.3 shows, more people said that Labour had been damaged most by the scandal compared with the other parties, but the clear winner was now 'all damaged equally'. These responses almost certainly reflected the conventional wisdom that had now taken root: the scandal had been a crisis for the whole political class, but it had been a particular problem for the incumbent government.

One of the interesting questions that can be asked about the pattern of responses reported in Figure 7.3 concerns the individual-level determinants of the judgements. It is generally accepted that most people seem to process political information on a continuous basis, their responses to new information being added to a 'running tally' of all prior evaluations (Lodge and Taber 2000). Just as important, this running tally is likely

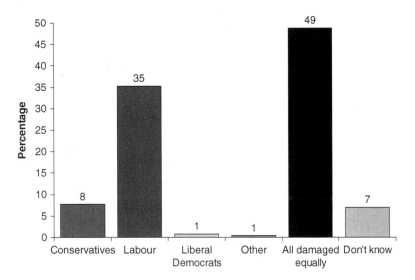

Figure 7.3 Who was damaged most by the scandal?
Source: BCCAP data.

to condition responses to any future information. What this means, in layman's terms, is that most individuals find it virtually impossible to evaluate any new piece of information in an even-handed way. Instead, they are likely to arrive at conclusions that they want to arrive at (Kunda 1990). They have pre-existing feelings about political objects – be they individual politicians, parties, institutions like Parliament or politicians as a class – and these feelings will almost inevitably bias their response to new information.

A very quick and easy way to demonstrate the bias that arises from individuals' prior beliefs and evaluations is to relate respondents' judgements about which party was most damaged with reported party identification at an earlier point in time (Wagner *et al.* 2012). Party identification in Britain has conventionally been understood as an enduring, psychological attachment to a political party (Butler and Stokes 1974), although more recently it has been understood as a 'heuristic' running tally of how individuals evaluate a party's performance (Clarke *et al.* 2009). Whatever the interpretation, we would still expect prior party identification to correlate with judgements about which party was most damaged by the expenses scandal.

Table 7.1 reports a simple cross-tabulation of respondents' reported party identification in December 2008 with their subsequent judgements of which party was most damaged by the expenses scandal. In line with the expectation that prior values matter, Labour identifiers were more likely than Conservative identifiers to judge that the Conservatives had been most damaged by the scandal (12% and 3% of each group respectively), whereas Conservative identifiers were much more likely than Labour identifiers to judge that Labour had been most damaged (55% and 22%). Labour identifiers were most likely to state

Table 7.1 'Who was most damaged' by prior party identification (%)

Party most damaged by the scandal (Sept 2009)	Party identification (Dec 2008)				
	Con	Lab	Lib Dem	Other	None
Conservative	3	12	23	4	2
Labour	55	22	30	38	34
Liberal Democrats	0	2	0	3	0
Others	1	0	4	0	0
All damaged equally	37	62	44	46	52

Source: BCCAP. Don't know figures not reported.

that all parties had been damaged equally. This last finding perhaps reflects Labour identifiers' awareness of the conventional wisdom, but it might also reflect a tendency to cope with the reputational damage done to Labour by believing that all other parties shared equally in the damage.

Marginal medium-term changes

The immediate responses to the expenses scandal were perhaps predictable, both in terms of the public's anger and, it seems, in terms of how individuals reconciled existing partisan preferences with the stories they read. The medium-term changes in public opinion were perhaps less predictable. In his analysis of changing levels of trust in institutions and attitudes towards different levels of political support in the aftermath of the expenses scandal, Oliver Heath (2011: 133) concludes: 'It seems that the expenses scandal may not have affected the public's underlying attitudes towards politicians, political institutions and democracy that greatly. Whatever backlash there was, it did not appear to last long.' Our own survey data offers additional evidence to support this claim.

An obvious advantage of the panel design that we employed is that it enables us to track the same respondents' answers to the same questions over time. All three of our surveys asked the same battery of questions designed to elicit individuals' perceptions of the prevalence of misconduct in British public life. One question, for example, asked respondents how they rated the standards of honesty and integrity of elected politicians in Britain today. The responses to this question are reported in Table 7.2. Very small proportions of respondents in all three waves rated British politicians as having very high or somewhat high

Table 7.2 Overall evaluations of the standards of honesty and integrity of elected politicians (%)

	April 2009	September 2009	April 2010
Very high	0	1	1*
Somewhat high	5	7	7
Neither high nor low	20	21	25
Somewhat low	39	40	39
Very low	29	29	22
Don't know	7	2	7

Source: BCCAP; * Less than 0.5%.

standards of honesty and integrity, and very large proportions rated them as having very low or somewhat low standards. At the aggregate level, the pattern of responses was virtually identical in both April and September 2009.

Another question asked respondents whether they thought that the standards of honesty and integrity of elected politicians had been improving or declining in recent years. Again, there seemed to be very little change at the aggregate level between April and September 2009. Just ahead of the expenses scandal, 62% answered that politicians' standards had been declining in recent years, a response repeated by 59% in September, and 24% said that their standards 'had stayed about the same', compared with 33% in September. The pattern of responses in April 2010 (see Table 7.3) suggests relatively little change over the subsequent months. For one reason or another, therefore, the *Telegraph*'s revelations do not appear to have had an enormous impact on people's judgements about the state of politicians' ethical standards.

A third question sought to ascertain changes in respondents' perceptions of the specific types of misconduct and wrongdoing that they thought might be occurring in Britain, including 'misusing official expenses and allowances', 'not giving straight answers to questions', 'accepting bribes' and 'making promises they know they can't keep'. In each case, respondents were asked to evaluate how much of a problem each type of behaviour was on a 0–10 scale, where a higher score indicated that the behaviour was perceived to be more of a problem. The answers to these questions, reported in Table 7.4, suggest that the misuse of expenses was seen as marginally more of a problem than other elite behaviours in April 2009, in particular not giving straight answers to questions and making promises they know they could not keep, yet it was seen as less of a problem than these two other features of political

Table 7.3 Changes in the standards of honesty and integrity of elected politicians in Britain (%)

	April 2009	September 2009	April 2010
Improving	2	2	4
Declining	66	60	57
Stayed about the same	25	33	31
Don't know	5	4	8

Source: BCCAP.

Table 7.4   Perceived problem of types of behaviour (average response)

	April 2009	September 2009	April 2010
Misusing official expenses and allowances	8.9	8.2	8.2
Not giving straight answers to questions	8.7	8.5	8.6
Making promises they know they can't keep	8.4	8.4	8.5
Accepting bribes	6.6	6.5	6.3

Source: BCCAP. Respondents were asked: 'In your opinion, how much of a problem is the following behaviour by elected politicians in Britain today? Please use the 0–10 scale, where 10 means it is a very big problem and 0 means it is not a problem at all'.

life in September 2009 and April 2010. In all three waves, the acceptance of bribes, usually an instance of unbridled corruption, was seen to be less of a problem than other elite behaviours.

Overall, therefore, the measures we employed suggest that the misuse of allowances and expenses was consistently a matter of concern to our respondents, but that the information released by the *Daily Telegraph* did not increase the concern felt by most members of the British public. This interpretation is further corroborated by an analysis of a new variable calculated by subtracting responses to this question in April 2010 from responses in April 2009. Among the 832 respondents who answered this question in both waves, the mean individual-level change was −0.59 (standard deviation 1.91), a small but not insignificant decrease that suggests the misuse of expenses came to be perceived as *less* of problem. While 40% of respondents gave the same response in both waves, 42% gave a more or less improved response in April 2010, compared with 17% whose perceptions were that conduct had deteriorated.

If perceptions of the scale and severity of the misuse of expenses and allowances were not greatly worsened by the expenses scandal, an even more surprising finding was that average evaluations of the honesty of politicians actually improved between April 2009 and April 2010. In these two waves of our study, respondents were asked whether they thought that different groups of people, including MPs, ministers, local councillors and journalists, were completely honest and trustworthy, or not at all honest and trustworthy. As with the question about perceived problems in political life, answers were recorded on a 0–10 scale, where 0 meant not at all honest and trustworthy, and 10 meant completely honest and trustworthy.

In line with previous studies of institutional trust (Pattie *et al.* 2004: 37–38), we found that actors associated with local government and the courts fared somewhat better than elected politicians. We also found that respondents tended to answer more favourably in respect of their own local MP compared with MPs in general. Insofar as we would expect responses to change as a result of the expenses scandal, our intuitive expectation would be for evaluations of politicians' honesty to deteriorate. However, as Table 7.5 shows, the opposite occurred. For every category of politician that respondents were asked to evaluate, the general trend was for people to judge them as being more honest and trustworthy nearly a year after the scandal compared with a month before. At the aggregate level, government ministers were the politicians whose ethical stock rose highest, followed by MPs in general, local councillors and then respondents' own local MP. Two other groups, judges and journalists, also witnessed an improvement in their perceived honesty and trustworthiness.

A similar story emerges when we look at how individuals' responses changed over time. Some respondents were almost inevitably more critical of politicians in April 2010 than in April 2009, but the average individual-level change in ratings of the honesty and trustworthiness of MPs in general was an increase of 0.76 points on the 0–10 scale. Just over half of respondents seemed to think more highly of MPs in general in the latter survey, compared with nearly a quarter whose reported judgement had worsened and a nearly identical proportion whose judgement remained the same.

To be sure, the verdict against all the actors was far from glowing. Only judges scored on average above the mid-point on the scale, and

Table 7.5   Perceived honesty of different groups (mean response)

	April 2009	April 2010	Change
Judges	5.9	6.3	+0.3
Your local MP	4.3	4.7	+0.3
Local councillors	3.8	4.3	+0.6
MPs in general	3.3	4.1	+0.8
Government ministers	3.0	3.9	+0.9
Journalists	3.0	3.4	+0.4

Source: BCCAP. All differences in means are significant at the .000 level. Respondents were asked: 'For each of the following groups, please say whether you think they are completely honest and trustworthy, or not at all honest and trustworthy. Please use the 0–10 scale where 10 means completely honest and trustworthy and 0 means not at all honest and trustworthy ... '.

perceptions of MPs' and ministers' ethics were decidedly unenthusiastic. Curiously, journalists were generally rated to be the least honest and trustworthy of the groups. This may or may not provide comfort to those politicians who felt unfairly treated by the *Daily Telegraph*. Nevertheless, a significant improvement can be observed in popular politicians' ethical reputations over the 12-month period beginning just before the expenses scandal. This finding is, on the face of it, curious. It deserves some attempt at an explanation.

Explaining the apparent 'improvement'

There are a number of possible factors that explain why members of our panel seemed to think, first, that politicians' ethical standards had not deteriorated significantly in the wake of the expenses scandal (and, if anything, had slightly improved); and, second, that the misuse of expenses was actually less of a problem, albeit still a problem in British politics. These factors are worth considering, partly because they reveal something about the nature of public responses to the expenses scandal and partly because they reveal something about the contemporary environment and culture that frames popular judgements of politicians' conduct.

One possible factor is that the media frenzy surrounding the publication of MPs' expenses claims was regarded by most members of the public as just that: a media frenzy. Most political journalists and editors tend to be far more engaged with day-to-day politics than their average reader (or viewer or listener), and it was always possible that the intense press interest in MPs' expenses claims was far greater than the public's. Certainly, very few members of the public expressed first-hand knowledge or experience of wrongdoing by an MP when we asked them in April 2009: just 3% of our sample answered 'yes'.

As one commentator in *The Guardian* noted two weeks into the scandal, most constituents were still flocking to their MPs with problems 'as though the expenses scandal exists in some parallel universe' (Smith 2009). Moreover, it was also possible that the hugely critical tone of many newspaper reports – with headlines like 'Give us a chance to boot out the fiddlers' (*The Sun*, 15 May 2009) and 'They don't mean "sorry"...And they are only paying back the money for one reason' (*Daily Mail*, 14 May 2009) – always reflected journalists' contempt for politicians (Barnett 2002) much more than the public's.

Yet, while public anger may well have been orchestrated by journalists, it was clear that many members of the public were angered by the allegations that were reported. Nor does it seem likely that the public thought the media frenzy was particularly unfair to MPs. In the September 2009 BCCAP survey, we asked respondents whether they thought the press coverage of MPs' claims under Parliament's second-home allowance scheme was fair and balanced or not. Responses to this question are shown in Figure 7.4. When we aggregate responses on the 0–10 scale, it becomes clear that most people were inclined to agree that they thought the press coverage had been fair and balanced. Some 55% of respondents came down on this side of the fence compared with 30% who said the coverage had not been fair and balanced. Another 15% located their answers at the mid-point. There was, therefore, some sympathy for the view expressed in certain quarters that the media frenzy had been unfair to MPs (we assume most respondents believed it was unfairly critical rather than unfairly positive), but most people were not unhappy with the messenger, even if they were unhappy about the message.

A second possible factor that may explain our findings is the prevailing and deep-rooted distrust that affects many people's responses

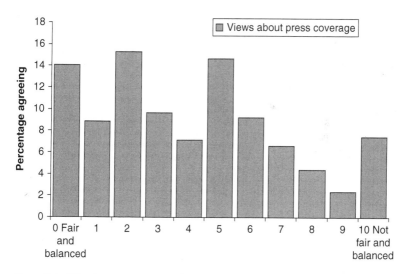

Figure 7.4 Was the press coverage fair and balanced?

Source: BCCAP data. Question wording was: 'You may have read or heard a lot earlier this year about MPs' claims under Parliament's second-home allowance scheme. Some people thought the press coverage was fair and balanced. Other people thought the coverage was not fair and balanced. Using the scale of 0 to 10, where 0 means the press coverage was fair and balanced and 10 means the press coverage was not fair and balanced, where would you place your views?'

to politicians and political institutions. Surveys have long shown politicians to be among the least liked and least trusted groups in British society (Mortimore 2003). Indeed, the standing of politicians is generally low in most democracies (Norris 2011). Suspicion about their motives and integrity is almost hard-wired into the public consciousness. It is likely that the *Daily Telegraph*'s revelations, when they came, simply provided evidence to justify these fears. A hint of these suspicions is suggested by responses to a question included in the April 2009 BCCAP survey. When asked whether they agreed with the view that 'the scandals involving elected politicians that are reported in the newspapers and on television are only the tip of the iceberg in terms of the misconduct that actually goes on', over three-quarters of respondents tended to agree. Further details of responses to this question are reported in Table 7.6, which shows the personal characteristics of those who answered either 'strongly agree' or 'agree'. In terms of age, older people were more likely to agree with the 'tip of the iceberg' sentiment than younger people, those who had left full-time education earlier in life were more likely to agree than those who had been in education for longer, and those who were not at all interested in politics were less cynical than

Table 7.6 Are reported scandals only the tip of the iceberg? (% agreeing)

	% agreeing		% agreeing
Age		**Household income**	
18–25	56	Less than £20,000	85
26–35	69	£20,000–£49,999	82
36–45	86	£50,000 plus	77
46–55	85	Won't say	65
56–65	81		
66 plus	86	**Interest in politics**	
		Very much	81
Gender		Somewhat	82
Men	80	Not that much	77
Women	78	Not at all interested	76
Social grade		**Age completed education**	
ABC1	77	15 or younger	85
C2DE	81	16–18	83
		19 or older	74
Total	**79**		

Source: BCCAP. Respondents were asked: 'The scandals involving elected politicians that are reported in the newspapers and on television are only the tip of the iceberg in terms of the misconduct that actually goes on'. % agreeing is the sum of those who answered either 'strongly agree' or 'agree'.

those who were interested in politics. Otherwise, however, the prevailing sense among all groups was that there was more misconduct going on than had yet been reported. When the *Daily Telegraph* began its run of detailed reports on 8 May, many readers may have been shocked, but very few were probably altogether surprised by the revelations.

A third factor that may explain our findings is the possibility that, while the public was initially angered by the *Daily Telegraph* allegations, the constant flow of information slowly desensitized citizens to the apparent wrongdoing and made them more critical of the media coverage as part of a process of 'scandal fatigue' (Kumlin and Esaiasson 2012). This fatigue may have set in much sooner because so many other allegations of impropriety, covering a range of misdemeanours, had been made against politicians in the preceding months (Heath 2011). The April 2009 BCCAP survey certainly suggested widespread awareness of these earlier allegations. We asked respondents whether they were familiar with a number of behaviours that had been reported in the newspapers or on television in recent years, including: MPs misusing their parliamentary allowances when employing members of their family (87% said this had been reported); MPs accepting money in return for asking questions in Parliament (71%); members of the House of Lords being prepared to accept money in return for attempting to change laws (66%); and party activists applying for postal votes using false names (48%).[7] As we have shown elsewhere, familiarity with past scandals has a significant impact on respondents' overall evaluations about the extent to which certain types of wrongdoing were problems in British politics (Allen and Birch 2011).

A fourth possible factor that may explain our findings is whether or not respondents' own MPs were personally implicated in the expenses scandal. Although media coverage tended to lump all MPs together, usually as sinners rather than saints, not all MPs were the subject of critical reporting, and not all MPs were obliged to repay any money. Sir Thomas Legg's audit of MPs' past claims made between April 2004 and March 2009 resulted in just 392 (out of 752) MPs and former MPs being required to repay some money, usually relatively small amounts (Curtis and Mulholland 2010). All things being equal, we might expect respondents whose own MP had been implicated to have become more critical of politicians' standards than those whose MP had escaped censure.

The April 2010 BCCAP survey asked respondents whether, from what they remembered, their own MP had been personally implicated in the expenses controversy of the year before. In response, some 26% answered 'yes', 47% answered 'no' and a further 27% replied 'don't know'. Table 7.7 relates these responses to answers to the question about

Table 7.7   Effect of MP being implicated or not on perceptions of standards (%)

	MP implicated	MP not implicated	Don't know
Standards have been improving	6	4	2
Standards have been declining	68	55	51
Standards have stayed about the same	24	38	26
Don't know	2	3	21

Source: BCCAP.

whether elected politicians' standards of honesty and integrity had been improving or declining in recent years. Among those respondents who said their MP had been implicated, 68% said that standards had been declining, whereas this figure was 55% among those who said that their MP had not been implicated. Although the differences are slight, it does add credence to the view that, while all politicians may be tarred by the same brush when one lapses, the public retains some ability to distinguish between those who transgress and those who do not.

One final factor that may have had a bearing on medium-term public responses to the expense scandal was the attempt by politicians to address the ethical failings by introducing new regulatory measures and by engaging in a collective round of blood-letting. Even as the *Daily Telegraph* continued its daily routine of publishing new details, the government announced plans for a new statutory Independent Parliamentary Standards Authority (IPSA) that would assume responsibility for administering and monitoring MPs' pay and expenses (Allen 2010). At the same time, the political parties began to investigate the claims made against some of the alleged offenders, which resulted in a number of forced retirements, and the Commons Speaker himself, Michael Martin, was forced from office. Such activity may well have gone some way towards restoring confidence in Parliament and moderating some of the anger felt by citizens, although our data do not enable us to shed any light on this matter.

A structural gap?

Broadly speaking, the expenses scandal lit up the sky of British political ethics but it did not greatly change the underlying terrain in terms of how citizens perceived their politicians' ethical standards of conduct.

As Pattie and Johnston (2012: 19) observe: 'Far from worsening an anti-politics mood in the country, therefore, the scandal seems only to have confirmed the public's already poor opinion of politicians.' Our own data incline us to agree. In this final section, we draw on some of the potential explanations identified in the previous section to explore the structural features that help to explain the public response to the expenses scandal.[8]

When it comes to citizens' perceptions of their politicians' standards of conduct, there is something akin to a structural 'expectations gap' (Flinders and Kelso 2011). Voters prefer their politicians to be honest; they are often disappointed by the reality (Birch and Allen 2010). This state of affairs can be explained by a number of factors, the first set of which relates to citizens. Most people tend to have a somewhat broader conception of political ethics than official and institutional preoccupations. Regulatory arrangements in most institutions, including the House of Commons, tend to be preoccupied with individual financial conflicts of interest and the potential use of public office for personal financial gain. One commentator, with an eye on regulatory practice in the US, describes this tendency as 'moral minimalism' (Jennings 1985: 151). Yet, most citizens tend not to think in such narrow terms; ethics tends to embrace veracity as well as probity. Thus, as Kellner (2004: 838, 840) notes, people are 'repelled by hypocrisy' and want 'authenticity'. Giving straight answers and making promises they can keep are often more important issues than MPs having extra-parliamentary jobs or employing their wives or husbands (Kellner 2004: 839). Needless to say, this broader conception of ethics means that there are more opportunities for politicians to appear unethical and dishonest, since empty or broken promises and evasive answers tend to be part and parcel of political life. Anyone who has ever watched *Prime Minister's Questions*, for example, will be quite familiar with how senior politicians seemingly ignore questions and make statements of their own choosing.

It may be, of course, that citizens have unrealistic expectations of the scope of ethics in politics. By no means should the public's preferences be discounted, but in the same way that doctors, lawyers and other professions need a distinct and functional code of ethics, so too may politicians. For instance, politics may well require an element of verbal flexibility that would not be acceptable in other walks of life. For instance, in the wake of the 2010 general election, both Conservative and Liberal Democrat politicians needed to explain to their respective supporters why they had compromised on their manifesto commitments in the course of producing the Coalition Agreement. Critics could easily paint the Agreement as a sell-out, but if neither party had been prepared to compromise, there may have been no government with a stable parliamentary majority. It may also be the case that politics requires certain bonds of commitment and loyalty that the public finds unpalatable, and which may mean appointing close friends and trusted associates to office, and which could even mean tolerating relatively minor ethical lapses such as, for example, a senior minister swearing at a police officer.

Another reason why citizens are almost certain to be disappointed by the perceived reality of politicians' conduct relates to the widespread cynicism surrounding their motives. Most individuals, when presented with new information about potential misbehaviour involving politicians, will almost inevitably respond in line with directional goals and the desire to reach a judgement that is consistent with prior beliefs and values (Lodge and Taber 2000: 186). Because those prior beliefs are likely to be of politicians being 'just in it for themselves', every new case of alleged misconduct will confirm most people's negative views; good conduct will be discounted and overlooked. In other words, citizens are psychologically inclined to project dishonesty and malign intentions onto politicians.

If psychology predisposes citizens to mistrust their politicians, another set of structural factors relate to the nature and organization of political life. Increasing numbers of politicians are career politicians (King 1981); politics may not be a matter of life or death, but it is a game that they very much want to win. As a result, they have every incentive to stretch ethical principles to the limit in their pursuit of career advancement.

There are also features of institutional political life that may further lead politicians away from the ethical expectations of citizens. On the one hand, institutional norms and socialization processes almost certainly exacerbate the tendency for politicians to see ethics in a narrow sense. Many institutional codes of conduct and standards focus primarily on financial conflicts of interest, as seen. On the other hand, membership of an institution like Parliament can have the effect of isolating politicians from public opinion, since it encourages them to mix with like-minded people (Atkinson and Bierling 2005). As a result, there are strong structural incentives that lead politicians away from what the public may regard as right and proper.

The last set of structural factors that explain the gap between public preferences and perceptions relate to the nature of the modern media.

The relationship between politicians and journalists, although always uneasy, has become increasingly antagonistic, even if both sides belong to the same political class (Oborne 2007). As a result of this antagonism, journalists take great delight in exposing political misconduct, partly because it sells newspapers and partly because they believe it is their democratic duty to hold politicians to account. At the same time, the gradual opening up of Parliament and other political institutions in recent years, together with initiatives like the Freedom of Information Act, has arguably increased the amount of potential 'dirt' that journalists can write about. Lastly, the rise of new media have altered the wider media ecology and allowed other actors to contribute to the 'political information cycle' with greater ease (Chadwick 2011). There are now many more access points that private individuals with information about alleged misconduct can use to get into the public domain.

These various structural factors make it virtually impossible for there to be any dramatic improvement in popular perceptions of politicians' honesty and integrity, either in the short term or the long term. They also go some way to explaining the prevailing anti-politics mood that provided such fertile ground for the *Daily Telegraph*'s expenses revelations, why they captured the public imagination, albeit briefly, and resulted in a mega scandal, and why their long-term impact was limited largely to reinforcing pre-existing sentiments.

To finish, it is instructive to compare the impact of the 2009 expenses scandal with the public response in the US to Bill Clinton's alleged affair with Monica Lewinsky. In a brief study of the initial allegations, Zaller (1998) explained the counter-intuitive bounce in President Clinton's approval ratings on the basis that issues of real substantive importance – chiefly the economy – were always going to trump alleged sexual indiscretions. Since most media frenzies tend not to be about substance, their 'lasting direct effect [...] tends to be nil' (Zaller 1998: 187). Yet, as Zaller (1998: 188) goes onto note, 'The closer media frenzies get to [...] political substance, the more likely the effects are to be lasting.' The 2009 expenses scandal was arguably 'substance' insofar as it was a reflection of the perceived ethical quality of the whole political class. Yet its impact, much like the Clinton–Lewinsky affair was also small. The reason why is because the substance it related to – the perceived low standards of honesty and integrity of Britain's politicians – was already an established feature of the public mood. Popular disillusionment with politics was already such that the expenses scandal could scarcely have undermined trust and confidence any further.

Notes

1. This paper reports findings from a wider project investigating popular understandings of politicians' conduct in Britain. We gratefully acknowledge financial support from the Economic and Social Research Council (RES-000-22-3459) and British Academy (SG-52322). Further details about the project can be found online at: http://www.essex.ac.uk/government/ethicsandintegrity/
2. An earlier baseline survey was carried out in December 2008.
3. The initial wave included 1,388 respondents of whom 890 took part in the second wave and 933 in the third. To control for compositional effects across the three waves, we limit our analysis to only those individuals who responded to all three surveys, a sample of 681.
4. Nexis UK is a comprehensive online database that contains the full text of all major UK national newspapers and many regional newspapers. For further information, see http://nexis.co.uk/pdf/NexisUK.pdf. Last accessed 30 March 2012.
5. As far as the authors can tell, opinion polls were published on considerably fewer than half of the 44 days between 8 May and 20 June.
6. ICM Poll for *The Sunday Telegraph*, 27–28 May 2009. Available from: http://www.icmresearch.com/pdfs/2009_may_suntele_euro_poll.pdf. Last accessed 30 March 2012.
7. In line with all the other BCCAP data in this chapter, these frequencies are of only those respondents who participated in all three waves.
8. These issues, and others, are analysed at length in a new monograph to be published by Cambridge University Press (Allen and Birch, forthcoming).

8
Singing from the Same Broad Sheet? Examining Newspaper Coverage Bias during the 2009 MPs' Expenses Scandal

Valentino Larcinese and Indraneel Sircar

To see whether UK media coverage during the MPs' expenses scandal followed partisan newspaper orientations, we analysed reporting from: a set of right-leaning (*Daily Mail*, *The Times* and *Daily Telegraph*) and left-leaning (*The Guardian*, *The Independent*) papers; the most widely read daily (*The Sun*); and a regional newspaper (*The Scotsman*). We found that, *ceteris paribus*, MPs received higher levels of coverage across all newspapers if they were on the front bench for one of the three major parties, misappropriated higher sums of money, received more media coverage before the scandal, or were female. However, there were no significant partisan differences between the newspapers under study. Thus, newspapers acted as watchdogs rather than in a partisan fashion during the expenses scandal.

Introduction

The mass media play a vital role in modern democracies, being the most important source of information about political affairs. This role is even more important during a scandal. While politicians have incentives to reach their voters to communicate their proposals and administrative activity, they clearly have no incentive to provide information about malfeasance. Hence, what citizens learn about their representatives' wrongdoing is mostly filtered through the media. Since the media, and particularly the press, often have ideological leanings, it is useful to ask whether the coverage of malfeasance can be biased by an outlet's political agenda.

In the UK, most newspapers have ideological orientations: right-leaning national (London-based) newspapers include the *Daily Mail*, *The Times* and *Daily Telegraph* (the latter of which first divulged the MP expenses story), whilst the *Daily Mirror*, *The Guardian* and *The Independent* tend to the ideological left. As in the US and other countries, major newspapers can also reveal political party preferences through the endorsement of a candidate, party or coalition prior to an election. Looking at the official endorsements of newspapers since 1945 (Stoddard 2010), the *Daily Telegraph* has endorsed the Conservatives in every post-war election, while the *Daily Mail* supported the Tories in all but one election since 1945 (preferring a Conservative–Liberal coalition in the October 1974 election). By contrast, the *Daily Mirror* has opted for the Labour Party in every post-war election, and *The Guardian* has not endorsed the Conservatives since 1955.

It is therefore legitimate to ask whether press coverage of the 2009 expenses scandal in the UK has been partisan, or alternatively, if newspapers traditionally leaning to the left or right have underreported wrongdoings of MPs of the left or right, respectively. Under and over-reporting here are not measured with respect to an unbiased or fair coverage. We are not in a position to say what fair coverage of each case would have been. We can, however, compare newspapers with each other in order to uncover systematic differences in their coverage patterns and then relate them to our prior knowledge of the newspaper political leaning.

We use a difference-in-differences methodology which is closely related to previous research on the US press by Larcinese *et al.* (2011) and Puglisi and Snyder (2011). The latter paper is particularly relevant for us since it analyses scandals on a large number of US newspapers and concludes that Republican-leaning newspapers give relatively more coverage to scandals involving Democratic politicians than scandals involving Republican politicians, while Democratic-leaning newspapers do the opposite. Our findings on the British press are instead more benign. We find no detectable partisan coverage, in the sense that patterns of coverage of specific newspapers do not appear to be influenced by their political leaning. Our conclusion is that the press, or at least the sample that we analyse, acted on average as a watchdog, by giving more coverage to scandals that involved members of the government and main opposition figures as compared to scandals involving backbenchers, irrespectively of their party affiliation: this is a pattern which is common to all of the newspapers we study.

An interesting feature of the UK expenses scandal, from a scholar's point of view, is that it comes with an accurate measure of monetary wrongdoing: following the scandal, an investigation was held that led to an accurate reconstruction of the amount misappropriated by each MP (the investigation led to the so-called Legg report).[1] This gives us a quite unique opportunity to compare newspaper reporting with actual wrongdoing. Reassuringly, and again on a positive note for the British press, we find that MPs who were recognized by the Legg report as more heavily involved in the scandal were also on average more heavily covered by the press, although many other factors contribute to explain coverage. We acknowledge that the seriousness of each individual misappropriation cannot be entirely captured by its monetary value. There were many symbolic cases that attracted attention independently of the intrinsic monetary value of the abuse. Two considerations, however, led us to use data from the Legg report as a benchmark: the first is that the amount of money misappropriated is an important dimension of the scandal and must be of concern for voters as taxpayers; the second reason is a practical one, that this is the only objective (to the extent that the review was conducted in an appropriate way) measure available.

Our conclusion is that personal characteristics explain press coverage, *ceteris paribus*, better than partisan affiliation. In particular, we uncover a systematic unfavourable treatment of female MPs who have, *ceteris paribus*, received more scrutiny than their male colleagues. Gendered coverage is common to all the papers in our sample, irrespective of their partisan leaning, and reflects what has been found more widely in other media studies. Research on the US has shown that female candidates receive less substantive media coverage than their male colleagues in presidential (Jalazai 2006) and gubernatorial (Kahn 1994) races. Furthermore, media coverage tends to portray female politicians in relation to their husbands or fathers (Romaine 1998: 136–137; Murray 2010: 15), and there is a greater media focus on fashion or physical appearance rather than policies (Romaine 1998; Murray 2010; Bligh *et al.* 2012). For example, UK Home Secretary Theresa May receives significant media coverage for her apparent preference for 'kitten heels' rather than her role on the ruling Coalition's front bench (Faulkner 2010; Rawi 2010).

Our contribution here is empirical: we aim to uncover patterns of coverage of the scandal and do not pretend to be able to provide an explanation for all our results. Above all, we hope that our findings, during a very delicate moment of the history of the British Parliament, will stimulate further thinking about the role played by the media in British democracy.

Data

On 8 May 2009, when the *Daily Telegraph* broke the story of the expenses scandal, there were 646 MPs in office in the UK House of Commons. This chapter brings together data from a number of sources in order to investigate relationships related to newspaper coverage on MPs between the publication of detailed expenses in May 2009 and the general election a year later.

Media

The first step in our analysis consists of selecting a sample of newspapers. We selected a set of daily newspapers (and their Sunday editions) that were widely read broadsheets and tabloids. To do this, we looked at the National Readership Survey (NRS) data for 2009–2010, which is summarized in Table 8.1. We then picked publications from both sides of the ideological spectrum. The large newspapers with national readership are based in London, so we also included one widely read regional broadsheet, *The Scotsman*, which did not endorse any party or coalition for the 2010 general election. It is interesting to note that *The Sun*, with the highest level of UK readership, endorsed the winning party in every election since 1979 – and endorsed the Conservatives in 2010 (Stoddard 2010). Using these criteria, the seven newspapers included in the analysis are: *The Sun, Daily Mail, Daily Telegraph, The Independent, The Guardian, The Times* and *The Scotsman*.

To operationalize the media coverage in the selected newspapers, we ran a series of searches on Nexis, a large online repository of news sources. The Nexis searches were conducted in two phases. First, to obtain a baseline measure, the frequency of mentions for each MP was collected for the seven newspapers in the three-month period before the *Daily Telegraph* disclosed detailed expenses (8 February 2009–7 May 2009). We use this baseline measure for two reasons: some newspapers carry more coverage on MPs in general; and some MPs have a pre-existing higher level of coverage, due to role in government, prominence in the political party or other factors. Second, we conducted Nexis searches for the MP name alongside the word 'expenses' in the period from the publication of the detailed MPs' expenses by the *Daily Telegraph* to the 2010 UK general election (8 May 2009–6 May 2010). In the following analysis, we will exclude the leaders of the three main political parties and the Speaker – Nick Clegg, Gordon Brown, David Cameron and Michael Martin – since they were often mentioned in newspaper reports independently of their own expenses.

Table 8.1 Newspaper readership (2009–2010)

National daily newspapers	Total copies (thousands)	Share
The Sun	7,700	15.5
Daily Mail	4,739	9.5
Daily Mirror/Record	4,004	8
The Daily Telegraph	1,751	3.5
The Times	1,613	3.2
Daily Star	1,551	3.1
Daily Express	1,423	2.9
The Guardian	1,130	2.3
The Independent	556	1.1
Financial Times	391	0.8
Regional daily newspapers (outside London)		
Press and Journal – Aberdeen	207	0.4
Yorkshire Post	177	0.4
Courier and Advertiser – Dundee	168	0.3
The Herald – Scotland	145	0.3
The Scotsman	131	0.3
Evening Times – Glasgow	151	0.3
Sunday Newspapers		
News of the World	7,628	15.3
The Mail on Sunday	4,974	10
Sunday Mirror	3,816	7.7
The Sunday Times	3,050	6.1
Sunday Express	1,518	3
The Sunday Telegraph	1,518	3
The People	1,291	2.6
Sunday Mail	1,109	2.2
The Observer	1,078	2.2
Daily Star Sunday	941	1.9
The Sunday Post	799	1.6
The Independent on Sunday	594	1.2
Scotland on Sunday	191	0.4
Sunday Herald-Scotland	142	0.3

Source: National Readership Survey.

MP data

We extracted the names and party affiliations of the 646 MPs in office on the date the *Daily Telegraph* published the expenses revelations (8 May 2009) using the *PublicWhip* database. The *PublicWhip* profiles also contain information about the roles that each individual has had during their time in Parliament, so we identified front-bench Members for the three main political parties by searching for roles that included the following terms: Minister of State, Foreign Secretary, Home Secretary, Chancellor, Prime Minister and Leader of the Opposition.[2] A list of front-bench Members for Labour, Conservatives and Liberal Democrats was compiled for 7 May 2009, the date before the *Telegraph* publication of detailed MPs' expenses.

Our analysis also includes control variables for individual MPs: gender; university degree; Oxford or Cambridge graduate; year MP was first elected to Parliament; and distance in miles from the MP constituency office to Westminster.[3] Summary statistics for all variables are reported in Table 8A in the appendix.

Legg report

The frequency of articles mentioning the MP name during the expenses scandal can be compared to a more objective measure of the amount of financial misappropriation for each MP through the Legg report audit of Additional Cost Allowance (ACA) payments from 2004 onwards, which non-London MPs could claim. We will be using the Legg report data compiled by Rogers (2010), who extracted information from the original Legg report and collected the following (in Pounds): total repayment recommended; amount reduced on appeal; total repayments received since 1 April 2009; and balance to be repaid. Our measure of monetary misappropriation consists of the total repayment recommended in the Legg report minus the amount reduced on appeal.[4] We use the natural logarithm of the resulting figure (*logLegg*).

The Legg report excluded any MP whose expenses had been investigated by the Parliamentary Commissioner for Standards or the police, so the four Members of the House of Commons among the 646 MPs identified who faced criminal trials due to their allowance claims – David Chaytor, Jim Devine, Eric Illsley and Elliot Morley – are not included in the report. It is for this reason that our analysis also excludes the four aforementioned MPs.

Analysis of media coverage

As mentioned in the introduction, UK newspapers tend to have traditions of right or left-leaning tendencies, which are evident in partisan reporting of day-to-day politics in the UK and endorsements during general election campaigns. As Larcinese *et al.* (2011) show in the US, newspapers aligned with the Democratic party dedicated more coverage to bad news when the incumbent was Republican and *vice versa*. Similarly, if there is significant partisan media bias in the UK, we would expect newspapers that have endorsed the Conservatives historically (e.g. *Daily Mail*) to highlight Labour misappropriation during the expenses scandal, and *vice versa* for left-leaning publications like *The Guardian*. Before proceeding to the analysis, however, it is instructive to examine some summary statistics of our main indicators.

Descriptive statistics

Pre-scandal levels of media coverage were calculated using the number of mentions of an MP name in the three-month period before the publication of the detailed expenses claims. The results are summarized in Table 8.2. Looking at the mean numbers of mentions, the selected newspapers vary significantly in their coverage of the Members of the House of Commons prior to the expenses scandal. Not surprisingly, the one newspaper without a nationwide readership, *The Scotsman*, has a lower mean of mentions for the MPs included in the analysis. Perhaps this is because there were only 59 MPs in Scotland, compared to 569 constituencies in England and Wales.

By contrast, *The Times* seems to have a higher default level of coverage of MPs compared to the other newspapers. We then divided the media coverage by political party; we present the mean levels of coverage for the three main political parties in tabular format (Table 8.3) and graphically (Figure 8.1).[5] We see that most newspapers focus more on Labour MPs compared to their Conservative and Liberal Democrat counterparts. This is particularly evident in the mentions in the left-leaning *Guardian*, where the mean frequency of Labour MPs is nearly double that of Conservative MPs, and also markedly higher than Liberal Democrats. There is a similar pattern in *The Independent* (also a left-leaning paper). The higher average level of newspaper coverage for the Labour Party is

Table 8.2 Frequency of total mentions of MP name between 8 February 2009 and 7 May 2009 (Pre-scandal coverage)

Newspaper	n	Mean	Standard deviation	Minimum	Maximum
Daily Mail	642	4.42	12.85	0	210
Daily Telegraph	642	3.76	12.07	0	171
The Times	642	9.52	27.08	0	307
The Sun	642	5.64	19.88	0	328
The Independent	642	3.58	10.87	0	126
The Guardian	642	5.62	16.02	0	192
The Scotsman	642	2.73	14.28	0	312

Table 8.3   Frequency of total mentions of MP name between 8 February 2009 and 7 May 2009 for Labour (n = 350), Conservatives (n = 194), and Liberal Democrats (n = 62)

Newspaper	Party	Mean	Standard deviation	Minimum	Maximum
Daily Mail	Labour	4.89	15.55	0	210
	Conservative	4.26	8.90	0	88
	Lib Dem	3.66	9.40	0	69
The Telegraph	Labour	4.23	14.04	0	171
	Conservative	3.56	10.22	0	117
	Lib Dem	2.44	7.19	0	54
The Times	Labour	9.96	27.94	0	301
	Conservative	8.40	25.37	0	307
	Lib Dem	7.00	19.88	0	153
The Sun	Labour	5.87	21.86	0	328
	Conservative	4.69	15.90	0	160
	Lib Dem	4.24	12.43	0	85
The Independent	Labour	4.11	12.25	0	126
	Conservative	2.84	9.18	0	111
	Lib Dem	3.35	9.95	0	77
The Guardian	Labour	6.82	19.14	0	192
	Conservative	3.62	9.85	0	107
	Lib Dem	5.40	15.59	0	117
The Scotsman	Labour	2.63	8.54	0	86
	Conservative	1.24	4.98	0	63
	Lib Dem	2.10	6.42	0	46

not entirely surprising, since they were the governing party during this period, though the differences in partisan coverage for each newspaper are not significant (see Figure 8.1).

If we now look at the frequencies of mentions of MPs alongside the word 'expenses' in the period after the *Daily Telegraph* published expenses claims, *The Scotsman* again appears to have less coverage compared to the other publications included in the analysis, while *The Times* has the highest average level of mentions. The mentions of the MP name alongside the word 'expenses' for the seven newspapers in our analysis in presented in Table 8.4a. We then divide the frequency of mentions of the MP name alongside the word 'expenses' for the three main parties, which we present in tabular format (Table 8.4b) and graphically (Figure 8.2). Compared to the patterns observed above for the pre-scandal period (in Table 8.3 and Figure 8.1), the partisan differences have changed slightly. In particular, with the right-leaning papers, *Daily Mail* and *Daily Telegraph*, Labour and Conservative MPs tend to have similar levels of coverage, while Liberal Democrats received less

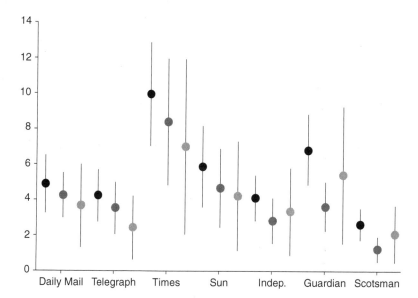

Figure 8.1 Means of total mentions of MP name between 8 February 2009 and 7 May 2009 for Labour (black), Conservatives (grey) and Liberal Democrats (light grey)

Note: The circle is the estimated mean, the line gives a 95% confidence interval.

coverage. *The Scotsman* had slightly higher levels of coverage for Labour MPs (the majority party in Scotland), and nearly identical mean levels of coverage for the Conservatives and Liberal Democrats. Although Liberal Democrats receive slightly less coverage at the 5% significance level specifically related to expenses *in The Sun* and *The Telegraph* compared with Labour MPs (Figure 8.2), there are no overall significant partisan patterns.

Table 8.4a Frequency of total mentions of MP name + 'expenses' between 8 May 2009 and 6 May 2010 (Scandal-related coverage)

Newspaper	N	Mean	Standard deviation	Minimum	Maximum
Daily Mail	642	3.02	8.04	0	87
The Telegraph	642	4.38	9.23	0	90
The Times	642	6.70	16.28	0	168
The Sun	642	3.40	9.32	0	118
The Independent	642	3.20	7.55	0	81
The Guardian	642	4.67	11.25	0	115
The Scotsman	642	2.34	5.55	0	54

Table 8.4b   Frequency of total mentions of MP name + 'expenses' between 8 May 2009 and 6 May 2010 for Labour (n = 350), Conservatives (n = 194), and Liberal Democrats (n = 62)

Newspaper	Party	Mean	Standard deviation	Minimum	Maximum
Daily Mail	Labour	3.52	9.67	0	87
	Conservative	2.92	6.22	0	43
	Lib Dem	1.85	4.02	0	22
The Telegraph	Labour	4.87	11.01	0	90
	Conservative	4.60	7.45	0	41
	Lib Dem	2.66	3.91	0	18
The Times	Labour	7.39	18.85	0	168
	Conservative	7.09	14.09	0	73
	Lib Dem	3.79	8.94	0	56
The Sun	Labour	4.11	11.52	0	118
	Conservative	2.96	6.10	0	38
	Lib Dem	1.53	3.84	0	23
The Independent	Labour	3.62	8.81	0	81
	Conservative	3.23	6.36	0	36
	Lib Dem	1.98	4.40	0	19
The Guardian	Labour	5.29	13.29	0	115
	Conservative	4.47	8.94	0	49
	Lib Dem	3.63	7.41	0	40
The Scotsman	Labour	2.53	5.98	0	54
	Conservative	1.96	4.08	0	22
	Lib Dem	1.95	3.91	0	21

Again we use logarithms for both indicators,[6] resulting in the following variables (in italics) for the analysis: the log of the frequency of mentions for each MP between 8 February 2009 and 7 May 2009 (*logpre*); and the log of the frequency of mentions for each MP alongside the word 'expenses' between 8 May 2009 and 6 May 2010 (*lognews*).

Regression analysis: Aggregate coverage

We start with an analysis of aggregate patterns of press coverage by adding up the number of articles of each newspaper. We first estimate equation (1), where the news variables refer to the total number of articles in the seven newspapers pulled together:

$$lognews_i = \alpha + \beta logpre_i + \gamma party_i + \delta X_i + \varepsilon_i \qquad (1)$$

where i indicates an MP, $party_i$ indicates the party of MP i, X_i is vector of control variables and ε_i is an error term. We do this to see whether

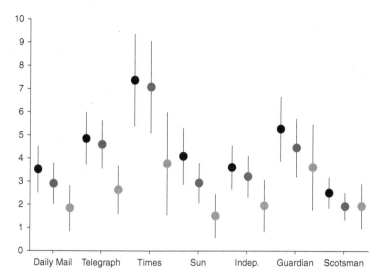

Figure 8.2   Means of total mentions of MP name + 'expenses' between 8 May 2009 and 6 May 2010 for Labour (black), Conservatives (grey) and Liberal Democrats (light grey)

Note: The circle is the estimated mean, the line gives a 95% confidence interval.

there is any overarching partisan bias in the media coverage if we take the seven selected newspapers together. The results of the regression analysis are given in Table 8.5, which includes the following models: no control variables (column 1); including *logLegg* and MP personal characteristics (column 2); including constituency characteristics (column 3). Not surprisingly, the level of newspaper coverage that an MP received after the expenses scandal story broke is, *ceteris paribus*, positively related to the level of newspaper coverage received in the period immediately before the scandal. In other words, MPs who were popular subjects for media coverage before the scandal continued to receive coverage during the scandal, whether or not they had been involved in perceived wrongdoing. We also found that the newspaper coverage focused more on more high-profile members of the House of Commons, that is front-benchers and those with more seniority, all other things being equal. Although there was no evidence of partisan bias, when we looked at the interaction effect with front bench, we found that there was increased newspaper coverage for Conservative and Labour front-bench Members, *ceteris paribus*, compared to other MPs (column 4). Moreover, newspaper stories involved Labour front-bench MPs more so than their Conservative counterparts. This suggests that the media took on a watchdog role during the coverage of the expenses scandal, focusing on the governing party (Labour) as well as the largest opposition party and potential government-in-waiting (Conservative).

Finally, in column 8.5 we focus on marginality. Although the marginality of a constituency does not appear, on average, to have had any significant impact on press coverage (see columns 3 and 4), column 5 shows that Labour-held marginal constituencies were significantly less covered than non-marginal constituencies, while Conservative and Liberal Democrat marginal constituencies are not statistically distinguishable from non-marginal constituencies.[7] Because of the extensive boundary changes that occurred between the 2005 and 2010 elections, we have included only constituencies whose boundaries changed by less than 10% in column 5. We have repeated all of our regressions restricting our sample by using various thresholds of percentage change in constituencies. Most of our conclusions, including those of the next sections, appear not to be affected by such restrictions. Results are therefore omitted in the interest of space.[8] Thus, we find that, controlling for other factors, the combined newspaper coverage on expenses is higher for: MPs with more experience in Parliament; those who had misappropriated higher amounts of money; and front-bench Members of the three main parties, particularly the governing Labour front bench.

We are now ready to exploit to a fuller extent the availability of a monetary measure of wrongdoing. Columns 2–5 of Table 8.5 show that repayments requested by the Legg report are, *ceteris paribus*, positively correlated with the amount of attention devoted to an MP. This suggests that media attention in the wake of the disclosure of detailed expenses claims published by the *Daily Telegraph* tended to be in line with the actual monetary misappropriation, as estimated in the Legg report. The coefficient indicates that on average a further scandal-related article on an MP appears for every 20 pounds of illegitimate expense claim.

An interesting question is now whether this average effect differed across the different parties. This amounts to estimating an equation with an interaction term:

$$lognews_i = \alpha + \beta logpre_i + \gamma_1 party_i + \gamma_2 legg_i + \gamma_3 party_i * legg_i + \delta \mathbf{X_i} + \varepsilon_i \quad (2)$$

Figure 8.3 displays the estimated $\hat{\gamma}_3$ for the various parties, showing that, for each pound that the Legg report recommended for repayment, *ceteris paribus*, Conservative MPs received more media coverage than Labour, Liberal Democrat and MPs from other parties.[9]

Table 8.5 Total news coverage (OLS coefficients)

Dependent variable	Natural log of total expenses news (May 2009–May 2010)				
	(1)	(2)	(3)	(4)	(5)
News February–April 2009	0.5319***	0.4729***	0.4731***	0.4518***	0.4580***
	(0.030)	(0.039)	(0.039)	(0.039)	(0.047)
Conservative MP	0.0258	0.0703	0.0520	0.1191	−0.3254
	(0.107)	(0.119)	(0.134)	(0.138)	(0.205)
Lib Dem MP	−0.2816*	−0.1336	−0.1476	0.0378	−0.1976
	(0.145)	(0.152)	(0.158)	(0.148)	(0.288)
Other MP	0.1974	0.2673	0.2222	0.2633	0.4845**
	(0.238)	(0.192)	(0.200)	(0.197)	(0.214)
Log of money owed (Legg)	0.0480***	0.0479***	0.0469***	0.0535***	
	(0.013)	(0.013)	(0.013)	(0.016)	
Female		0.3916***	0.4103***	0.4157***	0.5788***
		(0.107)	(0.110)	(0.109)	(0.156)
Age		0.0016	0.0026	0.0039	0.0049
		(0.007)	(0.007)	(0.007)	(0.009)
Seniority		0.0288***	0.0265***	0.0255***	0.0306***
		(0.008)	(0.009)	(0.008)	(0.010)
Degree		0.1467	0.1469	0.1382	0.2918**
		(0.107)	(0.107)	(0.106)	(0.133)
Oxbridge		−0.0555	−0.0554	−0.0295	0.0103
		(0.114)	(0.114)	(0.114)	(0.148)
Marginal in 2005			−0.1410	−0.1480	
			(0.116)	(0.116)	
Turnout in 2005			−0.0003	−0.0008	0.0129
			(0.009)	(0.009)	(0.013)
Distance from Westminster			0.0011	0.0012	−0.0001
			(0.001)	(0.001)	(0.001)
Front bench		0.5589***	0.5545***		0.5244**
		(0.178)	(0.179)		(0.245)
Conservative front bench				0.4414*	
				(0.259)	
Labour front bench				0.9641***	
				(0.239)	
Labour marginal					−0.4794**
					(0.194)
Conservative marginal					0.2753
					(0.235)
Lib Dem marginal					−0.0097
					(0.337)
Other marginal					−0.7656**
					(0.355)
Constant	1.0439***	0.2950	0.2042	0.1617	−0.6603
	(0.091)	(0.397)	(0.682)	(0.678)	(0.910)
Sample	All	All	All	All	Restricted
Observations	600	600	600	600	370
R-squared	0.3452	0.4375	0.4408	0.4527	0.4733

Note: Data do not include MPs from Northern Ireland and other MPs (details in the text). The restricted sample only includes MPs whose constituency boundaries changed by less than 10% according to Rallings and Thrasher (2007). Robust standard errors in parentheses. *** $p < 0.01$, ** $p < 0.05$, * $p < 0.1$. OLS coefficients reported.

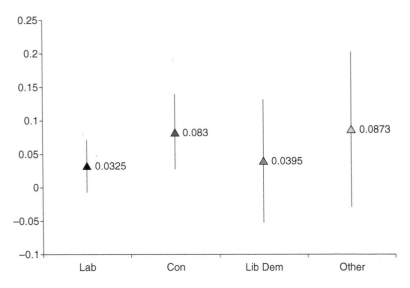

Figure 8.3 Aggregate press responsiveness to misappropriated money ($\hat{\gamma}_3$ in equation 2)

Note: The triangle is the estimated coefficient, the line gives a 95% confidence interval. Black is for Labour, grey is for Conservative, medium grey is for Liberal Democratic, light grey is for all the other parties combined.

Before concluding this section we would like to emphasize that our analysis also shows evidence of a gendered effect, although this was not initially a focus of the models. As can be seen from Table 8.5, females tended to receive more media coverage in the wake of the expenses scandal compared to their male counterparts, controlling for the other variables in the analysis, including party, seniority, money to be repaid according to the Legg report and whether the MP was on the front bench. Female MPs may have received higher media coverage during the expenses scandal compared with their male counterparts, since the media (and readers) may have seen their misbehaviour as 'unnatural' or 'unfeminine' while it is expected of ruthless masculine politicians. For example, in the wake of expenses revelations, one commentator referred to Jacqui Smith as 'a uniquely revolting figure, even in the grim annals of mean-minded, despotic home secretaries' and launched a personal attack addressed to her husband: 'One should have nothing to do with such a person, and if that means the cessation of intimate relations with her, then so be it.' (Lezard 2009) Smith felt that she had been targeted for being a female politician, commenting that 'it was my expenses people looked at first because I was a woman and should have been at home looking after my husband and children' (*Evening Standard* 2011).

Regression analysis: Individual newspapers

Drawing on this initial analysis, we now examine the coverage for the seven selected newspapers individually, which means that equation (1) must be analysed separately for each media outlet. The seven resulting equations are treated as a system of seemingly unrelated equations (SURE), which provides more efficient estimates than seven separate Ordinary Least Squares (OLS) regressions. The results are displayed in Table 8.6. Interestingly, there are no marked differences across the different newspapers regarding the relative values of the variables of interest, and there seems to be little evidence of partisan coverage among the selected newspapers for this chapter. The significant relationships across newspapers after the expenses scandal story was revealed are the same as in the previous analysis and are as follows: *ceteris paribus*, MPs recommended to repay more money in the Legg report tended to receive more media coverage; front-bench MPs from the three main parties tended to receive more media coverage; and MPs who have been in the House of Commons for longer tended to have more media coverage. As with the previous analysis, there is a gendered effect with more media coverage for female MPs during the expenses scandal in all newspapers with the exception of *The Scotsman* where there is no difference between male and female MPs.

We present the coefficients for the interaction between front-bench status and political party for the Conservatives and Labour (Figure 8.4). We see that the newspaper coverage is greater for Labour front-bench MPs compared to their Tory counterparts across all seven sources.[10] However, the gap between Labour and Conservative coverage in the right-leaning *Daily Mail* is more marked compared to the other newspapers included in the analysis. In any event, there is not a straightforward partisan pattern in the coverage: the left-leaning *Guardian* also had a large gap in coverage between the front-benchers of the two largest political parties, devoting many more articles to the Labour front bench. The other newspapers largely exhibited similar coefficients for the interaction between party and front-bench status, with the exception of *The Scotsman*, which had a smaller gap between the Labour and Conservative front-bench MPs. Thus, although there are some differences among the newspapers regarding the focus on front-bench MPs during the expenses scandal, and possible partisan behaviour in *Daily Mail* coverage, there are nonetheless no significant patterns among the sources that suggest an overarching partisan bias.

Table 8.6 Total expenses news reporting (SURE Estimates)

Variable	Natural log of total expenses news (May 2009–May 2010)						
	(1)	(2)	(3)	(4)	(5)	(6)	(7)
Newspaper	The Telegraph	The Times	The Guardian	The Independent	The Scotsman	The Sun	Daily Mail
News February–April 2009	0.1243***	0.1768***	0.2410***	0.1836***	0.1709***	0.1807***	0.1821***
	(0.023)	(0.024)	(0.026)	(0.024)	(0.025)	(0.022)	(0.024)
Log of Legg money	0.0353***	0.0578***	0.0334***	0.0364***	0.0337***	0.0394***	0.0405***
	(0.008)	(0.011)	(0.010)	(0.009)	(0.008)	(0.009)	(0.009)
Conservative	0.0712	0.0083	0.0746	-0.0231	0.0447	0.1027	0.0008
	(0.089)	(0.120)	(0.107)	(0.094)	(0.087)	(0.100)	(0.091)
Lib Dem	-0.0424	-0.1797	0.0504	-0.1650	-0.0307	-0.2550**	-0.0136
	(0.114)	(0.155)	(0.137)	(0.120)	(0.112)	(0.128)	(0.117)
Other	-0.1675	0.1592	0.3994*	0.1455	0.2311	-0.0479	-0.0057
	(0.175)	(0.238)	(0.210)	(0.184)	(0.172)	(0.196)	(0.179)
Front bench	0.7533***	0.9404***	0.8294***	0.7835***	0.6653***	0.6843***	0.7294***
	(0.099)	(0.134)	(0.118)	(0.104)	(0.094)	(0.111)	(0.100)
Female	0.1415*	0.2409**	0.2403**	0.1470*	0.1105	0.2316***	0.1486*
	(0.078)	(0.106)	(0.093)	(0.082)	(0.076)	(0.087)	(0.080)
Age	0.0008	-0.0057	-0.0051	-0.0074	-0.0089**	0.0016	0.0016
	(0.005)	(0.006)	(0.005)	(0.005)	(0.004)	(0.005)	(0.005)
Seniority	0.0185***	0.0333***	0.0315***	0.0266***	0.0237***	0.0159***	0.0120**
	(0.005)	(0.007)	(0.006)	(0.006)	(0.005)	(0.006)	(0.005)

Degree	0.0835	0.1039	0.1146	0.0258	0.0868	0.1516*	0.0610
	(0.080)	(0.109)	(0.096)	(0.085)	(0.079)	(0.090)	(0.082)
Oxbridge	0.0996	0.1113	0.0202	0.1024	0.0722	0.0153	0.0275
	(0.074)	(0.101)	(0.089)	(0.078)	(0.072)	(0.083)	(0.076)
Marginal in 2005	−0.0314	−0.1178	−0.1275	−0.0762	−0.0534	−0.0781	−0.1525**
	(0.075)	(0.102)	(0.091)	(0.080)	(0.074)	(0.085)	(0.077)
Turnout in 2005	−0.0056	0.0011	−0.0020	−0.0032	−0.0015	0.0050	−0.0035
	(0.006)	(0.008)	(0.007)	(0.007)	(0.006)	(0.007)	(0.006)
Distance from Westminster	0.0011*	−0.0004	−0.0003	0.0004	0.0006	0.0010	0.0004
	(0.001)	(0.001)	(0.001)	(0.001)	(0.001)	(0.001)	(0.001)
Constant	0.7206	0.1742	0.3941	0.6360	0.3569	−0.6898	0.3734
	(0.459)	(0.624)	(0.553)	(0.485)	(0.450)	(0.518)	(0.471)
Observations	600	600	600	600	600	600	600
R-squared	0.3041	0.3328	0.3581	0.3336	0.3430	0.3404	0.3216

Note: Standard errors in parentheses; *** p< 0.01, ** p< 0.05, * p< 0.1.

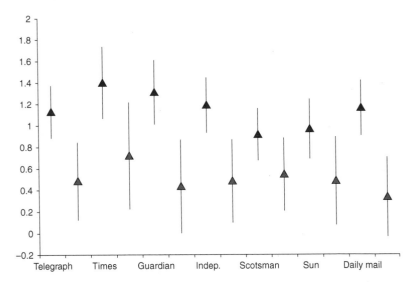

Figure 8.4 Coefficients of Labour (grey) and Conservative (light grey) front bench in individual newspapers regressions (interaction term for front-bench multiplied by party)

Note: The triangle is the estimated coefficient, the line gives a 95% confidence interval. Grey is for Labour, light grey for Conservative.

We can now re-estimate equation (2) using the same method, that is as a seemingly unrelated system of equations, one for each newspaper. Figure 8.5 reports the coefficients of the interaction term between *logLegg* and *party*. The pattern now changes. Conservative front-benchers receive more media coverage for each pound recommended for repayment compared to their Labour counterparts across all newspapers included in the analysis, all other variables being held constant, though we did not find evidence of a significant difference between these two parties. For the two left-leaning newspapers in the analysis, *The Guardian* and *The Independent*, the coefficients in the regression analysis were not significant, perhaps suggesting some under-coverage of Labour Party front-bench MPs given a level of misappropriation of ACA claims as determined by the Legg report. However, the overall pattern remains across newspapers and, again, there is no evidence of significant partisan media coverage across the newspapers.

To conclude, we find no clear evidence of partisan coverage of the expenses scandal across newspapers. For the seven papers examined, a number of patterns were evident, controlling for other explanatory

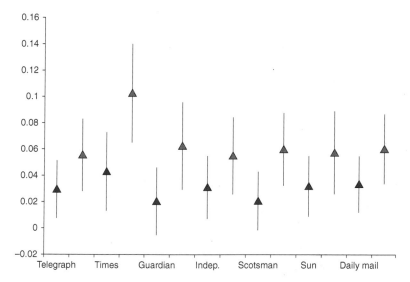

Figure 8.5 Responsiveness to misappropriated money ($\hat{\gamma}_3$ in equation 2) by newspaper

Note: The triangle is the estimated coefficient, the line gives a 95% confidence interval. Grey is for Labour, light grey for Conservative.

variables: more senior MPs, front-bench MPs from the three main parties and female MPs were mentioned more frequently. The interaction effect with the *logLegg* variable (γ_3) is positive for Labour and Conservatives MPs and a possible under-coverage of Labour MP by *The Guardian* and *The Independent* was uncovered. In general, however, the patterns we found hold equally for all newspapers with little variation. In particular, there is no more favourable coverage of MPs of a party closer to the editorial position of the newspaper. Given the substantially higher coverage of front-benchers belonging to Labour (the party in government), and in second place, of the front-benchers of the main opposition party (potential government members), we can conclude that the role of the press was rather that of a watchdog placing under closer scrutiny the government and its potential replacement.

Conclusions

In this chapter, we provide quantitative evidence on the press coverage of the UK expenses scandal. Our main conclusion is that the British press, or at least the seven newspapers we study, acted as watchdogs rather than in a partisan fashion. Other things being equal, government members and, to a less extent, front-benchers of the opposition received more coverage than other MPs. This result takes into account the natural tendency of the press to focus on front-benchers by controlling for pre-scandal press coverage levels. Responsiveness of coverage to amounts misappropriated (according to the Legg report) is instead higher for Conservative than for Labour MPs. In any event, all newspapers followed broadly similar patterns, irrespective of whether their ideological leaning and of whether they are tabloids or broadsheets.

Overall, it appears that personal characteristics explain press coverage better than party affiliation or other political variables like marginality. In particular, we uncover a non-negligible gender bias in press coverage. Other things equal, the British press has devoted substantially more attention to female MPs involved in the scandal than to their male colleagues. Once again, this pattern is shared by all newspapers, irrespective of their ideological leaning or their tabloid/broadsheet status.

The remarkable similarity in the numbers of articles devoted to each MP by different newspapers can be due to the fact that they shared the main source of information, namely the *Daily Telegraph* revelations. Still, there could have been scope for selective coverage, as for example found for the coverage of US scandals (Puglisi and Snyder 2011). The fact that this did not happen is good news about the British press although, on the other hand, the gender bias is certainly less encouraging.[11]

Appendix

Table 8A   Description of variables and summary statistics

Indicators of involvement in the scandal	N	Mean	Std. dev.	Min.	Max.
Lognews (MP name + expenses, May 2009–May 2010)	642	2.24764	1.36137	0	6.56
Logpre (MP name, February–May 2009)	642	2.29186	1.50682	0	7.23
Loglegg (money owed according to Legg report minus amount reduced in appeal)	642	3.67271	3.71583	0	10.65
Individual characteristics of MPs					
Age in years in 2009 [age]	646	55.1254	9.30257	29	83
Years in Parliament in 2009 (seniority)	646	13.2461	8.03885	1	45

Variables referred to electoral constituency					
Distance from constituency office to Parliament (distance)	646	153.56	134.216	0	702
Voter turnout in MP constituency in 2005 election (turn05)	608	60.8985	6.32085	37.6	76.42
% boundary change since 2005 election	626	15.4251	22.5315	0	135.89

Binary variables	**0 (no)**	**1 (yes)**
Front bench on 7 May 2009	570	76
Female MP	520	126
MP has university degree	133	513
MP graduated from Oxford or Cambridge	477	169
Constituency with < 10% majority in 2005 election (marginal)	453	155
Constituency boundary change since 2005 election	132	476

Note: Variables related to constituencies with a sample size of 608 exclude abolished constituencies (n = 18), constituencies where retiring MPs were replaced by sitting MPs for the 2010 election (n = 2), and Northern Ireland constituencies (n = 18).

Table 8B Summary of repayments from Legg report

	N	Mean	Std. Dev.	Min.	Max.
Repayment recommended	344	3,426.34	6,467.04	104.48	63,250.00
Amount reduced upon appeal	39	4,603.30	8,493.68	126.74	41,057.36
Repayments received since 1 April 2009[12]	328	3,069.92	5,735.95	0	42,674.13
Balance recommended to be repaid[13]	344	573.52	2,223.83	0	23,569.69

Note: in £ – only MPs with positive repayment are reported.

Notes

1. 'Review of past ACA Payments', February 2010. The review was conducted by Sir Thomas Legg, so it will be referred to hereafter as the Legg report.
2. This also includes Shadow equivalents, such as the Shadow Chancellor.
3. We updated the data of Besley and Larcinese (2011), which were collected for MPs who were elected at the 2001 general election. The distances between the constituency office addresses and the postcode of the Houses of

Parliament (SW1A 0AA) were estimated using a number of queries on Google Maps.

4. Detailed summary statistics of repayments recommended by the Legg report are provided in Table 8B in the appendix.
5. In addition to the MPs included in Table 8.3, there were 36 MPs who were not from one of the three main political parties.
6. log(n+1), where n is the number of articles for an MP in the selected newspaper.
7. The same is true of marginal constituencies held by SNP and PC, which are classified as 'Other marginal'.
8. We will report cases where sample changes made a difference. Boundary changes were calculated by using the data of Rallings and Thrasher (2007).
9. This result is robust to restricting the sample to constituencies with less than 10% boundary change. We find a similar effect for Labour MPs but it is both smaller and non-robust to sample variations.
10. The bars in Figure 8.2 refer to estimated coefficients for Conservative and Labour front-benchers. Hence, they capture the difference in coverage with respect to all other MPs.
11. In a separate paper, we try to uncover whether and how the media might have contributed to the removal from Parliament of MPs involved in the scandal (Larcinese and Sircar 2012).
12. If the amount of the recommended repayment is reduced to zero on appeal, MPs are not included in data for repayments received.
13. Of the 646 MPs examined in this chapter, the Legg report includes 344, of whom 62 are recommended to pay back any money from their ACA expense claims.

9
The New Regime: The Role of IPSA

Oonagh Gay

This chapter traces parliamentary reaction to the MPs' expenses crisis, which led to the creation of the Independent Parliamentary Standards Authority (IPSA). The Parliamentary Standards Act 2009 was rushed through both Houses in July 2009, the same time the Committee on Standards in Public Life undertook its review of MPs' allowances. IPSA was established in record time, and had a stormy initial reception from the new Parliament in 2010. The body was seen as unaccountable and remote from MPs' daily lives, administering an inflexible and unresponsive expenses scheme. IPSA is both regulator and administrator, and the dual role has caused tension with its customers, and there are continuing questions about its long-term viability, given the administrative overheads.

Introduction: The creation of IPSA

For members of the public, the *Daily Telegraph's* revelations appeared to come from nowhere. However, since 2007, there had been growing concern within the House of Commons that the system of Members' allowances was not fit for purpose and that reform was needed. Attempts by the Commons authorities to resist the release of information on individual Members' allowances in response to Freedom of Information (FOI) requests were attracting high levels of criticism from the media, and alongside this, via a resolution of the House, was a growing conviction that Members should no longer be responsible for setting their own pay. Thus, the stage had already been set for radical reform. The scale of public outrage however dictated a speedy response from the government and the opposition. In the process, the views of ordinary Members who would have to live under the new system were largely ignored.

A brief word about the governance of the House, which is complex and not well-understood, is warranted. The House of Commons Commission is responsible for the strategic direction of the House and is chaired by the Speaker. Other members are the Leader of the House, the Shadow Leader of the House, and three backbench members, Conservative, Labour and Liberal Democrat. The front bench, therefore, does not have a majority. In any case, decisions are normally taken by agreement, without votes. The Commons budget is set independently, is agreed by the Commission and covers the cost of Commons administration, upkeep of buildings, etc. Until 2010 the Commission also met as a select committee of the House, the Members' Estimates Committee, to consider policies on expenses for Members, which was taken from a separate budget or parliamentary vote. The Leader of the House is a member of Cabinet and is so able to communicate government wishes to the House, via the Commission. However, the Leader must also contend with a myriad of special committees established to administer the House, these range from Works of Art to Finance and Services. Moreover, the personality of the Speaker and his style of chairing the Commission were factors outside the control of the government. The complex administration arrangements for the House were a major factor in the expenses crisis, since decision-making was located in a number of different areas and those Members determined to influence change had various fora in which to make their voice heard.

The senior officials of the House form the Board of Management, chaired by the Clerk of the House, which reports to the Commission.[1] The administration of pay and allowances for MPs were the responsibility of the Department of Resources (formerly known as the Fees Office). The then director, Andrew Walker, therefore reported to the Board of Management, as well as sitting on it. He became more widely known when he appeared for the House in the Information Tribunal hearing over the release of detailed information on Members' allowances to FOI requesters. He first publicly revealed the existence of the 'John Lewis list' on 7 February 2008, used to decide whether claims for furnishing second homes were reasonable. The list was published on 13 March 2008 following a FOI request from the Press Association.

The Members Estimate Committee (with the same membership as the Commission) agreed a series of recommendations to reform both allowances and their audit in June 2008, which were rejected by the Commons when put forward for formal approval on 3 July 2008. A determined minority of backbench Members in both major parties opposed the changes as moving too far too fast and the audit arrangements as unworkable in practice; the Labour backbencher Don Touhig tabled an amendment to the MEC report which was carried by 172 votes to 144. The amendment was designed to reduce the scope of auditing. Press coverage of the debate and decisions of 3 July 2008 portrayed them as ignoring public concerns about the allowances system.

The Leader of the House, Harriet Harman, was strongly associated with the reform camp, but changes could not be pushed through without Labour backbench support, as shown in the 3 July vote. The Shadow Leader of the House, Theresa May and the Liberal Democrat leader, Nick Clegg quickly indicated that their respective parties would increase transparency on allowances, and so the front bench response to the *Telegraph*'s revelations was already foreshadowed as a bidding war for public support (Kelly 2009). Faced with the lack of consensus in the House, Ms Harman and the Commission attempted to find a way forward, which would provide a measure of transparency to the public, while retaining the support of Members. New proposals tightening audit requirements and requiring more detailed information to be published on Members' allowances were put to the House and agreed on 22 January 2009. But there remained much more intensive work on the details of new allowances and auditing. As public concern mounted, the Committee on Standards in Public Life (CSPL) announced a full review of Members' allowances in March 2009, and by the end of April the Prime Minister, Gordon Brown urged the body to act quickly in his ill-fated YouTube video.

The *Telegraph* began publishing its leaks on 8 May 2009, inviting increased public and media focus and outrage on allowances. Party leaders felt impelled to respond quickly. Mr Brown proposed a series of reforms, beginning with flat rate allowances. This was rapidly shot down in the media as outrageous, and the package of reforms brought forward by Harriet Harman on 29 April was rapidly supplanted by a commitment to legislate. Speaker Martin was impelled to resign on 19 May, clearing the way for action by the front benches of each major party. In many ways, the Commons had only itself to blame; there had been a failure to reach consensus on what to do about Members' allowances, leaving a vacuum of decision-making.

The future shape of the IPSA was foreshadowed in a statement from the Leader, Harman on 20 May. Responsibility for allowances and for the Code of Conduct for Members would be outsourced to an expert body, which would implement the recommendations from the CSPL. The Commons would lose control of setting the rate of allowances and of responsibility for their auditing. IPSA would also take on the role of paying Members, although not setting the rate. The outlines of the new body became clearer with the publication of the Parliamentary Standards Bill on 23 June 2009. The changes were more sweeping than expected within Westminster, since the system of regulating conduct and the registration of financial interests was also to pass to the new body, the IPSA.

IPSA: Phase one

The bill passed rapidly through both Houses, completing its passage by the rising of the House in July. There were arcane, but determined battles about its contents in the interim, led by senior parliamentary staff and Members concerned to ensure that the traditional boundary between legislature and judiciary was not weakened. In the end, the right of the Commons to design and approve its own code of conduct was maintained, although a statutory post of Commissioner for Parliamentary Investigations was established to investigate failure to register interests and misuse of allowances. This post would have co-existed with the existing non-statutory post of Parliamentary Commissioner for Standards.

The new body, the IPSA, was to be a regulator and an administrator. A statutory Speaker's Committee would provide oversight, but its board would be independent and accountability mechanisms were weak. A new criminal offence of misusing allowances was applied specifically to MPs, despite the existence of the Theft Acts, subsequently used in 2010 and 2011 to prosecute five MPs and former MPs.

But backbenchers remained muted in their scrutiny, as individual Members were pilloried in the media for their expenses claims. An additional inhibitor was the announcement that the former senior civil servant, Sir Thomas Legg, would review all allowances claims from existing Members for the past four years. The bill met more opposition in the Lords, where a sunset clause was inserted to force Ministers to renew the legislation on the Commissioner for Parliamentary Investigations in two years. However, the Lords gave way, once amendments were inserted to make clear that the legislation would not be used at a future date to regulate the upper House preserving the principle of self-regulation for the Lords. The Bill received royal assent on 21 July. In the event, the clauses on the Commissioner for Parliamentary Investigations never came into effect, due to criticism from the CSPL, discussed below.

The haste was understandable, given the intense public criticism of Parliament. But this was poor policy-making. IPSA was created with an extremely tight timetable, it was to become operational by the time of the next general election, widely expected to be May 2010. The new body had to be brought into existence, and following the appointment of a board, had to develop a new scheme of allowances and deal with an administratively complex transfer of systems from the Commons. Moreover, the CSPL had yet to report with its recommendations for reform. Its chairman, Sir Christopher Kelly made clear that it would continue to develop its recommendations despite the existence of the new law.

IPSA: Phase two

The CSPL report was published in November 2009. It disagreed with the decision to outsource regulation of financial interests and the creation of a new statutory Commissioner. Instead, the Committee recommended retaining the role of the Parliamentary Commissioner for Standards and creating a new Compliance Officer, who would be housed within IPSA, but act as an independent investigator. However, in one respect the CSPL went further than expected in its initial issues and questions paper in accepting the arguments of Andrew Tyrie, an influential Conservative backbencher, and others, that IPSA should be responsible for setting the pay of Members, as well as administering it.[2] With pay went the pensions scheme, hitherto administered by MPs who were pension trustees.

CSPL also had concerns about the governance of IPSA, arguing that there needed to be lay members on the Speaker's Committee for IPSA, to restore public trust. It also suggested that IPSA's role in supporting Members to carry out their duties needed to be made explicit in the legislation. The government accepted these recommendations, expanding IPSA's role, and made the legislative changes in the Constitutional Reform and Governance Act 2010. IPSA was now in charge of setting Members' pay, pensions and allowances; yet, it had barely been established as a body by the time these new clauses came into effect in April 2010.

IPSA implementation

The task facing IPSA was daunting. The new board had to set the direction, but in conjunction with staff seconded from the Ministry of Justice, who had to meet staff from the Commons Department of Resources to understand the old system, before designing a new one which would be demonstrably different. Moreover, there was no time to pilot the new scheme for allowances before the general election in May 2010. IPSA was fortunate to be given an exceptional civil servant,

Andrew McDonald, from the Ministry of Justice, as Interim Chief Executive. It was noticeable that senior staff from Resources were not invited to transfer, since there were concerns that IPSA's independence might be compromised by association with former practices (with only a very few junior staff electing to move). Following internal decision by the Board of Management, the Commons administration was reformed, the Department of Resources abolished in favour of new departments of Finance and Human Resources. There was no appetite among senior Commons officials for any further involvement in pay and allowances. The IPSA Board was appointed in December 2009. In January 2010, it published a consultation paper on its expenses scheme and on 29 March 2010, IPSA's *MPs' Expenses Scheme* was laid before the House of Commons by the Speaker. It came into force on the day after the 2010 general election (7 May 2010).[3]

IPSA rapidly ran into trouble with Members. There was immediate uproar that the scheme was over-complex and difficult to use. IPSA reacted quickly and issued a revised expenses scheme in July 2010 that offered some more flexibility on travel, staffing expenses and loans until Members had fully established their offices, but this was not enough to stem the tide of criticism. Particular exception was taken to the fact that IPSA's chief executive, Andrew McDonald, would not meet MPs to discuss their claims in detail and that all claims had to be submitted electronically. Instead of the friendly guidance from in-House officials that MPs were accustomed to, MPs were faced with employees from an external body, which saw its main duty as restoring public trust. MPs claimed that genuine mistakes would lead to public criticism, since details of expense claims would be published every two months. The administration of the scheme had also in effect been outsourced to MP's staff as each claim, with accompanying documentation had to be uploaded, replacing a system where a bundle of receipts could be sent for processing to staff within the House.

The speed and vitriol of the attacks on IPSA by MPs which surfaced after May 2010 were surprising to outsiders, but not to those who worked in Parliament. The new body was always going to have a high profile for MPs. The 2010 Parliament was jittery in the first weeks, as the question of the longer term implications for public trust of the expenses scandal in the last Parliament, remained unanswered. MPs who had escaped censure for their individual expense claims were able to take the lead in criticizing the complexity of the claims machinery.

A series of confrontations followed. MPs launched savage attacks on the competence of the new body and were horrified at the lack of opportunity to hold IPSA to account. The bureaucracy and lack of direct channels of communication were the main sources of complaint. It was an independent body, so no minister was accountable for its actions. Nor was the House of Commons Commission, which was no longer responsible for any form of expenses system. Little attention had been paid to this design factor during the passage of the legislation the previous year, as MP were cowed by the public outrage. Monthly written questions to the Speaker's Committee were instituted, but were inadequate to meet the number and frequency of demands for explanations to MPs. So MPs' attention turned to the first public meeting of the Speaker's Committee on 30 June 2010 where the budget of IPSA was due for approval. Committee members immediately focused on the costs (£6.5m) of administering IPSA. The atmosphere at the meeting was fraught with MPs in the audience shouting out their comments, and at times, IPSA witnesses struggling to be heard. In some senses, MPs were articulating the frustration of media attack felt over the past year, but for others, the complexity of the new scheme was a source of real anger.

MPs against IPSA

Over the next 18 months backbench MPs tried to use a series of forums to highlight continuing concerns about the cost and complexity of IPSA. They received no support from the front benches of major parties, which had no stomach for further legislative action on allowances so soon after the expenses crisis. Nor did the MPs seek or achieve significant public support as this was unlikely to be forthcoming. This was an internal conflict. MPs' first strategy turned to securing debates to criticize IPSA and its processes. On 16 June the veteran MP David Winnick (Labour, Walsall North) and fervent supporter of more transparency in the previous Parliament, initiated a debate in Westminster Hall on the subject of IPSA, complaining that it was deeply bureaucratic and complex and that Members could not communicate easily with its officials. IPSA issued a robust response to the debate that did nothing to calm passions.[4]

A minority of MPs had begun to consider radical reform. Adam Afriyie (Conservative, Windsor), a backbencher with an unblemished allowances record came forward with a private Member's bill, the *Parliamentary Standards (Amendment) Bill 2010–11*. As a presentation bill there was no automatic access to parliamentary time so that it could be progressed, but it served as a vehicle for an alternative approach of a much simpler flat rate system of allowances regionally adjusted, and a requirement to ensure that the administration costs of IPSA represented no more than 2.5% of the overall cost of payments made under the scheme. The details of the scheme would have once again operated by decision of MPs. Government whips blocked any progress despite voices of support from fellow MPs in the debate.

Afriyie's next move was to take advantage of a new mechanism introduced in the 2010 Parliament to enable backbenchers more control over the days devoted to non-government business. The Backbench Business Committee had established a 'Dragon's Den' type system allowing MPs to bid for a particular topic to be debated. Afriyie was able to demonstrate support from the parliamentary Labour Party, the 1922 Committee and the Liberal Democrat Party. He secured a debate on 2 December, on a motion criticizing excessive bureaucracy and calling for a simpler system. Afriyie pressed for radical change to be enacted before the beginning of the new financial year in April 2011, but this was never a likely scenario. Although David Cameron had expressed concerns about IPSA,[5] no new government would so quickly overturn a flagship policy and face a media storm. But the whips were wise enough not to fight the terms of the motion, knowing that the Commons could not enforce the will of a passionate minority against the government.

The most vocal discontent peaked in December 2010, when Cameron reassured the 1922 Committee that changes would be made to IPSA to make the regime more family friendly and less bureaucratic.[6] Backbenchers continued to criticize the organization as bureaucratic and unresponsive, failing to return phone calls, and requiring paperwork to be submitted electronically, but much of the energy was gone, as IPSA responded to criticism by making procedures more flexible, merging separate budgets and making more use of payment cards. However, at the July 2011 Speaker's Committee meeting to set the IPSA budget, concern over transaction costs and inflexibilities in the scheme was still evident. MPs were supported by the lay members, one of whom, Anthony Holland, complained of insufficient attention to value for money. IPSA argued that the requirement to reassure the public and so carefully audit, as well as the operational costs of being a small independent body were the factors behind the supposed extravagance. The Speaker's Committee took action, issuing a statement under the name of the Speaker stating that 'it is not satisfied that the estimate [for the budget of IPSA] is consistent with the efficient and cost-effective discharge by the IPSA of its functions'.[7]

Outside of Parliament, there was further pressure from the National Audit Office (NAO) for reform, which had undertaken an enquiry in early 2011. This noted that 83% of MPs thought the time required to comply with IPSA hindered them from doing their own work. The report spoke of the need to move to a risk-based system of validation and offering advice to Members on appropriate procurement. The NAO emphasized that the scheme ultimately existed in order to enable MPs to do a proper job. In effect, IPSA had failed to take account of its customers' needs.[8] The NAO recommended that IPSA take action by December 2011 to address the amount of time being spent on interacting with the scheme and make advice more consistent and accessible.

Following a hearing and evidence-taking, the Public Accounts Committee issued its own report on 23 September 2011, taking into account the NAO's recommendations.[9] It noted that 38% of claims cost more to process than the amount of money at issue and that IPSA had failed to adopt a risk-based approach to validation, instead insisting on validating all items of expenditure. A more common approach in auditing expenses is to focus on areas where misuse is most likely. Although the report was measured in tone, it was clear from the content that MPs felt unsupported by IPSA in terms of a public acknowledgement of their probity. The new body had failed to emphasize that 99.7% of claims submitted were within the rules and that of the 38 initial investigations undertaken by the Compliance Office, so far, no fraud had been found. IPSA was not therefore helping to restore public confidence, nor explaining to the public at large that the great majority of expenses were in fact staff salaries.

Adam Afriyie's next move had been to call for the creation of a Committee on Members' Expenses with the remit of reviewing the operation of the Parliamentary Standards Act 2009. The deadline of April 2011 for reform of the system which had been set by the Commons motion passed had not been met and the new Committee would offer another way in which to hold IPSA to account. In a series of hearings in the autumn of 2011, culminating in a report and debate in December 2011, the Committee continued to highlight the difficulties caused to Members by IPSA's mode of operation. It found that dissatisfaction among MPs had been less about what is covered and the sums available than about the process of claiming, the damage caused by the system to the reputations of individual MPs and to Parliament, and about MPs' time taken away from their constituents and parliamentary duties. The report was referred to IPSA, and once again the party leaders blocked the legislative reform called for by Afriyie's committee to ensure that the primary duty of IPSA was to support Members.

IPSA's response

IPSA's Chief Executive, Andrew McDonald, acted in the first year to review IPSA's system of allowances and claims procedure to reduce complexity. By the end of 2011, 77% of claims were being dealt with by direct payments to suppliers and by payment cards. However, he was wrestling with managing the expectations of a generation of MPs who had been used to a very personal service from Commons officials, who were now faced with online claims, backed up by detailed receipts, with a working week of often 70 or 80 hours a week, as they shuttled back and forth from constituency home to Westminster abode.

Many MPs said that they were frightened to claim for legitimate expenses, for fear of ridicule in the local or national press if mistakes were made. Moreover, IPSA's standardized forms didn't allow much flexibility in accounting for expenses. For example, the chair of a select committee has travel expenses to claim if asked to address a conference, but might want to combine this with a trip home to see a child perform at a school concert. This does not make for easy form-filling and IPSA were at first erring on the side of caution in interpreting their own allowance schemes. As the scheme matured, IPSA became more prepared to return to some of the flexibility of the Fees Office, combining budgets, and allowing MPs the choice of a taxi or a hotel for a late night sitting, for example. But this was accompanied by a strong emphasis on audit and transparency and an arm's length approach, discouraging detailed advice.

The IPSA Board reacted strongly to external criticism. By the summer of 2011, Sir Ian Kennedy (IPSA Chair) had begun to weary of the various accountability mechanisms that MPs had found to examine IPSA. In response to a request from the Speaker's Committee for more frequent meetings and a six monthly review of IPSA's budget, he said:

> We have very limited capacity for further iterations with the Speaker's Committee while we are simultaneously under the scrutiny of the National Audit Office, the Committee on Members' Allowances and the Public Accounts Committee. My hope is that, once these various exercises are completed, we will be able to give our undivided attention to the Speaker's Committee which is, after all, the body Parliament set up to oversee the cost-effective discharge of our responsibilities. As I said at our recent meeting, our ability to deliver cost savings has a relationship with the level of scrutiny to which we

are subject. The Board is strongly of the view that the current level is disproportionate.[10]

The desire to hold demanding MPs at arm's length was understandable. However, it is surprising that the first time that the full board of the IPSA met the Speaker's Committee was in the spring of 2012. A letter from the Speaker to Sir Ian Kennedy on 23 June 2011 proposed such a meeting in September 2011 as a way of understanding the operation of the board.[11] While there may well have been timetabling issues with agreeing a suitable date, it may also indicate IPSA's lack of willingness to build a close relationship with MPs.

In 2012 there appeared to be stalemate. The MPs did not have the power to bring forward amending legislation, since this was blocked by the party leaders, who were concerned that even modest changes might again provoke hostile media coverage. Polling suggested that the public remained hostile to any suggestion that MPs would regain control over allowances. This paralysed the political party leaders who feared any recurrence of the *Daily Telegraph* onslaught, and were also concerned that backbenchers might make unrealistic legislative proposals. The issue offered no political benefits at all. However, the ferocity of attacks by MPs had provoked a response from IPSA, which acted to make the allowances system more in line with the needs of Members. In particular, IPSA significantly increased the allowances for staff in the new scheme from £115,000 to £137,200 for non-London area MPs and £144,000 for London area MPs issued from April 2012. Ironically, many of the features it introduced were similar to the pre-2010 system; more flexibility, direct payments to suppliers and payment cards.

At the third annual meeting of the Speaker's Committee to review the IPSA budget on 22 May 2012, Sir Ian and Andrew McDonald were keen to emphasize that public trust on expenses had been restored and that the next issue to be resolved was the question of the appropriate pay and pensions for Members.[12] This is likely to be a tricky area for IPSA. It will stand accused of attempting to assess the work and value of Members without fully understanding their role and there is some danger that the majority of backbenchers will not consider that IPSA is the most appropriate body to do this.

The allowances scheme in detail

The legislation required IPSA to design and implement an allowances scheme, with provision for annual revision. The body was required to consult a number of stakeholders, including MPs. The outline of the scheme that IPSA brought forward for use from May 2010 bore some similarities with the allowances scheme it replaced. Pre-2010, there was a staffing allowance, an office allowance, winding-up and travel allowances and the notorious Additional Costs Allowance (ACA), from which housing and furniture costs were taken. The ACA allowance was designed to compensate Members for costs incurred staying overnight away from home while performing parliamentary duties.[13] There was a small London allowance designed to compensate London members ineligible for ACA. MPs could employ family members, provided that they were listed in a separate part of the Register for Members' Financial Interests. A communications allowance, covering the cost of regular newsletters etc., was frozen before the 2010 general election, since it had incurred criticism as being too party political. Finally, MPs were entitled to a resettlement grant following retirement or defeat at an election.

The new IPSA scheme also included an accommodation allowance, but only for rent and not mortgage interest. MPs who had incurred mortgages prior to 2010 had transitional arrangements until 31 August 2012 to meet the cost of mortgage interest. The allowance was sufficient for a one-bedroom flat in London or equivalent in the constituency. As of April 2013, household utility bills are allowable and there is a small allowance of up to £2,425 for costs for each dependant living with the MP. Only dependants under five (or 21 if the Member was a single parent) initially counted for this allowance. Each region has a rental budget and rents above these limits have to be met by the MP. For Members renting in the London area, the annual accommodation budget is £20,100.[14] MPs with London area constituencies may not claim for accommodation, but can claim the London Area Living Payment, capped at £3,760.

The travel rules are less flexible than before. Travel between Westminster and the constituency is allowable but not for party political or ministerial purposes. Dependants can, as before, claim for a number of journeys to and from Westminster. Office costs expenses may be claimed for any costs required to support the set-up and ongoing running of the constituency office, where these are necessary for the performance of parliamentary functions. Standard job descriptions and pay rates were specified for types of staff, such as senior caseworker. MPs employing more than one relative (connected party) when IPSA began could continue to do so, as long as they are registered. New MPs may employ one connected party. The outlines of the new scheme were perfectly recognizable to Members, but the flexibility of the old scheme had been lost. The new scheme required much more detail, receipts for each item of expenditure and had much stricter rules on accommodation; the latter having an impact on family life as it was no longer possible to claim for family homes in both Westminster and the constituency.

Under the pressure of criticism and with more experience of the complex needs of MPs, IPSA changed a number of details. Direct payments to suppliers and payment cards became available for common expenses, such as travel and utility bills. By the end of 2011 IPSA considered that 77% of costs could be met in this way.[15] These facilities had been in use under the pre-2010 regime and in many ways the alterations to the scheme brought the expenses closer to the pre-scandal Commons model. There were limited accommodation and travel improvements to aid MPs with caring responsibilities to families; provision was now made for dependants up to the age of 18; the definition of the London area was adjusted so that the number of London constituencies was reduced from 128 to 96 (these MPs were expected to commute to Parliament). The option of direct payments to landlords became available; modest bonuses could be paid to staff as long as they were not relatives; a start-up budget of £6,000 was available to new MPs to establish a constituency office; and receipts were not necessary for each regular payment (i.e. utilities).

There was more flexibility on website content, for instance allowing some party political material. The two office budgets were amalgamated into one Office Costs Expenditure (a name which recalled the pre-2010 Office Costs Allowance) allowing much more discretion for Members to claim according to their particular needs.[16] MPs were now allowed to choose whether to pay for a taxi or a hotel when the House sat late – allowing MPs to use their judgement – a distinct change in attitude from IPSA. Finally, the question of reintroducing a one-off resettlement payment to defeated MPs was brought forward by IPSA itself, as a valid payment to meet legitimate costs of redundancy over and above staff costs and ending leases on offices, already met by the winding up allowance. This is in force for any general election held before the expected date of the next election in 2015.[17]

There were fewer changes in the administration of the scheme. Information still had to be uploaded by MPs and their staff and the advice line operated only in the afternoons, although plans were developing for more drop-ins to provide a personal service. Details of claims made and paid were made available every two months on the IPSA website. However, IPSA did not change its rhetoric: its role was to reassure the public, not to improve its performance vis-a-vis its customers, and consequently, the IPSA Board appeared reluctant to give any ground to its critics. Tough regulation was required as well as transparency and audit.

Structure of IPSA

What of the body which was so hastily created as a political fix to a problem which had become uncontrollable by usual political means? IPSA is both a regulator and an administrator, and at times, this has been an uneasy mixture. The pronouncements of the chair of IPSA, Sir Ian Kennedy, have focused on its role as a guardian of public trust, yet for MPs it is principally a service deliverer, with an overgrown bureaucracy. IPSA was designed to be independent, to withstand any undermining of its principles and practices by MPs, but the flip-side of independence is non-accountability and, as we have seen above, this was a charge thrown at IPSA from the beginning of its existence.

IPSA is a public body with a board and chief executive and senior management team. It maintains about 50 staff, who are public servants, recruited directly by IPSA. Staff numbers peaked at 81 staff in July 2010, and Mr McDonald promised that they would be down to about 42 by April 2014.[18] For start up, there were nine senior managers, but this reduced to five by the summer of 2012. The body has no formal relationship with House of Commons staff. It has offices separate from Parliament and it does not maintain a physical presence in the Palace of Westminster. The key senior staff mostly came from a civil service background rather than from commercial facilities management. This has affected the overall culture of IPSA. It is firmly a public sector organization, with values different from an external payroll contractor, such as Capita. Some junior staff transferred from the Commons, but care was taken to build a different ethos from the Department of Resources.

IPSA is a quango or arm's-length body. Its independence gives its strength to withstand pressure both from Members and the House authorities. But it suffers from the usual perceived weakness of ethical watchdogs – it is an unelected body which may consult on appropriate arrangements for MPs' pay, allowances and pensions but ultimately has the responsibility of designing a scheme without having to justify it through any form of democratic accountability. Nor can the Commons easily challenge the operational decisions of IPSA, since the main oversight mechanism, the Speaker's Committee on IPSA, considers only appointments and the budget. We have seen above how the Committee has used control over the budget to persuade IPSA to cut running costs.

Its independence, generally seen as a strength, is also a weakness, since MPs have no ownership in its success. In the long run does IPSA need the support of its clients; or will the memory of the expenses scandal or the threat of bad publicity mean IPSA doesn't need to enjoy its customers' approval?

As an independent body, IPSA is vulnerable to criticism over the expense of its back-office functions. Previously the costs of public relations and administrative staff were shared across the whole of the Commons administration budget. The NAO review noted above made plain that IPSA had failed to adopt a risk-based approach to validation. The NAO report did not find that the direct costs of IPSA were excessive, being close to the average for other UK national legislatures, and the cost per item had fallen from £40 in August 2010 to around £16 in May 2011, partly through reduced checking once it became clear that rejection rates were low.

This was a fundamental question for IPSA. What was its role? Was it to ensure that nothing like the MPs' expenses scandal ever occurred again? Or was it to ensure that MPs had an efficient responsive service, with a risk-based system of validation as recommended by the NAO? This would mean that auditing would focus only on high-risk areas or individuals. The legislation had been amended during its passage through Parliament to ensure that IPSA had a duty to assist MPs, but this had to be balanced against the wider public interest.

There are also difficulties in designing a regulatory system where those regulated have so few opportunities to take ownership of the scheme. Most professionals are regulated by a mixture of internal and external bodies, but any oversight by Members had been discredited during the expenses scandal. Moreover, there was a relatively successful regulatory model in Parliament itself. The Parliamentary Commissioner for Standards is semi-independent. He initiates an investigation in response to a complaint, or where he suspects that there has been a breach of the rules. The Commissioner reports to a parliamentary committee, the Standards and Privileges Committee which reviews and then publishes the report. It is the Committee that recommends sanctions to the House, and the House has to agree these sanctions.

The CSPL accepted the viability of this model in its November 2009 report, which recommended that the regulation of financial interests should remain with the House. Outsourcing the regulation of expenses made the role of the Standards Commissioner more straightforward, as he had been under-resourced to tackle the multiple cases of misuse of expenses uncovered in 2009. Political reality dictated the (form and) survival of IPSA. The front benches resisted any reform in 2010 and 2011, arguing that the expenses scheme itself had been so discredited that public and press would not stand for any form of an in-house scheme. One problem is that the more the expenses scheme disappears into history, the less valid the argument becomes, particularly if there remains a strong independent regulator and a guarantee of transparency. If IPSA has solved the problem of public trust, does its existence need to be permanent? Alternatively, if the public distrust of politicians in general remains high, does IPSA make any different to that perception?

Barry Winetrobe, an independent parliamentary consultant, highlighted the confusion of purpose at the heart of IPSA during the inquiry carried out by Adam Afriyie's Committee on Members Expenses in 2011:

> A fascinating debate, within and out with the Inquiry, has been raging on what sort of body IPSA actually is, and what its primary function should be. While MPs and the Committee on Standards in Public Life see IPSA mainly as a body to administer schemes of financial support for MPs in carrying out their parliamentary duties, IPSA sees itself primarily as an independent regulator, and as such, its fundamental purpose is 'to serve the public interest'.[19]

Sir Ian himself set out the difficulties in a speech in 2010:

> The I in IPSA stands for independent. That's what Parliament legislated for. Yet, the regulator's means of operation is controlled by a Committee of the regulated. This is very uneasy territory. And the terms of reference of the Committee do allow it to interpret its brief in such a way as to use consideration of the cost-effectiveness of the estimate, so as to challenge aspects of the scheme or its operation on the ground that doing things a different way would be more cost-effective. It then requires a very little jump to saying that there should be a different scheme. At that point, IPSA has lost its independent ability to devise the scheme it believes best meets the needs and concerns of the public and MPs, both of whose interests we exist to serve.[20]

IPSA prides itself on its unique model, as independent regulator and policy maker. The model is exceptional in comparative terms. Many parliaments have wrestled with robust regulation of allowances, where parliamentarians have been resistant to outside scrutiny. For example, French National Assembly members voted in July 2012 against plans for external scrutiny of their £5,000 monthly expenses allowances.[21] In Australia, the executive controls the setting of pay and allowances, but administration rests with the Parliamentary Service.[22] The US Congressional Committee on House Administration is in charge of administering expenses but any citizen may initiate a suit under the False Claims Act by alleging that false or fraudulent allowances claims have been made.[23] Legislatures in Scotland and Wales both acted as a result of the scandal in Westminster, establishing independent commissions to create externally devised allowances schemes, but left payment in-house, through parliamentary staff.

Independent regulation of pay and allowances is almost unknown in European legislatures. In Germany, Article 48(3) of the Basic Law stipulates that Members of the Bundestag are entitled to remuneration which is adequate to ensure their independence. The amount of the remuneration must reflect the importance of the special position held by a Member of the Bundestag and the responsibility and burdens accompanying that office. It must also take account of the status attaching to tenure of a parliamentary seat within the constitutional system. Since its judgment of 5 November 1975 on the remuneration of Members of the Bundestag (reference 2 BvR 193/74), the Federal Constitutional Court has repeatedly invoked this principle.[24] However, staff of Members of the Bundestag are paid directly by the legislature, which provides office equipment for its Members, rather than paying flat rate allowances. Reforms have been instituted at the European Parliament with the flat rate travel allowance replaced by provision of receipts for actual journeys made. However, the British media regularly highlight continuing problems with the allowances systems for MEPs.

Can IPSA be successful at combining the roles of regulator and administrator?

The NAO found that the IPSA model was unique in terms of regulating and processing Members' allowances. Although in Scotland and Wales the task of setting the rate of allowances had been outsourced, parliamentary staff are still responsible for the payment (Bush 2012). It is not inherently impossible to combine both functions, but the purposes are different. For administration and auditing, cost is paramount: is the system easy to use, user-friendly, with risk-based auditing built in; for the regulator, probity and transparency are the important issues, as well as restoring public trust. It is difficult to combine in a single body.

This point was made forcefully by Afriyie's Committee on Members' Expenses. Lack of transparency had been the root of the MPs' expenses scandal. If there was transparency, did we need intensive regulation? The Committee did have its concerns about the detail of transparency, arguing that providing data every two months was excessive and needed commentary to put the differences between individual Members in context. IPSA itself noted that the number of hits on its website had declined considerably since it had become clear that the information was available and that regulation was robust. On the other hand, the CME presented impressive evidence from the NAO and surveys it conducted, that up to 90% of MPs were not claiming the allowances they were entitled to, due to concerns about bureaucracy but also transparency, that the total claim would attract opprobrium from local media and constituents. IPSA acknowledged in its oral evidence to the Speaker's Committee in May 2012 that it was making active attempts to persuade more Members to claim allowances to which they were entitled.[25]

The (CME) report, however, illustrated that some major arguments had been won over recalcitrant backbenchers. No MP was prepared to argue that FOI should not apply to allowances. The issue that convulsed the Commons before the crisis was over. The CME also accepted that independent setting of allowances should continue and considered that MPs should not set their own pay. Some of its members believed that a system of flat rate allowances would resolve the question of regulation, others thought that this would not be acceptable to the public. It was hard to argue against the overall conclusion of the CME, that administration of allowances is best done in-house due to economies of scale, provided there is independence of regulation and transparency.

Setting members' pay and pensions

Having established a more flexible allowances system, IPSA's next challenge is to set the rate of MPs' pay. Responsibility to determine pay was passed to the body in May 2011. In March 2011, under government pressure, the House passed a resolution to freeze pay for a further year[26] and in February 2012, IPSA announced that it would freeze salaries in 2012/2013 at £65,738 and would consult on increasing salaries by 1% in 2013 and 2014. Pension contributions were increased by 1.85% from April 2012.[27] Pension contributions would be subject to consultation and IPSA would complete a review of pay and pensions by the end of 2013. Sir Ian commented, 'while we address the longer term changes which are needed, I believe it is right that we act in the interim so that MPs' circumstances more closely reflect those experienced by others'.[28]

The pay consultation began formally in the autumn of 2012 and included both the public and stakeholders. Initial evidence-taking from the public was attempted on the IPSA website, following by citizens juries. Anonymized surveys of Members revealed that many believed that their pay needed significant uplift, but few MPs were prepared to say this publicly. The moral authority to make decisions on pay is likely to become a battleground in the final years of the 2010 Parliament.

Has IPSA solved the problem?

IPSA may be an unsatisfactory temporary solution for MPs but has its creation solved the problem of a crisis in public trust? Curtice and Park's (2010) research has demonstrated that public trust in MPs had been low for some time before the MPs' expenses scandal and that the explosion of disgust seen among the electorate in the summer of 2009 when faced with evidence that MPs had misused their parliamentary allowances. They found that 'trust in politicians has never been particularly high in Britain; in most years, well under a half (and often well under a third) say they trust governments or politicians "just about always" or "most of the time" '.[29] The damage done by the expenses scandal, though very severe in terms of the public's assessment of the honesty and trustworthiness of politicians, failed to inspire a deeper and wider cynicism about our political institutions. Nevertheless commentators and opinion formers continue to cite the dishonesty of MPs as an underlying justification for other social evils such as the riots in England in August 2011.

There is evidence that the existence of IPSA did restore trust, and almost immediately. In January 2011, an IPSA poll showed that 30% of respondents 'trust MPs to claim only for legitimate expenses'. A further 35% said they had 'some trust, but not very much'.[30] Just six months later, in July 2011, the National Audit Office was able to report 'an increase in public confidence regarding MPs' expenses during the past year'.[31] The NAO had commissioned a question in a recent Ipsos-MORI General Public Omnibus Survey showing that '55% of people thought the situation with expenses had improved'. A lot of the credit was to IPSA: 'Although other factors such as high-profile prosecutions will have played their part, we believe that IPSA has significantly contributed to this improvement, which has been achieved in an impressively short period.'[32]

This improvement may have been as much a sign of the expenses issue dropping off the public's radar, as any indication of rising public warmth towards MPs. IPSA told the Public Accounts Committee in July

2011 that when it first published Members' claims in full in 2010, the number of hits on the website was over 10,000. On the fifth cycle, in the summer of 2011, the number of unique hits had fallen to 83. This fall-off in public interest may also be seen as vindication of IPSA's policy of full transparency about Members' claims.

So would transparency without regulation have been enough? Did we need payment of expenses and pay to be carried out by an independent body? Here polling evidence is hard to interpret. A series of polls in May 2009 by Ipsos MORI showed significant support, at 85%, for a judicial-type body to regulate expenses. But Ipsos MORI did not test whether an independent body was needed to pay MPs' expenses, so evidence as to the potential popularity of IPSA is lacking. Regular media confusion about its set-up and role suggests almost complete public ignorance about its work.

One scenario is that after another Parliament, the rationale for a stand-alone (and therefore expensive) body to pay remuneration and expenses will come under challenge and that the payroll function will either return to the Commons, or be undertaken by a commercial body under contract. IPSA may therefore be a victim of its own success. It remains a unique model in terms of administration of parliamentary allowances but there are no signs that it will be an international comparator.

Notes

1. The Board comprised the Clerk of the House, the Clerk Assistant, and the Head of Resources, Information Services and Facilities, with two external board members. In 2013 it has an additional external member, and the heads of the Department of Finance and Department of Human Resources and Change. The Department of Resources was abolished in 2010.
2. Committee on Standards in Public Life Issues and Questions Paper 23 April 2009.
3. IPSA, *The MPs' Expenses Scheme*, 29 March 2010, HC 501 2009–2010; House of Commons, *Votes and Proceedings*, 29 March 2010, Appendix, Item 31.
4. *Public Service* 'IPSA Compromises After Rudeness' 16 June 2010.
5. See for example HC Deb 14 July 2010 c946.
6. Cameron Condemns Expenses Watchdog. (2010) *Press Association*, 16 December 2010; see also Nicholas Watt and Allegra Stratton, 'MPs' Expenses Body Must Change or be Changed, says David Cameron', *Guardian*, 16 December 2010.
7. SCIPSA Statement under Schedule 1 of the Parliamentary Standards Act 2009 23 June 2011.
8. See National Audit Office, Independent Parliamentary Standards Authority: The Payment of MPs' Expenses.

9. House of Commons (2011), Public Accounts Committee, 51st Report.
10. Sir Ian Kennedy's letter to Right Honourable John Bercow, Speaker, 4 July 2011.
11. Speaker's letter to Sir Ian Kennedy on the IPSA draft budget 23 June 2011.
12. Speaker's Committee for IPSA, Oral Evidence 22 May 2012.
13. House of Commons Library Research Paper 08/31 Parliamentary Pay Allowances and Pensions.
14. For details of allowances payable in 2012/2013, see Commons Library Research Paper 12/29 *Members' Pay and Expenses – Current Rates and a Review of Developments Since 2009* 22 May 2012.
15. Evidence to Members' Expenses Committee December 2011.
16. IPSA, 'The Guide: What You Can Claim and How You Can Go about It', April 2012.
17. IPSA, 'The MP's Scheme of Business Costs and Expenses' 4th edition, April 2012.
18. Speaker's Committee on IPSA Oral Evidence 22 May 2012 Q23.
19. MPs Expenses, IPSA and Parliamentary Watchdogs: A Parliamentary Committee Inquiry Lite?
20. Speech by Sir Ian Kennedy at the Institute for Government, 22 July 2010.
21. *The Times* 25 July 2012 'Look at Our Expenses? No You Don't say French MPs'.
22. Australian Government: Parliamentary Services accessed July 2012.
23. See House of Representatives House Ethics Manual 2008 edition.
24. See House of Commons Library Standard Note 5050 Members' Pay and Allowances: Arrangements in other Countries.
25. Speaker's Committee on IPSA Oral Evidence 22 May 2012 Q14.
26. HC Deb 21 March 2011 c824.
27. 'IPSA Increase MP Pension Contribution Rates' 19 March 2012.
28. See IPSA, MPs' pension scheme letter to Members 8 February 2012 and 'Prime Minister responds to IPSA announcement on MP pension consultation', 8 February 2012.
29. See Curtice and Park 2009.
30. IPSA Annual Review of the MPs' Expenses Scheme Consultation, Annex C January 2011 and IPSA press release 5 January 2011.
31. Report by the Comptroller and Auditor General 2011: 7.
32. Public Accounts Committee, Corrected Transcript of Oral Evidence from Sir Ian Kennedy and others, Wednesday 13 2011. To be published as HC 1426-i, Q 35.

10
Conclusions: A Very British Episode?

Justin Fisher and Jennifer vanHeerde-Hudson

The word 'scandal' is much over-used in British politics, but in the case of the expenses scandal, it was entirely appropriate. It shook Westminster to the core, yet while the scandal has had long-term implications for Parliament, the impact on life outside Parliament has been much more limited. Beyond the political causalities, the most significant development was the creation of the Independent Parliamentary Standards Agency (IPSA). This removed the processing and regulation of expenses from Parliament and created more transparency. Yet, IPSA's rule-bound interpretation of its role may well have more negative longer term consequences, arguably creating an unreasonable burden on MPs (the vast majority of whom did not abuse the system) and, perhaps most seriously, creating perverse incentives so that the only non-permissible actions become only those rules that are not expressly forbidden.

The word 'scandal' is predictably over-used by politicians and some media commentators, but often unthinkingly by analysts, including academics. The slightest misdemeanour is often referred to as a scandal in much the same way as many political incidents acquire a '-gate' suffix. This is not helped by its rather vague dictionary definition, which refers to 'general public outrage', which may well be triggered by simple public misunderstanding. Yet, overuse of the term 'scandal' can render the term meaningless. Many political incidents are not the result of systematic and intentional wrongdoing, which could reasonably be described as being scandalous. Rather, things like reporting irregularities or minor infractions are better described as episodes, since they do not involve any desire to seek personal material gain or breach regulations to any significant extent. Thus, in defining scandal, one might reasonably point to intent and scale as indicators of something that moves beyond error and minor misdemeanour. Debates surrounding party finance are

196

dogged by the over-use of the word 'scandal', when the term 'episode' is more appropriate and this is brought into sharp relief when one compares party finance episodes in Britain with what are genuine scandals in other European countries (Fisher 2009).

Yet, the expenses scandal was just that – a *bona fide* scandal where both the rules and the spirit of the rules were well and truly broken by some (but by no means a majority) within Parliament. It resulted in public figures standing trial and being convicted, and others calling premature time on their political careers. As affairs go, there was some genuinely scandalous behaviour. This point is worth raising because it may help us to understand why the reaction of both Westminster and the wider public was as it was. The expenses scandal resulted in rapid change; episodes, which some have (mistakenly) referred to as scandals such as in party finance, have not generated change in such a rapid manner. Of course, whether that change has been productive and whether it is sustainable is another matter.

The chapters in this book detail the scandal itself and the aftermath with real clarity. The scandal, as a number point out, shook Westminster to the core. But the overriding findings are that while the scandal has had long-term implications for Parliament, the impact on life outside Parliament was much more limited in scope and lifespan. As both Birch and Allen, and Pattie and Johnston, point out, the impact on public opinion was not as large as one might expect. For a variety of reasons, the public was not especially enamoured with politicians before the scandal, and this scandal added little in the long term to that assessment. Perhaps more critically for our understanding, as vanHeerde-Hudson and Pattie and Johnston show very clearly, the electoral effects were negligible. Of course, there were a number of retirees, who opted for the political equivalent of being left alone with the Service revolver, but the impact on turnout and those who chose to remain was insignificant. Perhaps we ought not to be surprised. As Cowley (2005) shows, there was no significant electoral impact in terms of MPs' parliamentary votes on the Iraq war in the subsequent general election, despite it being the major issue of that Parliament. Whatever MPs and commentators would like to think in respect of voters rewarding or punishing parliamentarians for their choices at Westminster, it would seem that, in general, voters are more concerned with issues that more directly affect them, such as the economy.

Of course, the lack of electoral impact could be taken as an indicator of success. If, scarcely a year after a genuine scandal, voters do not abandon politics or crucify those who are alleged to have transgressed at the ballot box, this could point to the success of both the press for highlighting and reporting the issue in a responsible way, and Parliament in its ability to respond. In terms of the former, Larcinese and Sircar show that the press both broke the story and reported it in a non-partisan manner, albeit with a stronger focus on women than on men. In terms of the latter, the ultimate response by Parliament – the creation of IPSA – coupled with the conviction of MPs in the most serious cases could appear to point to a responsive and functioning system. Why would voters continue to hold a grudge if Parliament and the courts had already responded to the issue?

Another conclusion is that this was of an issue of great importance to Parliament, but not to the general public to any great long-term extent. If that is the case, then the reaction of Parliament may not have been measured as was appropriate, resulting in outcomes that may not provide the best long-term solutions. Of course, it is impossible to say at the time of writing whether the solutions will be effective in the long term, and that is true of any policy. But policy made in haste is more vulnerable to the problem of failing to adequately consider the potential pitfalls of different proposals. As Gay points out, Parliament had to be seen to do *something*. The question is whether the actions taken were well thought through.

The most significant development resulting from the scandal was the creation of IPSA itself. This removed the processing and regulation of expenses from Parliament and created more transparency. The IPSA scheme also introduced some beneficial changes such as the accommodation allowance, which effectively dealt with abuses of mortgage interest payment, as well as flexibility over taxi or hotel costs for late sittings, and one-off re-settlement payments for defeated MPs.

But as Gay shows, IPSA also established procedures that were mechanistic and inflexible, which caused significant consternation among MPs. It was also effectively unaccountable to any democratic body and contained some ill thought out measures, for example, the bar on paying bonuses to relatives. Here, there is a clear inconsistency, since the issue is the abuse of payments in favour of those close to you rather than whether they are related through blood or marriage. At the most extreme end, it would be problematic, for example, to pay a bonus to your wife, but not to your mistress. And one might reasonably assume that if abuse was to occur, it would be more likely to be the case in an illicit relationship. Coupled with the fact that the families of MPs frequently act as unpaid helpers and of course suffer from the long hours and low pay that MPs endure, this double whammy seems all the more ill thought out.

As a related point, David Cameron's pledge to reduce the number of MPs as a partial response to the expenses scandal seems similarly ill thought through. This would, it was argued, reduce the cost of politics. This provision was included in Parliamentary Voting System and Constituencies Act 2011, which also contained provisions for equalizing the population in constituencies as well as the referendum on the use of the Alternative Vote for Westminster elections. Yet, while there was an intellectually defensible case for the equalization of constituencies, the case for the reduction of MPs had little basis to it, beyond a populist response to the scandal. And as a measure of how ill thought out this proposal was, the whole re-drawing of the boundaries has now been shelved until at least after the 2015 election.

In the aftermath of the scandal, which was of course of MPs' own making, one might make the case that none of these concerns mattered. The previous system was not fit for purpose and being outside of Parliament did at least mean that IPSA was more able to withstand pressure from within it. Moreover, public opinion often tends to support rule-bound approaches. Dunleavy and Weir (1995: 610) found in a 1995 survey that reliance on self-regulation by Parliament was supported by only 26% of the public while 67% preferred rules enforced from outside. Moreover, 78% felt that questions of ministerial misconduct should be dealt with either by an independent commission or the courts, rather than by the Prime Minister or Parliament (Dunleavy and Weir 1995: 611). And, in that vein, there is some suggestive evidence that the creation of IPSA did indeed go some way to improving public confidence in the conduct of processing MPs' expenses. Yet as Gay highlights, improving confidence may also have been driven by high-profile prosecutions and the issue having fallen off the public's radar.

Of course, changes in public opinion may suggest some level of success, but this measure does not fully capture whether any new system of regulating parliamentary expenses is fit for purpose as the sustainable success of IPSA is also a function of its relationship with other audiences like MPs. IPSA has generally taken the line that its primary role is to reassure the public rather than to service the needs of its principal client group. Yet this model of regulation is unlike the successful one pursued by the Electoral Commission, which sees its role both to regulate parties but also to provide guidance, interacting with parties on a regular basis. It is likely that any regulator will face significant difficulties if its principal stakeholders – especially ones as potentially powerful as MPs – continue to regard it with such suspicion and in some cases, with outright contempt. IPSA needs to ensure that MPs' work can continue. Yet, the report of the National Audit Office in 2011 suggested that IPSA's concern with addressing public confidence was at the expense of supporting MPs in fulfilling their duties. Coupled with ongoing concerns by MPs of the regulation of their activities being undertaken by an extra-parliamentary body, it is not yet clear that IPSA has been successful, since its permanence is not assured. That said, as Gay remarks, IPSA's success in effectively diminishing concern about abuses may be that the prospect of returning regulation of expenses to Parliament is no longer the unthinkable long-term solution that it was in 2009 and 2010. This may be viewed as the mark of a successful regulator – that it creates an environment where those it regulates can again be trusted to act responsibly.

An important consideration is also to understand how politicians themselves react to such affairs. Here, the political finance literature can be instructive. One of the dominant approaches used to understand the behaviour of parties and their representatives has been Katz and Mair's cartel model (1995). From this perspective, parties protect their interests in respect of the provision of state support by colluding with each other to determine how resources are distributed. The result is that whether or not a party is in power, its resources are protected. As Fisher (2009) points out, this is a rational and predictable response in a game of coordination, since it ensures that new entrants are disadvantaged, while reducing the risk of punitive action by the other party when it enters power. Wright's discussion of how he was treated when he queried the rules surrounding expenses provides an excellent example of this kind of coordination.

However, as the chapter by Gay shows, when the scandal broke, the reaction of MPs was not one of coordination. Here, the insights of Scarrow (2003), provide a clue as to why this may have occurred. She shows that rational parties may, in fact, pursue different strategies from those predicted by Katz and Mair. Her 'electoral economy' model suggests that parties may seek to gain competitive electoral advantage by actively opposing state subventions to parties, even if such a move would be financially damaging. Equally, they may advocate enhanced regulation for similar motives. In the context of the expenses scandal, this may explain why parties rushed to endorse new rules and ultimately create a body (IPSA) that was arguably not in their interests as this was deemed to generate potential electoral benefits. Yet, just as Katz and Mair's cartel model highlights the potential to create bad practice through rational collusion, Scarrow's model shows how the rush to create IPSA through a different rational desire for electoral popularity can also potentially produce bad policy.

Gay's chapter illustrates that the haste with which IPSA was created led to a body that was arguably too concerned to appease (un)reasonable public concern. Of course, some public concern was entirely appropriate and legitimate. But as with many incidents in politics, much concern was either ill-informed or not reasonable. And so, in moving to complex and rule-bound procedures, where suspicion was implied through the validation of all items of expenditure, rather than through a risk-based approach, IPSA might be said by some to have followed the logic of the lynch mob. That is not in any way to say that some reform was not appropriate. Rather, that by creating IPSA and its rules with so much haste and arguably so little thought, Parliament risked creating its own 'Dangerous Dogs Act' – a set of procedures created in response to an outcry, which are ill thought out and very difficult to implement.

Hindsight is, of course, a wonderful thing, and there may have been greater risks in moving too slowly in response to the scandal. The scandal required some kind of quick response, but in rushing to legislate and establishing IPSA so quickly, the perhaps inevitable elements of over-reaction to the problems were not sufficiently debated or reflected upon by MPs, who in the febrile atmosphere of May to July 2009 were unable or unwilling to scrutinize and challenge the proposals to any significant degree. A useful comparison here is with the introduction of the Political Parties, Elections and Referendums Act 2000. Responding to rising concerns about party finance, the then Prime Minister, Tony Blair asked the Committee on Standards in Public Life to examine the issue. The result was an extensive report published in 1999, which was passed into law a year later. While not a flawless piece of legislation, it did nevertheless deliver extensive and sustainable reform, in part because of the measured approach taken in its development.

Ultimately, however, it is culture rather than rules that will protect Parliament from future scandals. The culture in Parliament, as Wright astutely observes, was formally one of tacit acceptance that expenses were a means of boosting the artificially low level of salaries. Now, it is one whereby many expenses are apparently not claimed for fear that they might be rejected with all the adverse publicity that this would create. Neither is a healthy state of affairs. The first generated a situation which allowed the worst excesses of the expenses scandal, such as the flipping of homes, to occur in the name of 'perks'. The latter risks creating a rule-bound approach, which has two potential adverse side effects.

The first is common to all areas of regulation, namely that excessive rule-making and procedure risks not creating more transparent and appropriate conduct, but rather a culture of threshold compliance. Standards of conduct can be reduced to a minimal level of compliance; a box-ticking exercise. This has been described as generating perverse incentives, behaving in accordance with only what the rules stipulate cannot be done, analogous to tax compliance. Such a culture deems only that which the rules determine is not permissible as being illegitimate. Any other behaviour is permissible. As it should be clear, this does little to avoid the risk of a serious disjuncture between public and media expectations and what the rules allow. Moreover, as Fisher, vanHeerde and Tucker (2010) show, trust in politicians is more likely to be generated through delivery of promises than the process through which politics is conducted. The latter is important, of course, but agency appears to have greater significance overall than the rules of the game on generating (or re-generating) trust. It's also worth pointing out that some regulations, however well-intentioned, can produce the opposite of their intended effect in the short term. Transparency is an excellent example, here. Few would argue against the principle of transparency in public life so long as a degree of personal privacy was protected. Yet, as the experience of the introduction of transparency regulation in party finance shows, the newly available data, published on a regular basis can actually produce more media stories with the potential to damage public confidence, simply because there are more data with which to generate these stories (Clift and Fisher 2005: 250).

The second adverse effect is to create an intolerable burden on MPs and make the job of an MP even more unattractive to many. While much is made of the salary of MPs relative to the average wage, this misses the point, since the real costs of being an MP (frequently including additional accommodation, staff, travel and so on), while funded mainly from the public purse, are not part and parcel of most jobs. Notwithstanding the fact that MPs' salaries do not compare at all favourably with jobs that demand the level of responsibility and commitment of an MP – let alone the potentially precarious job security of those who do not enjoy large majorities – the real costs of representative democracy are much higher than most realize. MPs are more rather than less responsive to constituents than in the past and more rather than fewer people contact their MP – made easier, of course, by electronic communications. Coupled with the fact that survey data reveal that many voters value the 'localness' of an MP above other traits (Cowley 2013), the costs of being the kind of representative that voters demand is high.

All of this is to say, that rather than engaging in self-flagellation on account of the bad behaviour of a minority of former members, Parliament (and indeed IPSA) might consider a more robust response in respect of the actual costs of being an MP, both in terms of salary sacrifices and, most critically here, the additional expenses that are necessary to perform the job that the public demands. Wright's chapter shows how successive governments have side-stepped this for fear of unpopularity. Yet the short-termism which can be a consequence produces the result of a further scandal waiting to happen. Moreover, the fears of unpopularity may be overstated. First, and most obviously, there is no evidence that there would be adverse electoral effects. If MPs were not punished for claiming illegitimate expenses, they are hardly likely to be so for seeking to address the underlying problem. Second, as vanHeerde-Hudson and Fisher (2013) show in an article about public opinion and party finance, there may be no reason to avoid potentially unpopular measures such as state-funding for fear of public backlash, when understanding of a topic is so limited.

So ultimately, was this a very British episode? In one sense, some of the claimed expenses deemed illegitimate (duck houses, moats and adult films) have a very British air about them – *Carry On Parliament*. Equally, while representing a clear disjuncture between public expectations and actual behaviour, the actions of many of the accused MPs would not compare with their counterparts in other countries. Yet, to reiterate a point made at the beginning, the difference between this and other affairs was that this represented a genuine scandal. Individuals were unlawfully enriched and the behaviour of many of those forced to repay expenses, while technically within the bounds of what was permissible, was so far in breach of the spirit and intention of the rules that the term 'scandal' is entirely appropriate. In that sense, the affair was not a very British episode, but a scandal; not necessarily comparable in scale with some scandals elsewhere, such as the Tangentopoli affair in Italy, but arguably on a par with ones such as the CDU party finance scandal in Germany. And, while the impact on public opinion was ultimately short-lived, we must hope that the measures introduced in the wake of the scandal are sufficient to prevent future problems. Unfortunately, the evidence to date is such that there is a danger that the problem may re-emerge through the perverse incentives often generated by over-regulation.

Bibliography

Abramowitz, A. (1991) 'Incumbency, Campaign Spending, and the Decline of Competition in U.S. House Elections'. *The Journal of Politics* 53: 34–56.

Ackerman, J. and Sandoval-Ballesteros, I. (2006) 'The Global Explosion of Freedom of Information Laws'. *Admin. L. Rev.* 58, 85.

Agnew, J. (1997) 'The Dramaturgy of Horizons: Geographical Scale in the "Reconstruction of Italy" by the New Italian Political Parties, 1992–95'. *Political Geography* 16: 99–121.

Ahuja, S., Beaver, S., Berreau, C., Dodson, A., Hourigan, P., Showalter, S., Walz, J. and Hibbing, J. (1994) 'Modern Congressional Election Theory Meets the 1992 House Elections'. *Political Research Quarterly* 47: 909–921.

Alford, J., Teeters, H., Ward, D. and Wilson, R. (1994) 'Overdraft: The Political Cost of Congressional Malfeasance'. *The Journal of Politics* 56: 788–801.

Allen, N. (2011) 'Dishonourable Members? Exploring Patterns of Misconduct in the Contemporary House of Commons'. *British Politics* 6(2): 210–240.

Allen, N. (2010) 'Keeping MPs Honest? Ethics Reforms in the British House of Commons'. *Public Integrity* 12(2): 105–123.

Allen, N. (2008) 'A New Ethical World of British MPs?'. *The Journal of Legislative Studies* 14(3): 297–314.

Allen, N. (2006) 'A Restless Electorate: Stirrings in the Political System'. In J. Bartle and A. King (eds.), *Britain at the Polls 2005*. Washington, DC: CQ Press, pp. 54–77.

Allen, N. and Birch, S. (Forthcoming) *Ethics and Integrity in British Politics: How Citizens Judge their Politicians' Conduct, and why it Matters*. Cambridge University Press.

Allen, N. and Birch, S. (2011) 'Political Conduct and Misconduct: Probing Public Opinion'. *Parliamentary Affairs* 64(1): 61–81.

Allen, N. and Birch, S. (2009) "On Either Side of a Moat? Elite and Mass Attitudes towards Right and Wrong". PSA Parliaments and Legislatures Specialist Group Annual Conference, June 2009, London.

Allern, S., Kantola, A., Ester, P. and Blachorsten, M. (2012) 'Increased Scandalization: Nordic Political Scandals, 1980–2010'. In S. Allern and E. Pollack (eds.), *Scandalous! The Mediated Construction of Political Scandals in Four Nordic Countries*. Gothenburg: Nordicom.

Allern, S. and Pollack, E. (2012) *Scandalous!: The Mediated Construction of Political Scandals in Four Nordic Countries*. Gothenburg: Nordicom.

Allington, N. and Peele, G. (2010) "Moats, Duckhouses and Bath Plugs: Members of Parliament, the Expenses Scandal and Use of Web Sites". *Parliamentary Affairs* 63(3): 385–406.

Atkinson, M. and Bierling, G. (2005) 'Politicians, the Public and Political Ethics: Worlds Apart'. *Canadian Journal of Political Science* 38(4): 1003–1028.

Australian Government: Parliamentary Services (2012) http://www.finance.gov.au/parliamentary-services/index.html [Accessed July 2012].

Banducci, S. and Karp, J. (1994) 'Electoral Consequences of Scandal and Reapportionment in the 1992 House Elections'. *American Politics Quarterly* 22(1): 3–26.

Barnett, S. (2002) 'Will a Crisis in Journalism Provoke a Crisis in Democracy?' *Political Quarterly* 73(4): 400–408.

Barrett, D. and Bloxham, A. (2010) MPs' Expenses: The Timeline. 3 October 2010. http://www.telegraph.co.uk/news/newstopics/mps-expenses/5335266/MPs-expenses-the-timeline.html [Accessed 14 January 2013].

BBC. (2012) 'MLAs "Out of Touch with People" – Taxpayers' Alliance. 19 April 2012. http://www.bbc.co.uk/news/uk-northern-ireland-17652717

BBC News. 'Voters Believe MPs Corrupt – Poll'. http://news.bbc.co.uk/1/hi_politics/8078159.stm [Accessed 25 February 2010].

BBC News Europe. (2012) 'French MPs Throw Out Proposal to Audit the Expenses'. 26 July 2012. http://www.bbc.co.uk/news/world-europe-19004353 [Accessed 12 March 2013].

Bell, M. (2009) *A Very British Revolution: The Expenses Scandal and How to Save Our Democracy*. London: Icon Books.

Bercow, J. (2011) Speaker's letter to Sir Ian Kennedy on the IPSA Draft Budget. 23 June 2011 http://www.publications.parliament.uk/pa/cm201012/cmselect/spcomipsa /110623.pdf [Accessed 21 January 2013].

Besley, T. and Larcinese, V. (2011) 'Working or Shirking? Expenses and Attendance in the UK Parliament'. *Public Choice* 147: 291–317.

Besley, T. and Valentino, L. (2005) 'Working or Shirking? A Closer Look at MPs' Expenses and Parliamentary Attendance'. Sticerd Political Economy and Public Policy Discussion Paper No. 15.

Birch, S. and Allen, N. (2010) 'How Honest Do Politicians Need to Be?' *The Political Quarterly* 81(1): 49–56.

Bless, H., Igou, E., Schwarz, N. and Wanke, M. (2000) 'Reducing Context Effects by Adding Context Information: The Direction and Size of Context Effects in Political Judgment'. *Personality and Social Psychology Bulletin* 26: 1036–1045.

Bless, H. and Schwarz, N. (1998) 'Context Effects in Political Judgement: Assimilation and Contrast as a Function of Categorization Processes'. *European Journal of Social Psychology* 28: 159–172.

Bligh, M., Schlehofer, M., Casad, B. and Gaffney, A. (2012) 'Competent Enough, But Would You Vote for Her? Gender Stereotypes and Media Influences on Perceptions of Women Politicians'. *Journal of Applied Psychology* 42(3): 560–597.

Bowler, S. and Karp, J. (2003) 'Politicians, Scandals and Trust in Government'. *Political Behavior* 26(3): 271–287.

Brace, P. (1985) 'A Probabilistic Approach to Retirement from the U.S. Congress'. *Legislative Studies Quarterly* 10(1): 107–123.

Brocklebank, C. (2012) 'Tory MP Nick Boles Claims Expenses to Learn His Civil Partner's Language'. 10 August 2012 http://www.pinknews.co.uk/2012/08/10/tory-mp-nick-boles-claims-expenses-to-learn-his-civil-partners-language/ [Accessed 4 December 2012].

Brooke, H. (2010) *The Silent State: Secrets, Surveillance and the Myth of British Democracy*. London: Windmill Books.

Brown, L. (2006) 'Revisiting Scandals in the U.S. House of Representatives, 1966–2002'. *Journal of Political Marketing* 5(1–2): 149–172.

Bush, K. (2012) 'A Tale of Two Cities – Legislating for Member Remuneration at Cardiff Bay and at Westminster'. *Statute Law Review* 33(2): 141–150.

Butler, D. and Stokes, D. (1974) *Political Change in Britain: The Evolution of Electoral Choice*. London: Macmillan.

Cabinet Office. (2012) *Open Data White Paper: Unleashing the Potential* (Cmd 8353). London: TSO.

Cain, B., Egan, P. and Fabbrini, S. (2010) 'Towards More Open Democracies: The Expansion of FOI Laws'. In B. Cain *et al.* (eds.), *Democracy Transformed? Expanding Political Opportunities in Advanced Industrial Democracies*. Oxford: Oxford University Press, pp. 115–139.

Cain, B., Ferejohn, J. and Fiorina, M. (1987) *The Personal Vote: Constituency Service and Electoral Independence*. Cambridge, MA: Harvard University Press.

Cameron, D. (2010) Prime Minister's Podcast on Transparency. 29 May 2010. http://webarchive.nationalarchives.gov.uk/20130109092234/http://number10.gov.uk/news/pms-podcast-on-transparency/ [Accessed June 2010].

Campbell, A., Converse, P., Miller, W. and Stokes, D. (1960) *The American Voter*. New York: Wiley.

Carey, J. and Shugart, M. (1995) 'Incentives to Cultivate a Personal Vote: A Rank Ordering of Electoral Formulas'. *Electoral Studies* 14(4): 417–439.

Castels, M. (2007) 'Communication, Power and Counter-Power in the Network Society'. *International Journal of Communication* 1(1): 238–266.

Chadwick, A. (2011) 'The Political Information Cycle in a Hybrid News System: the British Prime Minister and the "Bullygate" Affair'. *The International Journal of Press/Politics* 16(1): 3–29.

Chang, E. and Chu, Y. (2006) 'Corruption and Trust: Exceptionalism in Asian Democracies'? *Journal of Politics* 68: 259–271.

Chang, E. and Golden, M. (2006) 'Electoral Systems, District Magnitude and Corruption'. *British Journal of Political Science* 37: 115–137.

Chang, E., Golden, M. and Hill, S. (2010) 'Legislative Malfeasanace and Political Accountability'. *World Politics* 62: 177–220.

Clark, B. and Logan, J. (2011) 'A Government of the People: How Crowdsourcing Can Transform Government'. SSRN: http://ssrn.com/abstract=1868283

Clarke, H., Feigert, F., Seldon, B. and Stewart, M. (1999) 'More Time with my Money: Leaving the House and Going Home in 1992 and 1994'. *Political Research Quarterly* 62: 67–85.

Clarke, H., Sanders, D., Stewart, M. and Whiteley, P. (2010) 'Public Reaction to the MPs Expenses Claims Scandal: Evidence from the BES-CMS'. University of Essex.

Clarke, H., Sanders, D., Stewart, M. and Whiteley, P. (2004) *Political Choice in Britain*. Oxford: Oxford University Press.

Clarke, H.D., Sanders, D., Stewart, M.C. and Whiteley, P. (2009) *Performance Politics and the British Voter*. Cambridge: Cambridge University Press.

Clift, B. and Fisher, J. (2005) 'Party Finance Reform as Constitutional Engineering? The Effectiveness and Unintended Consequences of Party Finance Reform in France and Britain'. *French Politics* 3(3): 234–257.

Committee on Standards in Public Life. (2009) *Background Paper Number 2: Timeline of Events*. http://www.public-standards.gov.uk/Library/Background_Paper_No_2._ Timeline_of_Events.pdf [Accessed XX]

Committee on Standards in Public Life. (2009) Issues and Questions Paper, 23 April 2009.

Cooper, J. and West, W. (1981) 'Voluntary Retirement, Incumbency and the Modern House'. *Political Science Quarterly* 96(2): 279–300.

Cowley, P. (2013) 'Why Not Ask the Audience? Understanding the Public's Representational Priories'. *British Politics* 8(2): 138–163.

Cowley, P. (2005) 'Being Policed? Or Just Pleasing Themselves? Electoral Rewards and Punishment for Legislative Behaviour in an Era of Localized Campaigning Effects: The Case of the UK in 2005'. Paper Presented at the American Political Science Association Annual Conference, Washington, DC, September 2005.

Criddle, B. (2010) 'More Diverse, Yet More Uniform: MPs and Candidates'. In D. Kavanagh and P. Cowley (eds.), *The British General Election of 2010*. Basingstoke: Palgrave Macmillan.

Curtice, J. and Park, A. (2010) 'A Tale of Two Crises: Banks, MPs' Expenses and Public Opinion'. In A. Park, J. Curtice, E. Clery and C. Bryson (eds.), *British Social Attitudes – the 27th Report: Exploring Labour's Legacy.* London: Sage, p. 144.

Curtice, J. and Seyd, B. (2012) 'Constitutional Reform: A Recipe for Restoring our Faith in Democracy?' In A. Park, E. Clery, J. Curtice, M. Phillips and D. Utting (eds.), *British Social Attitudes: The 29th Report.* London: NatCen Social Research, pp. 45–63.

Curtice, J., Fisher, S. and Ford, R. (2010) 'Appendix 2: An Analysis of the Results'. In D. Kavanagh and P. Cowley (eds.), *The British General Election of 2010*. Basingstoke: Palgrave Macmillan.

Curtis, P. and Mulholland, H. (2010) 'MPs' Expenses: System "Deeply Flawed", says Sir Thomas Legg'. *The Guardian*, 4 February 2010.

Daily Telegraph. (2012) 'MPs' Expenses: Denis MacShane Resigns'. 3 November 2012.

Daily Telegraph. (2012) 'John Bercow Has Not Kept His Word on MPs' Expenses'. 18 October 2012.

Daniel, A. and Flew, T. (2010) "The Guardian Reportage of the UK MP Expenses Scandal: A Case Study of Computational Journalism". *Communications Policy and Research Forum*, 15–16 November, Sydney.

Darch, C. and Underwood, P. (2010) *Freedom of Information in the Developing World: Demand, Compliance and Democratic Behaviours.* Chandos: Oxford University Press.

Denver, D. (2010) 'The Results: How Britain Voted'. In A. Geddes and J. Tonge (eds.), *Britain Votes 2010*. Oxford: Oxford University Press.

Dimock, M. and Jacobsen, G. (1995) 'Checks and Choices: The House Bank Scandal's Impact on Voters in 1992'. *The Journal of Politics* 57(4): 1143–1159.

Dunion, K. (2011) *Freedom of Information in Scotland in Practice.* Dundee: Dundee University Press.

Dunleavy, P. and Weir, S. (1995) 'Media, Opinion and the Constitution'. In E. Ridley and A. Doig (eds.), *Sleaze: Politicians, Private Interests and Public Reaction.* Oxford: Oxford University Press, pp. 54–68.

Dunleavy, P. and Weir, S. (1995) 'Sleaze in Britain: Media Influences, Public Response and Constitutional Significance'. *Parliamentary Affairs* 48(4): 602–616.

Eggers, A. and Fischer, A. (2011) 'Electoral Accountability and the UK Parliamentary Expenses Scandal: Did Voters Punish Corrupt MPs?' *Political Science and Political Economy Working Paper* 8/11, LSE Department of Government, available at: http://www2.lse.ac.uk/government/research/resgroups/PSPE/pdf/PSPE_WP8_11.pdf [Accessed 14 October 2011].

Electoral Commission. (2010) *General Election Results 2010*. London: Electoral Commission.

Farrell, D., McAllister, I. and Studlar, D. (1998) 'Sex, Money and Politics: Sleaze and the Conservative Party in the 1997 Election'. In D. Denver, J. Fisher, P. Cowley and C. Pattie (eds.), *British Elections and Parties Review 8: The 1997 General Election*. London: Frank Cass, pp. 80–94.

Faulkner, K. (2010) 'So Theresa, What's your Policy on Glamour? Home Secretary Mrs May Leaves her Kitten Heels at Home for Fashion Awards'. *Daily Mail*, 10 June 2010.

Fenno, R. (1978) *Home Style: House Members in the Districts*. Boston: Little Brown.

Fenno, R. (1975) 'If, As Ralph Nader Says, Congress Is "The Broken Branch" How Come We Love Our Congressmen So Much?' In N. Ornstein (ed.), *Congress in Change: Evolution and Reform*. New York: Praeger.

Ferejohn, J. (1986) 'Incumbent Performance and Electoral Control'. *Public Choice* 50: 5–20.

Ferejohn, J. (1990) 'Information and the Electoral Process'. In J. Ferejohn and J. Kuklinski (eds.), *Information and the Democratic Process*. Urbana, IL: Illinois University Press, pp. 1–22.

Ferraz, C. and Finan, F. (2008) 'Exposing Corrupt Politicians: The Effects of Brazil's Publicly Released Audits on Electoral Outcomes'. *The Quarterly Journal of Economics* 123: 703–745.

Fisher, J. (2009) 'Hayden Phillips and Jack Straw: The Continuation of British Exceptionalism in Party Finance?' *Parliamentary Affairs* 62(2): 298–317.

Fisher, J., vanHeerde, J. and Tucker, A. (2010) 'Does one Trust Judgement Fit All? Linking Theory and Empirics'. *British Journal of Politics & International Relations* 12(2): 161–188.

Flinders, M. and Kelso, A. 'Mind the Gap: Political Analysis, Public Expectations and the Parliamentary Decline Thesis'. *British Journal of Politics and International Relations* 13: 249–268.

Frantzich, S. (1978) 'Opting Out: Retirement from the House of Representatives, 1966–74'. *American Politics Quarterly* 6(3): 251–273.

Gay, O. (2004) 'The Development of Standards Machinery in the Commons'. In O. Gay and P. Leopold (eds.), *Conduct Unbecoming: The Regulation of Parliamentary Behaviour*. London: Politico's, pp. 91–139.

Gay, O. and Rush, M. (2004) 'Introduction'. In O. Gay and P. Leopold (eds.), *Conduct Unbecoming: The Regulation of Parliamentary Behaviour*. London: Politico's, pp. 1–27.

Giannetti, D. and Laver, M. (2001) 'Party System Dynamics and the Making and Breaking of Italian Governments'. *Electoral Studies* 20: 529–553.

Gillis, R. (1998) 'Freedom of Information and Open Government in Canada'. In A. McDonald and G. Terrill (eds.), *Open Government*. Basingstoke: Palgrave, pp. 143–168.

Gronbeck, B. (1997) 'Character, Celebrity, and Sexual Innuendo in the Mass-Mediated Presidency'. In J. Lull and S. Hinerman (eds.), *Media Scandals: Morality and Desire in the Popular Culture Marketplace*. New York: Columbia University Press, pp. 122–142.

Groseclose, T. and Krehbiel, K. (1994) 'Golden Parachutes, Rubber Checks, and Strategic Retirements from the 102d House'. *American Journal of Political Science* 38(1): 75–99.

Guardian. (2012) 'Speaker John Bercow Tries to Block Release of MPs' Expenses'. 18 Oct 2012. http://www.guardian.co.uk/politics/2012/oct/18/mps-expenses-john-bercow [Accessed 22 January 2013].

Guardian. (2012) 'MPs Dodge Expenses Rules to Get First-Class Rail Travel'. 21 October 2012. http://www.guardian.co.uk/politics/2012/oct/21/mps-dodge-expenses-first-class [Accessed 22 January 2013].

Guardian. (2010) 'David Laws' Resignation over Expenses Scandal Leaves Coalition in Turmoil'. 29 May 2010. http://www.guardian.co.uk/politics/2010/may/29/david-laws-quits-expenses-scandal [Accessed 14 December 2012].

Guardian. (2009) 'David Cameron Claimed over £1,000 a Month on Second Home'. 10 December 2009. http://www.guardian.co.uk/politics/2009/dec/10/david-cameron-mps-expenses [Accessed 14 December 2012].

Hall, R. and van Houweling, R. (1995) 'Avarice and Ambition in Congress: Representatives' Decisions to Run or Return from the U.S. House'. *American Political Science Review* 89(1): 121–136.

Hammarlin, M. and Jarlbro, G. (2012) 'From Tiara to Toblerone. The Rise and Fall of Mona Sahlin'. In S. Allern and E. Pollack (eds.), *Scandalous! The Mediated Construction of Political Scandals in Four Nordic Countries*. Gothenburg: University of Gothenburg.

Hansard Society. (2013) 'Audit of Political Engagement 10: The 2013 Report'. London: Hansard Society.

Hansard Society. (2011) 'Audit of Political Engagement 8: The 2011 Report'. London: Hansard Society.

Hansard Society. (2010) 'Audit of Political Engagement 7: The 2010 Report with a Focus on MPs and Parliament'. London: Hansard Society.

Hastings, R. (2012) 'Speaker John Bercow Reportedly Attempts to Block Publication of MPs' Expenses over Security Risk'. 18 October 2012. http://www.independent.co.uk/news/uk/politics/speaker-john-bercow-reportedly-attempts-to-block-publication-of-mps-expenses-over-security-risk-8215817.html [accessed 4 December 2012].

Hay, C. (2007) *Why We Hate Politics*. Cambridge: Polity Press.

Hazell, R., Bourke, G. and Worthy, B. (2012) 'Open House? Freedom of Information and its impact on the UK Parliament'. *Public Administration* 90(4): 901–921.

Hazell, R., Worthy, B. and Glover, M. (2010) *The Impact of the Freedom of Information Act on Central Government in the UK: Does FOI Work?* Basingstoke: Palgrave Macmillan.

Heath, O. (2011) 'The Great Divide: Voters, Parties, MPs and Expenses'. In N. Allen and J. Bartle (eds.), *Britain at the Polls 2010*. London: Sage, pp. 120–146.

Herrick, R. (2000) 'Who Will Survive?: An Exploration of Factors Contributing to the Removal of Unethical House Members'. *American Politics Research* 28: 96–109.

Hibbing, J. (1982) 'Voluntary Retirement from the U.S. House of Representatives: Who Quits?' *American Journal of Political Science* 26(3): 467–484.

Hibbing, J. and Theiss-Morse, E. (1995) *Congress as Public Enemy: Public Attitudes toward American Political Institutions.* Cambridge: Cambridge University Press.

High Court. (2008) [2008] EWHC 1084 (Admin) Case No: CO2888/2008.

Hirano, S. and Synder, J. (2012) 'Primary Elections and Political Accountability: What Happens to Incumbents in Scandals'?' Working Paper. http://scholar.harvard.edu/files/jsnyder/files/primaries_scandals_qjps_note.pdf   [Accessed 06 March 2013].

Holmberg, S. (2009) 'Candidate Recognition in Different Electoral Systems'. In H.-D. Klingemann (ed.), *The Comparative Study of Electoral Systems.* Oxford: Oxford University Press, pp. 158–170.

House of Commons. (2008) Debates for 3 July 2008 (pt 0016) c1102.

House of Commons. (2008) 'Freedom of Information Request Log 2008' (tables). http://www.parliament.uk/site-information/foi/request-foi/commons-foi-request-log [Accessed 13 March 2009].

House of Commons Library. (2012) Research Paper 12/29: Members' Pay and Expenses – Current Rates and a Review of Developments Since 2009. 22 May 2012.

House of Commons Library. (2009a) Research Paper 09/60 Members' Allowances. http://www.parliament.uk/briefing-papers/RP09-60 [Accessed 25 November 2012].

House of Commons Library. (2009b) Standard Note 5050 Members' Pay and Allowances: Arrangements in other Countries. http://www.parliament.uk/documents/commons/lib/research/briefings/snpc-05050.pdf   [Accessed 25 November 2012].

House of Commons Library. (2008) Research Paper 08/31 Parliamentary Pay Allowances and Pensions. London: The Stationary Office Limited.

House of Commons, Members Estimate Committee. (2010) *Review of Past ACA Payments.* London: The Stationary Office Limited.

House of Commons Reform Committee. (2009) *Rebuilding the House,* HC 1117, November 2009, p. 7.

House of Commons, Standards and Privileges. (2012) *Second Report-Denis MacShane* [HC 635]. London: The Stationary Office Limited.

House of Representatives House Ethics Manual. (2008) http://ethics.house.gov/sites/ethics.house.gov/files/documents/2008_House_Ethics_Manual.pdf

Independent Parliamentary Standards Authority. (2012) *Reviewing MPs' Pay and Pensions: A Consultation,* October 2012.

Independent Parliamentary Standards Authority. (2012a) IPSA MPs' pension scheme letter to Members 8 February 2012 and "Prime Minister responds to IPSA announcement on MP pension consultation" 8 February 2012.

Independent Parliamentary Standards Authority. (2012b) IPSA The Guide: What you Can Claim and How You Can Go About it. April 2012. http://www.parliamentarystandards.org.uk/TheGuide/Pages/Default.aspx

Independent Parliamentary Standards Authority. (2010) *The MPs' Expenses Scheme,* 29 March 2010, HC 501 2009–10; House of Commons, *Votes and Proceedings,* 29 March 2010, Appendix, Item 31.

Independent Parliamentary Standards Authority. (2010) *The MPs' Expenses Scheme*, 29 March 2010, HC 501 2009–10.

Information Commissioner's Office. (2007) Freedom of Information Act 2000 (Section 50) Decision Notice Reference: FS500704691, 13 June 2007.

Information Tribunal. (2008) *Information Tribunals Appeals* EA/2007/0060 and others, 26 February 2008 http://image.guardian.co.uk/sys-files/Politics/documents/2009/05/29/infoTribunalJudgment.pdf

Information Tribunal. (2007). *Decision Notice* EA/2006/0074/0075/0076. http://www.informationtribunal.gov.uk/DBFiles/Decision/i84/HoC2.pdf

Institute of Government. (2010) Speech by Sir Ian Kennedy at the Institute for Government, 22 July 2010.

Irish Times. (2012) 'TDs Paid 6m in Expenses since March, 2 February 2012'.

Irish Times. (2009) 'Department Defends Expenses of over €100,000 by O'Donoghue'. 28 July 2008.

Jacobson, G. and Dimock, M. (1994) 'Checking Out: The Effects of Bank Overdrafts on the 1992 House Elections'. *American Journal of Political Science* 38(3): 601–624.

Jacobson, G. and Kernell, S. (1983) *Strategy and Choice in Congressional Elections.* New Haven: Yale University Press.

Jalazai, F. (2006) 'Women Candidates and the Media: 1992–2000 Elections'. *Politics and Policy*, 34(3): 606–633.

James, S. (2006) 'The Potential Benefits of Freedom of Information'. In R. Chapman and M. Hunt (eds.), *Open Government in a Theoretical and Practical Context.* Aldershot: Ashgate Publishing, pp. 17–132.

Jennings, B. (1985) 'Legislative Ethics and Moral Minimalism'. In B. Jennings and D. Callahan (eds.), *Representation and Responsibility: Exploring Legislative Ethics.* New York: Plenum Press, pp. 149–166.

Jiminez, F. and Cainzos, M. (2006) 'How Far and Why do Corruption Scandals Cost Votes'. In J. Garrard and J. Newell (eds.), *Scandals in Past and Contemporary Politics.* Manchester: Manchester University Press, pp. 192–212.

Kahn, K. (1994) 'The Distorted Mirror: Press Coverage of Women Candidates for Statewide Office'. *Journal of Politics* 56(1): 154–173.

Kam, C. (2009) *Party Discipline and Parliamentary Politics.* Cambridge: Cambridge University Press.

Katz, R. and Mair, P. (1995) 'Changing Models of Party Organization and Party Democracy: The Emergence of the Cartel Party'. *Party Politics* 1(1): 5–28.

Kellner, P. (2004) 'Britain's Culture of Detachment'. *Parliamentary Affairs* 57(4): 830–843.

Kelly, C. (2009) 'MPs' Expenses and Allowances'. (CM 7724). London: Committee on Standards in Public Life.

Kelly, R. (2009) Members Allowances: House of Commons Library Research Paper 09/60. London: House of Commons Library.

Kelso, A. (2011) 'New Parliamentary Landscapes'. In P. Cowley, R. Hefferman and C. Hay (eds.), *Developments in British Politics 9.* London: Palgrave, pp. 52–70.

Kelso, Alexandra. (2009) 'Parliament on its knees: MPs' expenses and the Crisis of Transparency at Westminster'. *Political Quarterly* 80(3): 329–338.

Kennedy, I. (2011) Letter to Speaker. http://www.publications.parliament.uk/pa/cm201012/cmselect/spcomipsa/110704.pdf [Accessed 21 January 2013].

Kennedy, I. (2010) Speech by Sir Ian Kennedy at the Institute for Government, 22 July 2010. London.

Kiewiet, D. and Zeng, L. (1993) 'An Analysis of Congressional Career Decisions, 1947–1986'. *American Political Science Review* 87: 928–941.

King, A. (1986) 'Sex, Money, and Power'. In R. Hodder-Williams and J. Caesar (eds.), *Politics in Britain and United States: Comparative Perspectives*. Durham, NC: Duke University Press.

King, A. (1981) 'The Rise of the Career Politician in Britain – and its Consequences'. *British Journal of Political Science* 11(3): 249–285.

Klasnja, M. (2011) 'Why do Malfeasant Politicians Maintain Political Support? Testing the "Uninformed Voter" Argument'. Working Paper https://files.nyu.edu/mk3296/public/files /working_papers/uninformed.pdf [Accessed 26 July 2011].

Kumlin, S. and Esaiasson, P. (2012) 'Scandal Fatigue? Scandal Elections and Satisfaction with Democracy in Western Europe, 1977–2007'. *British Journal of Political Science* 42(2): 263–282.

Kunda, Z. (1990) 'The Case for Motivated Reasoning'. *Psychological Bulletin* 108(3): 480–498.

Lafay, J. and Servais, M. (2002) 'The Impact of Political Scandals on Popularity and Votes'. *Homo Oeconomicus* 19: 153–170.

Lafay, J. and Servais, M. (2000) 'The Influence of Political Scandals on Popularity and Votes'. In M. Lewis-Beck (ed.), *How France Votes*. New-York and London: Chatham House Publishers, pp. 189–205.

Larcinese, V. and Sircar, I. (2012) Crime and Punishment in the UK: Accountability Channels Following the MPs' Expenses Scandal. Unpublished working paper, London School of Economics.

Larcinese, V., Puglisi, R. and Snyder, J. (2011) 'Partisan Bias in Economic News: Evidence on the Agenda-Setting Behavior of U.S. Newspapers'. *Journal of Public Economics* 95(9–10): 1178–1189.

Lezard, N. (2009) 'Pity Jacqui Smith's Poor Husband'. *The Guardian*, 30 March 2009. URL: http://www.guardian.co.uk/commentisfree/2009/mar/30/jacqui-smith-mps-expenses1 [Accessed 28 October 2012].

Lodge, M. and Taber, C. (2000) 'Three Steps Toward a Theory of Motivated Political Reasoning'. In A. Lupia, M. McCubbins and S. Popkin (eds.), *Elements of Reason: Cognition, Choice, and the Bounds of Rationality*. Cambridge: Cambridge University Press.

London Evening Standard. (2011) 'I Was Targeted for Being a Woman': Jacqui Smith on Expenses Porn Shame. 22 February 2011. http://www.standard.co.uk/news/i-was-targeted-for-being-a-woman-jacqui-smith-on-expenses-porn-shame-6569676.html [Accessed 28 October 2012].

Lull, J. and Hinerman, S. (1997) *Media Scandals: Morality and Desire in the Popular Culture Marketplace*. New York: Columbia University Press.

Mail on Sunday. (2002) 'MP Took £100,000 in Bogus Home Claims'. 15 December 2002.

Mair, P. (2010) 'The Parliamentary Peloton'. *London Review of Books*, 25 February 2010.

Mair, L. and Kelly, R. (2009) House of Commons Library. Standard Note 5050 Members' Pay and Allowances: Arrangements in Other Countries. http://www.parliament.uk/documents/commons/lib/research/briefings/snpc-05050.pdf [Accessed 17 January 2013].

Major, J. (2000) *The Autobiography*. London: HarperCollins Publishers.

Malone, A. (2011) 'Empire of the Spivs: We Fret about our MPs' Expenses, but in Italy the Awesome Corruption of Politicians is Frankly Beyond Belief'. Mail Online. http://www.dailymail.co.uk/news/article-2021982/UK-frets-MPs-expenses-corrupt-politicians-belief.html [Accessed 14 June 2013].

Marsh, M. and Tilley, J. (2010) 'The Attribution of Credit and Blame to Governments and its Impact on Vote Choice'. *British Journal of Political Science* 40(1): 115–134.

Mayhew, D. (1984) *Congress: The Electoral Connection*. New Haven: Yale University Press.

Members Expenses Select Committee. (2011) Evidence to Members Expenses Committee, December 2011.

Mendel, T. (2005) 'Parliament and Access to Information: Working for Transparent Governance'. Washington DC: World Bank Institute.

Moore, M. and Hibbing, J. (1998) 'Situational Dissatisfaction in Congress: Explaining Voluntary Departures'. *Journal of Politics* 60(4): 1088–1107.

Moran Diary. (1966) '21 May 1954'. In *Winston Churchill: The Struggle for Survival 1940–1965*. Constable.

Mortimore, R. (2003) 'Why Politics Needs Marketing'. *International Journal of Nonprofit and Voluntary Sector Marketing* 8(2): 107–121.

Murray, R. (2010) 'Introduction: Gender Stereotypes and Media Coverage of Women Candidates'. In R. Murray (ed.), *Cracking the Highest Glass Ceiling: A Global Comparison of Women's Campaigns for Executive Office*. Santa Barbara: Praeger Press, pp. 3–27.

mySociety. They Work for You. (2010) http://www.theyworkforyou.com/mps/. [Accessed 7 July 2010].

National Audit Office. (2011) 'Report by the Comptroller and Auditor General'. *The Payment of MPs' Expenses*, [the NAO Report] HC (2010–12) 1273, (London: National Audit Office, 2011). http://www.nao.org.uk/publications/1012/ipsa. aspx [Accessed 7 July 2011].

New York Times. (2012) 'Corruption Rattles Already Shaky Italians' Trust in Politicians', 17 October 2012. http://www.nytimes.com/2012/10/18/world/europe/italys-political-scandals-rattle-public-trust.html?pagewanted=all&_r=0 [Accessed 12 March 2013].

Niven, D. (2004) 'A Fair Test of Media Bias: Party, Race, and Gender in Coverage of the 1992 House Banking Scandal'. *Polity* 36: 637–649.

Nord, L. (2001) *Statsråden och Dreven: Rainer-affären 1983 och Freivalds-affären 2000*. Institutet för Mediestudier.

Norris, P. (2011) *Democratic Deficit: Critical Citizens Revisited*. Cambridge: Cambridge University Press.

Norris, P. (2010) May 6th 2010 British General Election Constituency Results Release 5.0, available at: http://www.hks.harvard.edu/fs/pnorris/Data/Data. htm

Norris, P. (1997) 'The Battle for the Campaign Agenda'. In A. King (ed.), *New Labour Triumphs: Britain at the Polls*. Chatham, NJ: Chatham House.

Oakley, R. (2009) 'Comment: Anger at MPs' Expenses Could Change Politics'. 11 May 2009 http://edition.cnn.com/2009/WORLD/europe/05/11/oakley.uk. mps.expenses/ [Accessed 3 December 2012].

Oborne, P. (2013) 'Have MPs Learned a Thing Since 2009? Their Greed Suggests Not'. 15 May 2013. http://www.telegraph.co.uk/news/newstopics/

mps-expenses/10059243/Have-MPs-learnt-a-thing-since-2009-Their-greed-suggests-not.html [Accessed 4 June 2013].

Oborne, P. (2007) *The Triumph of the Political Class*. London: Simon and Schuster.

Parker, G. and Davidson, R. (1979) 'Why Do Americans Love Their Congressmen So Much More Than Their Congress?' *Legislative Studies Quarterly* 4(1): 53–61.

Patterson, K. and Magleby, D. (1992) 'Poll Trends: Public Support for Congress'. *Public Opinion Quarterly* 56: 539–551.

Pattie, C. and Johnston, R. (2001) 'A Low Turnout Landslide: Abstention in the British General Election of 1997'. *Political Studies* 49: 286–305.

Pattie, C. and Johnston, R. (2004) 'Party Knowledge and Candidate Knowledge: Constituency Campaigning and Voting and the 1997 British General Election'. *Electoral Studies* 23(4): 795–819.

Pattie, C. and Johnston, R. (2012) 'The Electoral Impact of the UK 2009 MPs' Expenses Scandal'. *Political Studies*, doi: 10.1111/j.1467-9248.2011.00943.x.

Pattie, C., Fieldhouse, E. and Johnston, R. (1994) 'The Price of Conscience: The Electoral Correlates and Consequences of Free Votes and Rebellions in the British House of Commons, 1987–92'. *British Journal of Political Science* 24(3): 359–380.

Pattie, C., Seyd, P. and Whiteley, P. (2004) *Citizenship in Britain: Values, Participation and Democracy*. Cambridge: Cambridge University Press.

Persson, T. and Tabellini, G. (2000) *Political Economics: Explaining Economic Policy*. Cambridge, MA: MIT Press.

Persson, T., Tabellini, G. and Trebbi, F. (2003) 'Electoral Rules and Corruption'. *Journal of the European Economic Association* 1(4): 958–989.

Peters, J. and Welch, S. (1980) 'The Effects of Charges of Corruption on Voting Behavior in Congressional Elections'. *American Political Science Review*, 74(3): 697–708.

Piotrowski, S. (2007) *Transparency in the Path of Administrative Reform*. New York: State University of New York Press.

Press Association. (2010) 'Cameron Condemns Expenses Watchdog'. 16 December 2010. http://article.wn.com/view/2010/12/16/Cameron_condemns_expenses_watchdog/#/video [Accessed 21 January 2013].

Przeworski, A., Stokes, S. and Manin, B. (1999) 'Elections and Representation'. In A. Przeworski, S. Stokes and B. Manin (eds.), *Democracy, Accountability and Representation*. Cambridge: Cambridge University Press, pp. 29–54.

Public Accounts Committee. (2011) Corrected Transcript of Oral Evidence from Sir Ian Kennedy and Others, Wednesday 13 2011. To be published as HC 1426-i, Q 35. http://www.publications.parliament.uk/pa/cm201012/cmselect/spcomipsa/110704.pdf, London: TSO.

Public Accounts Committee. (2011a) Fifty First Report 2010–12 Independent Parliamentary Standards Authority. http://www.publications.parliament.uk/pa/cm201012/cmselect/cmpubacc/1426/142602.htm

Public Administration Select Committee. (1998) 'Your Right to Know: The Government's Proposals for a Freedom of Information Act – Volume I'. HC 398-1. London: House of Commons.

Public Service. (2010) 'IPSA Compromises after Rudeness'. 16 June 2010. http://www.publicservice.co.uk/news_story.asp?id=13265 [Accessed 14 November 2010].

Puglisi, R. and Snyder, J. (2011) 'Newspaper Coverage of Political Scandals'. *Journal of Politics* 73: 931–950.

Rallings, C. and Thrasher, M. (2007) *Media Guide to the New Parliamentary Constituencies*. Plymouth: Local Government Chronicle Elections Centre.

Rawi, M. (2010) 'Home Secretary Theresa May Turns Heads in Turquoise Sari at Asian Awards (with Matching Kitten Heels of Course)'. *Daily Mail*, 20 May 2010.

Reed, S. (1999) 'Punishing Corruption: The Response of the Japanese Electorate to Scandals'. In *Political Psychology in Japan: Behind the Nails Which Sometimes Stick out (and Get Hammered Down)*. Commack, NY: Nova Science, pp. 131–148.

Reed, S. (2005) 'Japan: Haltingly Toward a Two-Party System'. In M. Gallagher and P. Mitchell (eds.), *The Politics of Electoral Systems*. Oxford: Oxford University Press, pp. 277–293.

Regner, I. and Le Floch, V. (2005) 'When Political Expertise Moderates the Impact of Scandal on Young Adults' Judgements of Politicians'. *European Journal of Social Psychology* 35: 255–261.

Report by the Comptroller and Auditor General. (2011) *The Payment of MPs' Expenses*, [the NAO Report] HC (2010-12) 1273. London: National Audit Office, p. 7.

Ridley, F.F. and Doig, A. (eds.). (1995) *Sleaze: Private Interests and Public Reaction*. Oxford: Oxford University Press.

Roberts, A. (2010) 'A Great and Revolutionary Law? The First Four Years of India's Right to Information Act'. *Public Administration Review* 70(6): 925–933.

Roberts, A. (2006) *Blacked Out: Government Secrecy in the Information Age*. New York: Cambridge University Press.

Rogers, S. (2010) 'MPs' Expenses: The Legg Report's Full List of MPs and Their Repayments'. *The Guardian*, 5 February 2010. http://www.guardian.co.uk/news/datablog/2010/feb/05/mps-expenses-repayments-legg-report [Accessed 14 March 2012].

Romaine, S. (1999) *Communicating Gender*. London: L. Erlbaum.

Rundquist, B., Strom, G. and Peters, J. (1977) 'Corrupt Politicians and their Electoral Support: Some Experimental Observations'. *American Political Science Review* 71(3): 954–963.

Rush, M. and Giddings, P. (2010) 'Worlds Apart: Explaining the MPs' Expenses Scandal'. Ninth workshop of Parliamentary Scholars and Parliamentarians, 24–25 July 2010, Wroxton College Banbury.

Russell, M. (2011) ' "Never Allow a Crisis Go to Waste": The Wright Committee Reforms to Strengthen the House of Commons'. *Parliamentary Affairs* 64(4): 612–633.

Sanders, D. (1999) 'Conservative Incompetence, Labour Responsibility and the Feelgood Factor: Why the Economy Failed to Save the Conservatives in 1997'. *Electoral Studies* 18: 251–270.

Sanders, D., Clarke, H., Stewart, M. and Whiteley, P. (2011) 'Downs, Stokes and the Dynamics of Electoral Choice'. *British Journal of Political Science* 41: 287–314.

Sanders, D., Clarke, H., Stewart, M. and Whiteley, P. (2007) 'Does Mode Matter for Modeling Political Choice? Evidence from the 2005 British Election Study'. *Political Analysis* 15(3): 257–285.

Scarrow, S. (2004) 'Explaining Party Finance Reforms: Competition and Context'. *Party Politics* 10(6): 653–675.

216   *Bibliography*

Schwarz, N. and Bless, H. (1992) 'Scandals and the Public's Trust in Politicians: Assimilation and Contrast Effects'. *Personality and Social Psychology Bulletin* 18: 574–579.

SCIPSA. (2011) Statement under Schedule 1 of the Parliamentary Standards Act 2009 23 June 2011. http://www.publications.parliament.uk/pa/cm201012/cmselect/spcomipsa/1337/133703.htm#a1 [Accessed 17 January 2013].

Seaward, P. (2009) 'A Summary of Members' Pay and Expenses', *The Operation of the Parliamentary Standards Act 2009*, First Report of session 2010–12, HC 1484-ii, Ev. 112–123.

Smith, J. (2009) 'I am Sick of My Country and This Hysteria over MPs'. *The Guardian*, 25 May 2009. http://www.guardian.co.uk/commentisfree/2009/may/25/mps-expenses-democracy [Accessed 14 March 2011].

Snell, R. and Upcher, J. (2002) 'Freedom of Information and Parliament: A Limited Accountability Tool for a Key Constituency?' *Freedom of Information Review* 100: 35–41.

Speaker's Committee for IPSA. (2012) Oral Evidence, 22 May 2012. http://www.publications.parliament.uk/pa/cm201213/cmselect/spcomipsa/uncorr/spcom2205.htm

Speaker's Committee for IPSA. (2011a) Statement under Schedule 1 of the Parliamentary Standards Act 2009, 23 June 2011.

Speaker's Committee for IPSA. (2011b) Speaker's Letter to Sir Ian Kennedy on the IPSA Draft Budget, 23 June 2011. http://www.publications.parliament.uk/pa/cm201012/cmselect/spcomipsa/110623.pdf

Speaker's Committee for IPSA, Oral Evidence 22 May 2012. http://www.publications.parliament.uk/pa/cm201213/cmselect/spcomipsa/uncorr/spcom2205.htm

Stevenson, R. and Vonnahme, G. (2009) 'Executive Selection and the Informed Electorate: How the Rules and Norms Governing Cabinet Formation Impact Citizens' Knowledge of Politics'. Paper presented at the Annual Meeting of the Midwest Political Science Association, Chicago, 2–5 April 2009.

Stoddard, K. (2010) 'Newspaper Support in UK General Elections'. *The Guardian*, 4 May 2010. http://www.guardian.co.uk/news/datablog/2010/may/04/general-election-newspaper-support [Accesed 23 October 2010].

Stoker, G. (2006) *Why Politics Matters: Making Democracy Work*. Basingstoke, Hants: Palgrave Macmillan.

Sunday Tribune. (2009) 'How O'Donghue Fell on His Sword', 11 October 2009.

Swaddle, K. and Heath, A. (1989) 'Official and Reported Turnout in the British General Election of 1987'. *British Journal of Political Science* 19: 537–551.

Theriault, S. (1998) 'Moving Up or Moving Out: Career Ceilings and Congressional Retirement'. *Legislative Studies Quarterly* 23(3): 419–433.

The Star. 2013. 'Senators and MPs likely Cheating on Expenses', Canadians Tell Pollsters. 14 June 2013. http://www.thestar.com/news/canada/2013/06/14/senators_and_mps_likely_cheating_on_expenses_canadians_tell_pollsters.html [Accessed 21 June 2013].

The Telegraph. (2010) 'British Social Attitudes Survey: Trust in Politics Hits New Low over MPs' Expenses Scandal. http://www.telegraph.co.uk/news/8197672/British-Social-Attitudes-survey-trust-in-politics-hits-new-low-over-MPs-expenses-scandal.html [Accessed 16 January 2013].

The Times. (2012) 'Look at Our Expenses? No You Don't Say French MPs'. 25 July 2012.

The Times. (2010) 'MPs Book House Banqueting Rooms for Lobbyists to Entertain Clients', 5 February 2010. http://www.timesonline.co.uk/tol/news/politics/article7015889.ece [Accessed 21 June 2010].

The Times. (2009) 'Poll Shows Public Revulsion at MPs' Conduct over Expenses'. 12 May 2009. http://www.timesonline.co.uk/tol/news/politics/article6269939.ece

The Times. (2007) 'Government Promises Action on Cash for Peers', 17 Jul 2007. http://www.timesonline.co.uk/tol/news/politics/article2090024.ece [Accessed 21 June 2010].

Thompson, J. (2000) *Political Scandal: Power and Visibility in the Media Age*. Cambridge: Polity Press.

Thompson, J. (1997) 'Scandal and Social Theory'. In J. Lull and S. Hinerman (eds.), *Media Scandals: Morality and Desire in the Popular Culture Marketplace*. Cambridge, UK: Polity Press, pp. 34–64.

Tilley, J. and Hobolt, S. (2011) 'Is the Government to Blame? An Experimental Test of How Partisanship Shapes Perceptions of Performance and Responsibility'. *Journal of Politics* 73(2): 316–330.

United States Congress. (2008) House of Representatives House Ethics Manual 2008 edition. http://ethics.house.gov/sites/ethics.house.gov/files/documents/2008_House_Ethics_Manual.pdf [Accessed 10 September 2012].

University College London, Constitution Unit. (2012) MPs Expenses, IPSA and Parliamentary Watchdogs – A Parliamentary Committee Inquiry Lite? http://constitution-unit.com/2011/10/28/mps%e2%80%99-expenses-ipsa-and-constitutional-watchdogs-a-parliamentary-committee-inquiry-lite/

Unlock Democracy. (2012) 'A Storm is Brewing'. 19 October 2012. Press Release.

vanHeerde-Hudson, J. (2011) 'Playing by the Rules: The 2009 MPs' Expenses Scandal'. In D. Wring, R. Mortimore and S. Atkinson (eds.), *Political Communication in Britain: The Leader Debates, the Campaign and the Media in the 2010 General Election*. Basingstoke: Palgrave Macmillan, pp. 241–260.

vanHeerde-Hudson, J. and Fisher, J. (2013) 'Parties Heed (with caution): Public Knowledge of and Attitudes towards Party Finance in Britain'. *Party Politics* 19(1): 41–60.

Viner, K. 'Interview with Gordon Brown', 20 June 2009, *The Guardian Online*. http://www.guardian.co.uk/politics/2009/jun/20/gordon-brown-interview/print [Accessed 18 August 2010].

Vivyan, N., Wagner, M. and Tarlov, J. (2012) 'Representative Misconduct, Voter Perceptions and Accountability: Evidence from the 2009 House of Commons Expenses Scandal'. *Electoral Studies* 31(4): 750–763.

Vleugels, R. (2009) 'Overview of All 90 FOIA Countries & Territories'. *Fringe*, Fringe Special.

Wagner, M., Tarlov, J. and Vivyan, N. (2012) 'Partisan Bias in Opinion Formation on Episodes of Political Controversy: Evidence from Great Britain'. *Political Studies* doi: 10.1111/j.1467-9248.2012.01002.x.

Watt, N. and Stratton, A. 'MPs' Expenses Body Must Change or be Changed, says David Cameron'. *Guardian*, 16 December 2010. http://www.guardian.co.uk/politics/2010/dec/15/cameron-mps-expenses-ipsa [Accessed 23 November 2013].

Watts, Robert. (2013) 'MPs Spend £500,000 on Business Class Flights'. 22 June 2013 http://www.telegraph.co.uk/news/uknews/10136603/MPs-spend-500000-on-business-class-flights.html [Accessed 24 June 2013].

Weibing, X. (2010) 'China's Limited Push Model of FOI Legislation'. *Government Information Quarterly* 27(4): 346–351.

Welch, S. and Hibbing, J. (1997) 'The Effects of Charges of Corruption on Voting Behavior in Congressional Elections, 1982–1990'. *Journal of Politics* 59: 226–239.

Wellhofer, E. (2007) 'Party Realignment and Voter Transition in Italy, 1987–1996'. *Comparative Political Studies* 34: 156–186.

Wheeler, B. (2011). 'Can UK Political Parties be Saved from Extinction'? BBC News Online, http://www.bbc.co.uk/news/uk-politics-12934148 [Accessed 3 March 2015].

White, N. (2007) *Free and Frank: Making the Official Information Act Work.* Wellington: Institute of Policy Studies, Victoria University.

Williams, R. (1998) *Political Scandals in the USA.* Edinburgh: Keele University Press.

Winetrobe, B. (2008) 'Precedent vs. Principle: The Convergence of the UK and the Scottish Parliaments'. Eighth Workshop of Parliamentary Scholars and Parliamentarians, 26–27 July, Wroxton College.

Winnett, R. and Rayner, G. (2009) *No Expenses Spared.* London: Bantam Press.

Wood, S. (2006) 'Parliament and FOI: How are MPs using the Act'. Constitution Unit FOI Seminar Series, 31 May, London.

Worthy, B. (2010) "More Open but Not More Trusted? The Effect of the Freedom of Information Act 2000 on the United Kingdom Central Government". *Governance* 23(4): 561–582.

Worthy, B. and Bourke, G. (2011) 'The Sword and the Shield: The use of FOI by Parliamentarians and the Impact of FOI on Parliament'. Constitution Unit: London.

Worthy, B. and Burke, G. (2011) 'Open House? The Impact of the Freedom of Information Act on Westminster'. Paper presented at the annual Political Studies Association Conference, April 2011, London.

Worthy, B. and Hazell, R. (2010) "The Sword: How MPs and Peers have Used Freedom of Information in the UK". Paper Presented at the Annual Meeting of the Political Studies Association, 31 March, Edinburgh.

Worthy, B., Hazell, R., Amos, J. and Bourke, G. (2011) *Town Hall Transparency? The Impact of FOI on Local Government in England.* Constitution Unit: London.

Wright, T. (2012) *Doing Politics.* London: Biteback Publishing.

Wright, T. (2010) "What Are MPs For?". *Political Quarterly* 81(3): 298–308.

Wright, T. (2004) "Prospects for Parliamentary Reform". *Parliamentary Affairs* 57(4): 867–876.

Wright, T. (2002) Committee on Standards in Public Life, Oral Evidence, 11 June 2002.

Wright, T. (1996) 'Palace of Low-grade Corruptions'. *New Statesman,* 9 August 1996.

YouGov. (2010) 'YouGov/The Sun: Survey Results'. http://today.yougov.co.uk/sites/today.yougov.co.uk/files/TheSun_BrokenBritain.pdf [Accessed 21 November 2010].

Zaller, J. (1998) 'Monica Lewinsky's Contribution to Political Science'. *PS: Political Science and Politics* 31(2): 182–189.

Index

Printed and bound in the United States of America